PRAISE FOR *EXCELLENCE IN PEOPLE ANALYTICS*

Jonathan Ferrar and David Green have hit the mark here with *Excellence in People Analytics*. This book is filled with topical case studies that can support any people analytics and HR team along their journey to become evidence-based in their pursuit of creating enterprise value.

Loren I Shuster, Chief People Officer and Head of Corporate Affairs, The LEGO Group

Excellence in People Analytics is exceptional and will become the standard for people analytics.

Dave Ulrich, Rensis Likert Professor, Ross School of Business, University of Michigan, and Partner, The RBL Group

There is a need for companies to become more human in our increasingly digital age. I have found, as a CHRO, that analytics provides equal benefit to both employees and the business, and *Excellence in People Analytics* dovetails these two very well. Using analytics is clearly one of the most valuable tools for becoming more human, enabling personalization and consumerization of the employee experience.

Leena Nair, Chief Human Resources Officer, Unilever

At long last, workplaces are recognizing the value of being as data-driven in managing people as they are with products. The question is how to do people analytics well, and *Excellence in People Analytics* has timely answers. Cutting-edge practitioners share insights that you can start putting into action right away.

Adam Grant, #1 *New York Times* bestselling author of *Think Again* and host of the TED podcast *WorkLife*

All eyes are on HR. It is time to seize the opportunity and become more strategic. HR is closer to the business than ever, and *Excellence in People Analytics* shows how people analytics is a business activity that drives substantial value. The authors have used brilliant case studies to highlight these points.

Katarina Berg, Chief Human Resources Officer, Spotify

People analytics provides business executives with another lever to improve their strategy and operations. Jonathan Ferrar and David Green have a deep understanding of this topic and its impact on people and performance. Their work with companies across the globe is now captured in this book, providing insight with a collection of terrific case studies and practical advice. It is an outstanding guide for executives wishing to create value using people analytics.

John Boudreau, Professor Emeritus, Marshall School of Business, University of Southern California

Excellence in People Analytics is a delightful journey of discovery through the field of people analytics, with 30 vivid case studies and practical models. Businesses have recognized that workforce data can unleash the potential of talent and create value for them. Yet people analytics is one of the biggest capability gaps for organizations. This book inspires me and is a great guide to implement people analytics beyond the 'buzz' term.

Rosa Lee, Executive Vice President, Bosch China, and Corporate HR, Head of Asia-Pacific, Bosch

Excellence in People Analytics will equip HR leaders and practitioners with the structures and use cases they need to keep up with technology and learn new skills. I have little doubt that this book will define HR's contribution to the workplace of the future.

Bernard Marr, bestselling author, futurist and strategic advisor

Brilliantly insightful and practically impactful. This is a foundational book in the field of people analytics that emphasizes a business-first approach for elevating human performance. The nine dimensions for success are complemented with powerful cases that will empower any practitioner to apply these concepts.

Michael J Arena, VP Talent and Development, AWS, and author of *Adaptive Space*

Excellence in People Analytics is a must-read for human resources leaders who want to create business value through workforce data. This groundbreaking book provides compelling case studies, methods and tools to help respond to critical questions such as what we should focus on, how to improve impact and how to create more value.

Alessandro Bonorino, Global Vice President of People, IT and Shared Services, BRF

Every HR professional needs to understand the value of workforce data and its impact on the organization and people engagement. *Excellence in People Analytics* is a superb guide, with practical case studies, that is relevant to every HR professional and business leader wishing to use data analytics for better decision making.
Low Peck Kem, Chief Human Resources Officer, Public Service Division, Prime Minister's Office, Singapore

Excellence in People Analytics shows how leading companies save money – a lot of it – by applying analytics to identify and then fix employee and business problems. This is the new source of competitive advantage for business.
Peter Cappelli, George W Taylor Professor of Management and Director, Center for Human Resources, The Wharton School, University of Pennsylvania

This book, written by two big influencers in the field of people analytics, is indispensable reading for anyone interested in data-driven approaches to harnessing human potential at work. Through a wide range of practical lessons and evidence-based recommendations, Jonathan Ferrar and David Green help us tackle today's critical issues in human capital, such as privacy, ethics and governance.
Tomas Chamorro-Premuzic, Professor, Columbia University and University College London

With *Excellence in People Analytics*, Jonathan Ferrar and David Green provide an incredible guide to companies and a helpful business-led framework for thinking about the potential impact of people data on employees and workers. If that isn't enough, they intersperse this guide with the greatest collection of practical cases studies I have ever seen in one book on this topic.
Frida Polli, CEO and Co-founder, pymetrics

HR has the fantastic opportunity to completely reinvent itself, like a phoenix, over the next 10 years, just as marketing has done in the past decade: data, analytics, personalization and a transformation of leadership will play a major role in this story. This book contains many case studies that will help guide its readers along this exciting journey.
Peter Hinssen, Visiting Lecturer, London Business School, Partner, nexxworks and author of *The Phoenix and the Unicorn*

As an educator, I welcome Jonathan Ferrar and David Green's *Excellence in People Analytics* as a requisite primer for all HR, talent and employee experience professionals. People analytics must enter the core curriculum of 21st-century management education. This book provides an excellent historical overview and a comprehensive set of case studies. I plan to adopt it for the classes I teach at NYU.
Anna Tavis PhD, Academic Director, Human Capital Management Department, New York University

Jonathan Ferrar and David Green have created an invaluable resource for people analytics professionals and business leaders. They break down complex topics with concise explanations and case studies, providing an easy point of entry for both people analytics beginners and experienced professionals. *Excellence in People Analytics* is an essential book at a critical time for people analytics.
Ben Waber, President and Co-founder, Humanyze

One of the things I love about *Excellence in People Analytics* is that it roots the value of people analytics in solving business problems. This book is a practical and clear guide for people analytics leaders and practitioners at any level, providing them with both insights on their own craft but also on how to make their work of the highest value to the businesses they serve. It provides a wonderful balance of real-life examples and useful frameworks that can help practitioners break down even the toughest challenges into solvable questions and efficient processes.
Stacia Garr, Co-founder and Principal Analyst, RedThread Research

If you are looking to create an extraordinary workplace, mastering people analytics is key. I can think of no better authorities on the topic than Jonathan Ferrar and David Green. *Excellence in People Analytics* provides the direction that business executives and human resources leaders need to transform data into insight and develop actionable strategies for moving the needle.
Ron Friedman PhD, author of *Decoding Greatness* and *The Best Place to Work*

Jonathan Ferrar and David Green provide not just a deep dive into what is state of the art in people analytics but the stories behind that destination – the different journeys leaders go on to get there and how they navigate both the internal and external challenges and opportunities in their organizations. *Excellence in People Analytics* is an invaluable road map for anyone going on this journey.
Didier Elzinga, CEO and Founder, Culture Amp

Excellence in People Analytics

How to use workforce data
to create business value

Jonathan Ferrar
David Green

KoganPage

First published in Great Britain and the United States in 2021 by Kogan Page Limited

2nd Floor, 45 Gee Street	122 W 27th St, 10th Floor	4737/23 Ansari Road
London	New York, NY 10001	Daryaganj
EC1V 3RS	USA	New Delhi 110002
United Kingdom		India
www.koganpage.com		

Kogan Page books are printed on paper from sustainable forests.

ISBNs

Hardback   978 1 78966 118 7
Paperback   978 0 7494 9829 0
eBook   978 0 7494 9830 6

British Library Cataloguing-in-Publication Data
A CIP record for this book is available from the British Library.

Library of Congress Cataloging-in-Publication Data
Names: Ferrar, Jonathan, author. | Green, David (David Richard), author.
Title: Excellence in people analytics : how to use workforce data to create business value / Jonathan Ferrar, David Green.
Description: London, United Kingdom ; New York, NY, USA : Kogan Page Limited, 2021. | Includes bibliographical references and index. |
Identifiers: LCCN 2021019061 (print) | LCCN 2021019062 (ebook) | ISBN 9780749498290 (paperback) | ISBN 9781789661187 (hardback) | ISBN 9780749498306 (ebook)
Subjects: LCSH: Personnel management–Data processing. | Personnel management–Statistical methods. | Personnel management–Planning.
Classification: LCC HF5549.5.D37 F47 2021 (print) | LCC HF5549.5.D37 (ebook) | DDC 658.30072/7–dc23

Typeset by Integra Software Services, Pondicherry
Print production managed by Jellyfish
Printed and bound by CPI Group (UK) Ltd, Croydon CR0 4YY

BRIEF CONTENTS

CONTENTS

05   Technology 141

06   Data 179

PART THREE The next steps for people analytics 293

ABOUT THE AUTHORS

Jonathan Ferrar is a globally respected speaker, author, influencer and business advisor in HR strategy and people analytics. He has worked in corporate business for over 25 years for companies like Andersen Consulting (now Accenture) and IBM, where he served as an executive for more than 10 years. He is a Board Member of the CIPD and advisor to the analytics company, TrustSphere. Currently, Jonathan is Chief Executive Officer and co-founder of people analytics and HR professional services firm, Insight222 (www. insight222.com). He is regularly cited in HR Influencer lists such as 'The 100 most influential people in HR' (*HR Weekly*, January 2021) and 'Top 100 HR tech influencers' (*HR Executive*, May 2020). Additionally, Jonathan is a co-author of the people analytics book, *The Power of People: Learn how successful organizations use workforce analytics to improve business performance* (Pearson, 2017).

David Green is recognized worldwide as one of the most influential leaders in the people analytics field. He is an award-winning writer, speaker and executive consultant on people analytics and the future of work. He is regularly invited to chair and speak at industry conferences. David's articles and the Digital HR Leaders Podcast he hosts have built up an extensive following. He is regularly cited in HR influencer lists, most recently in 'The 100 most influential people in HR' (*HR Weekly*, January 2021) and 'Top 100 HR tech influencers' (*HR Executive*, May 2020). As Managing Partner at Insight222, David works with chief human resources officers and people analytics leaders in global companies to help them create more value and impact from people analytics. David has accumulated over 20 years of experience in the human resources and technology fields including at IBM, Cielo, Capita, Amadeus and Reed, and is also a board advisor at TrustSphere.

With

Kirsten Levermore is a business storyteller and neuroscientist. She is an expert on cross-functional and multicultural communications and has provided input as a storytelling consultant on numerous global initiatives. Kirsten has contributed to several books on leadership psychology, managing humans in a technology-enabled workforce and internal communications, and previously spent two years as deputy editor of international leadership and management magazines *Dialogue Review* (Duke Corporate Education) and *Edge* (Institute of Leadership & Management), and the official journal of the Chartered Institute of Marketing, *Catalyst*.

LIST OF CASE STUDIES

Listed in the order that they appear in the book:

FOREWORD

Think back over your last 24 hours. How many decisions did you make about your personal life: Where to spend your time? Who to spend time with? How to manage yourself (grooming, food, situation and so forth)? Research says that 60 to 75 per cent of our choices are made out of habit; the other choices are consciously made to realize our personal goals.

Likewise, business and HR leaders make daily decisions about how to provide human capital services. While many of these decisions are organizational routines (like individual habits) embedded in policies and procedures, others are conscious choices made to deliver and accelerate business goals.

People analytics adds enormous value to make informed conscious choices about human capital investments. I often ask business and HR leaders why they choose one human capital initiative over another. Their answers include: 'we have always done it this way', 'others are doing it', 'we want to be as good or better than another organization', and 'because someone said we should'.

Thank goodness for *Excellence in People Analytics*!

Jonathan Ferrar and David Green are two thoughtful colleagues who have spent much of their recent esteemed professional careers helping business and HR leaders use people analytics to create value. What is particularly impressive is that their work on people analytics models the research on using information to improve decision making.

The 30 remarkable case studies in this book offer deep perspectives into some of the most innovative analytics work in the world today. The insights from these leading companies offer example after example of what can be done to use people analytics to inform human capital decisions. They also provide valuable opportunities to discover and share broad ideas.

Then, Jonathan and David use their model – Insight222 Nine Dimensions for Excellence in People Analytics® – to go beyond these delightful case studies and offer a logical and measurable framework for delivering people analytics work and developing a sustainable analytics capability.

Combined, the unstructured case studies and structured Nine Dimensions model offer business and HR leaders an incredible book along with specific practical tools that will lead to business impact.

Jonathan and David's insights will evolve 'people analytics' from collecting data to using information to make informed choices. Their work has informed and paralleled mine in so many ways, including:

1 HR is not about HR, but about the business. People analytics is not about measuring HR activities found in scorecards or dashboards, or even about fascinating insight or tidbits, but about helping deliver results.

2 People analytics starts by defining desired stakeholder results. Any organization has some version of a balanced scorecard with outcomes in five areas: employee, strategy, customer, financial and community results. Being clear about these desired outcomes offers a clear proclamation of what matters most (dependent variables in analytics terms).

3 People analytics requires an understanding of the pathways or initiatives to deliver desired stakeholder outcomes. In my own work on human capital, we have identified four domains (talent, leadership, organization and the HR department) where initiatives can be designed and delivered (independent variables in analytics terms).

4 The human capital initiatives can be prioritized based on their relative impact on the five key outcomes. The Organization Guidance System (www.rbl.ai) offers a disciplined methodology to make informed choices about how to accelerate the five results by investing in human capital initiatives that add the most value.

People analytics done well moves beyond merely benchmarking how a company compares to others and beyond best practice to adopt what someone else does, to personalized guidance for what business and HR leaders *should* do to create sustained value for all stakeholders. As readers will discover in *Excellence in People Analytics*, the correct answer to 'why choose this initiative?' is because it delivers value to results that matter!

While organization routines, like personal habits, continue to affect how organizations think, act and feel, *Excellence in People Analytics* will inform organizational choices to make the right things happen. This book dramatically shifts the entire human capital profession to align with, and accelerate, results that matter.

Dave Ulrich,
Rensis Likert Professor, Ross School of Business,
University of Michigan,
Partner, The RBL Group
dou@umich.edu
April 2021

THE CHIEF HUMAN RESOURCES OFFICER'S PERSPECTIVE

Of the companies discussed in this book, one that stands out is Microsoft.[1] It is one of the best examples of how people analytics and insights have been infused into the company's operations and strategies. Analytics has allowed Human Resources to unlock value for employees and the business. A detailed case study of Microsoft's approach to people analytics is included in Chapter 5 (Technology). We are very grateful that Microsoft's Chief People Officer Kathleen Hogan[2] also generously shared her insights on the topic during our research:

'Our mission as Human Resources is to empower the people who empower the planet. To support our mission, it's important to hear from our employees. Microsoft analyses more than one million employee comments every year. We use data to help set context, drive understanding of trends we're seeing within the organization and, ultimately, deliver insights that help us make good decisions. It is often said that "people are the most important asset in business". In Microsoft, that is absolutely true. So, decisions regarding our talent have a unique impact on our business.

People analytics can deliver deep value in so many areas of the business. These include more obvious things like reducing attrition, improving diversity or improving the hiring funnel. One example of how we are leveraging data is in the area of recruiting. Historically, we focused on a set of top schools[3] for computer science talent. Engineering leaders and hiring managers saw these schools as the indicator on whether we were getting the best computer science talent. After analysing the data two years post-hire, we realized that many other schools yielded equally successful employees. We shared that data with our Chief Executive Officer and their executive team and agreed that we would expand the list of universities where we recruited. This not only yielded greater options for talent, but it also offered us a much more diverse talent pool.

In the area of employee experience, we've used data to better understand the moments that matter to an employee's career – and have done specific analysis in the onboarding space to identify areas that we can focus on to ensure employees are productive on day one. Additionally, we see many opportunities to leverage data and analytics in the important topic of employee well-being. Understanding behaviors that can impact the perception of work–life balance is just the beginning. And correlated to that is empowering our employees and managers with their own data. By understanding behaviors that create positive experiences for their teams and their colleagues, we're putting the insights at their fingertips to enable them to self-correct ineffective behaviors and amplify positive ones.

But less obvious areas where people analytics makes a real difference include influencing productivity and enhancing manager effectiveness. In partnership with our sales organization, Microsoft's HR Business Insights team has been able to identify certain behaviors that make sales professionals more productive, thereby influencing more positive sales outcomes.

People analytics is not just important internally, it's important to our external customers. With Workplace Analytics, LinkedIn, Glint, Power BI, and Azure, we are making it easier for our customers to embrace people analytics and benefit from the value that understanding your workforce can provide. When talking with external customers, we find it really helps to explain how these technologies assist us internally to bring value.

Like many companies and internal functions, Human Resources is experiencing a renaissance due to digital transformation. As companies embrace more digital systems, they gain more data. I think we're just at the beginning of an incredibly exciting time for HR leaders who increasingly have more of a strategic role and are able to use more empirical data to inform decisions around performance, talent management, agility, employee experience and productivity.

This can and will change the trajectory of the business, for the better.'

Kathleen Hogan,
Chief People Officer, Microsoft,
Redmond, WA, USA
September 2020

Notes

1 The Microsoft Corporation is a multinational corporation headquartered in Redmond, Washington, US, that develops, manufactures, licenses, supports and sells computer software, consumer electronics and personal computers and services (see https://www.microsoft.com/en-gb/about/ (archived at https://perma.cc/SXU4-3EV2), last accessed 30 March 2021).

2 Kathleen Hogan has served as Chief People Officer and Executive Vice President of Human Resources at Microsoft since 2015. Previous to that, Kathleen served as corporate vice president of Microsoft Services, and was a partner at McKinsey & Co. and a development manager at Oracle Corp. She holds a bachelor's degree in applied mathematics and economics from Harvard University and an MBA from the Stanford University Graduate School of Business. Kathleen also sits on the board of directors of Alaska Air Group and the National Center for Women & Information Technology.

3 In the USA, the term 'school' is used to describe institutions of higher education. The words 'university' or 'college' are often used in other countries.

PREFACE: A WORD FROM THE AUTHORS

It was a crisp and bright February morning in London in 2015 when two people met in the shadow of the Tower of London to talk about people analytics.

Jonathan Ferrar was a human capital management executive at IBM. David Green was in recruitment process outsourcing at Cielo. One wore a suit, and one wore jeans. In terms of human resources, we could not have worked in more different spheres – but a shared passion for analytics and a fateful social media connection brought us together.

Ultimately, this connection led to us working together at IBM and (with others) founding Insight222, a company dedicated to putting people analytics at the centre of business. Our shared passion for the field of people analytics gelled quickly in these early years and the genesis for this book started on a warm and pleasant evening at the Beach Club in Watson's Bay, Sydney in May 2016.

Since that evening, we've worked together and conducted research with over 100 organizations on people analytics. We are fortunate to have seen it in practice in every major country and industry, globally.

In almost every one of these organizations, we have repeatedly come across three themes: focus, impact and value.

- **What should I focus on?** Practitioners who focus on challenges linked to the company's business strategy are more successful in their endeavours.

- **How can I improve my impact?** Organizations that build solid foundations and don't dive into solving technology and data issues create more impact on a long-term basis.

- **How can I create more value?** Leaders who prioritize their work with the end goal in mind deliver more value for the business and the employees themselves.

We reviewed all the work over the prior few years in the context of these three questions during a business retreat in Hamburg in May 2018. Hamburg has played a critical role in creative thinking for bands such as The Beatles – and it was no different for us: it was an inspiring place, as we developed the framework discussed in this book.

The answers to those three commonly asked questions – What should I focus on? How can I improve my impact? How can I create more value? – can be summarized into nine dimensions, grouped into three categories: foundation, resources and value.

We call it the Insight222 Nine Dimensions for Excellence in People Analytics® model (see Figure A.1).

The most successful organizations in people analytics seek excellence in each of the nine dimensions and address them in a way that is suitable (and in whatever order is appropriate) for their company. We find that organizations that have delivered the most impact focus on all three categories simultaneously. The Nine Dimensions model is not sequential. It does not need to be 'done' in a particular order. And it does not imply that moving from one dimension to the next cannot happen without achieving a certain level of 'maturity'.

Figure A.1   Insight222 Nine Dimensions for Excellence in People Analytics®

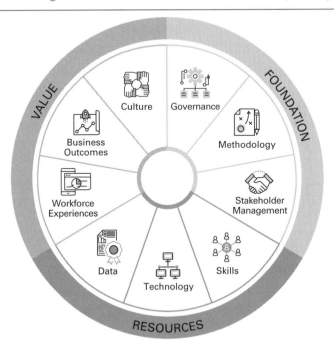

As you read this book, ask yourself one question: How can I use workforce data to improve the value for my people and my company?

We aim to help business leaders, chief human resources officers and analytics practitioners make their companies and organizations a better place for their people, and deliver more value to all of their stakeholders. So, between the summer of 2019 and early 2021, we searched for the best examples of people analytics in the world and crystallized many of these into 30 case studies.

While the model and frameworks provide theoretical guidance, the case studies bring the topics to life. We are sure the practical advice in this book will inspire business leaders and human resources executives to invest in people analytics. If that happens, we are confident that their people analytics teams will have more focus, provide more impact and deliver more value to their organizations.

NINE DIMENSIONS FOR EXCELLENCE IN PEOPLE ANALYTICS

Foundation

People analytics needs a solid foundation with the right elements in place to enable success in the future before the work becomes too complex. This is rooted in having strong governance, clear methodologies and effective stakeholder management.

Dimension One – Governance

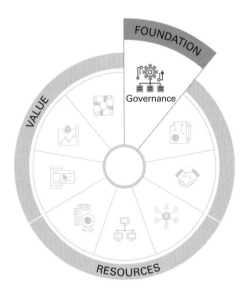

Governance, as one of the Nine Dimensions, refers to the mechanisms, processes and procedures by which people analytics operates. It underpins all analytics and ensures the right people provide direction for work, that the structure and stewardship for managing data and projects are implemented and applicable, and that risks are managed appropriately.

We emphasize the practice and value of strong governance and steward-ship with case studies from:

- **Novartis International A.G.,** on aligning people analytics to the business strategy;

- **Trimble, Inc.,** on how creating a brand for people analytics enhances credibility;

- **Lloyds Banking Group,** on establishing ethical standards for people analytics.

Dimension Two – Methodology

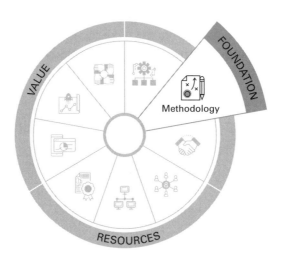

Methodology, as one of the Nine Dimensions, focuses on the processes and frameworks that should be established for repeatable and dynamic people analytics. These include the way in which the prioritization of work occurs, and the use of effective and transparent criteria, plus the involvement of sponsors and how to provide focus to the team, while creating impact and delivering value.

We explore practical applications of implementing effective methods and sponsorship with case studies from:

- **Merck & Co., Inc.,** on how to be agile when prioritizing in a pandemic;

- **American Eagle Outfitters®,** on developing a people analytics manifesto;

- **Swarovski A.G.,** on delivering top-line growth with the right sponsor.

Dimension Three – Stakeholder Management

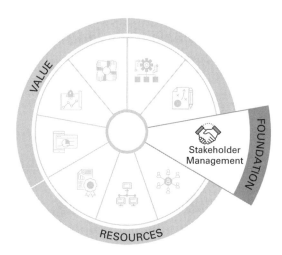

Stakeholder Management, as one of the Nine Dimensions, discusses the different types of stakeholders that people analytics teams will interact with to create impact and deliver value. In particular, it focuses on building a purposeful stakeholder map, how to engage and conduct effective meetings and what to do in the long term to build effective and sustainable relationships across all stakeholders.

We learn from the experiences of three senior leaders on how they secured stakeholder commitment in case studies from:

- **Johnson & Johnson,** on developing great stakeholders at the very top;
- **The Viessmann Group,** on the value of being an analytical CHRO;
- **Syngenta A.G.,** on the importance of having stakeholder engagement.

Resources

People analytics must have impact to be credible. This requires balancing the right resources, including expertise in the team itself, appropriate technologies and robust and extensive data.

Dimension Four – Skills

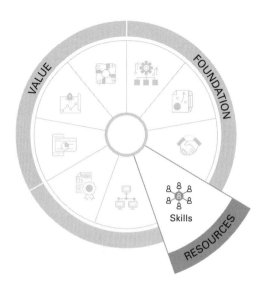

Skills, as one of the Nine Dimensions, focuses on the people analytics team itself. It discusses the responsibilities and skills of the people analytics leader in particular, plus the operating model for the team and the key skill set for translating the business and human resources language into analytical language, and vice versa.

We gain insights from companies that have built successful people analytics teams with case studies from:

- **Standard Chartered Bank**, on the people analytics leader;
- **Capital One**, on scaling the people analytics team;
- **Royal Caribbean Cruises Ltd.**, on the importance of great translators.

Dimension Five – Technology

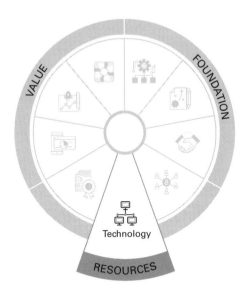

Technology, as one of the Nine Dimensions, consists of all types of analytics technology needed for successful people analytics. In particular, it outlines the topic of 'build versus buy', using technology to scale analytics solutions and emerging technologies to accelerate data gathering, analysis, insights and the democratization of data.

We provide practical examples of experiences in harnessing technology for people analytics with case studies from:

- **Vertex Pharmaceuticals,** on buying technology;
- **Bosch GmbH,** on building a technical architecture for workforce planning;
- **Microsoft Corporation,** on scaling analytics across the enterprise.

Dimension Six – Data

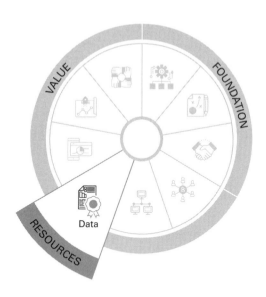

Data, as one of the Nine Dimensions, consists of data stewardship, data management and how to use data to deliver more value to the business. Of particular importance is the use of data sources, especially emerging data, that will add incremental value and expand people analytics far beyond the focus on human resources policies and process, to those that address the most complex business issues.

We highlight outstanding examples of how data governance and data management have created impact with case studies from:

- **HSBC,** combining the role of the chief data officer for HR with people analytics;
- **Nokia Corporation,** on leveraging a burning platform for data management;
- **Tetra Pak,** on partnering with finance to standardize data for a key business objective.

Value

People analytics has a responsibility to deliver value to the organization and its workforce. This is derived by providing enhanced experiences to the workforce, creating impact through business outcomes and developing a data-driven culture for analytics.

Dimension Seven – Workforce Experiences

Workforce Experiences, as one of the Nine Dimensions, describes how key audiences across any organization benefit from people analytics. It outlines topics such as consumerization and personalization of employee experiences, the democratization of data to all managers, how to excite executives with interactive analytics and how to change organizational processes for improving the entire workforce experience.

We share compelling stories of how people analytics can deliver powerful experiences with case studies from:

- **ABN AMRO Bank N.V.**, on measuring employee experiences;
- **FIS (Fidelity National Information Services, Inc.)**, on using data to change the performance management system across the company;
- **Santander Brasil S.A.**, on bringing analytics to life in front of executives.

Dimension Eight – Business Outcomes

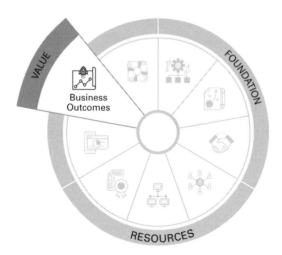

Business Outcomes, as one of the Nine Dimensions, describes the rationale and techniques that lead to delivering outcomes as a result of people analytics activity. These outcomes are actionable insights and recommendations, financial value, and tangible business improvement across the enterprise.

We also hear about how people analytics delivers business outcomes and scales solutions with case studies from:

- **MetLife, Inc.,** on securing investment for people analytics;
- **Nestlé S.A.,** on speaking the language of the business;
- **IBM (International Business Machines Corporation),** on scaling for value with advanced analytics and technologies.

Dimension Nine – Culture

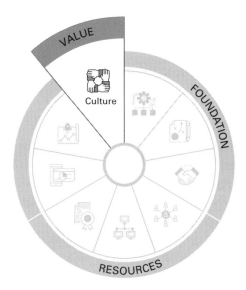

Culture, as one of the Nine Dimensions, is focused on building analytically willing and savvy people across the human resources function. It considers the skills and mindset needed for the future HR professional and how these can be developed and instilled to provide a basis for innovation, curiosity and delivering value to the organization.

We spotlight the attributes of analytical cultures that enable sustainability in people analytics with case studies from:

- **Merck KGaA,** on the adoption of a culture of people analytics across the enterprise;

- **Rabobank,** on how to engage and enable HR to kick-start a data-driven culture;

- **PepsiCo,** on building collaboration between global and local teams.

ACKNOWLEDGEMENTS

This book has taken over three years to bring from proposal to publication. During that time, we have been fortunate to work with and research well over 100 global organizations on people analytics. We have spoken and collaborated with scores of executives, leaders and practitioners in every major country and industry worldwide on the topic. We would like to thank all our colleagues, friends, clients and partners plus all our followers on social media. Every interaction – from the smallest online comment to the most extensive interaction with clients – in these three years has helped to shape our thinking and contributed to this book.

We wish to thank all the people who agreed to be interviewed for this book. In particular, we thank those companies and the people in them that helped define the case studies that are included. These case studies provide a practical example of excellence in people analytics and bring the book to life. We are grateful to those companies and leaders for their confidence in us and our work.

We are ever grateful to Kirsten Levermore. Without her persistence, dedication and inspiration, this book would still be 'in draft'. Kirsten wrote first versions of much of the book, shaping our ideas and converting them to text. She was especially helpful in shepherding each of the 30 case studies from idea to manuscript and worked tirelessly with each company to perfect those stories.

We would like to thank all of our colleagues at Insight222, who helped us with much of our research and in completing the manuscript. We pay particular thanks to Anastasia Ktena, who helped us with figures, Ian Bailie, who reviewed our chapters on Technology and Data, and Naomi Verghese, who, as an ex-practitioner in people analytics, wrote much of the glossary.

Finally, we'd like to thank all of our clients – both current and former – for providing inspiration through their enthusiasm for the field of people analytics.

Jonathan Ferrar and David Green

I would like to thank Elena for her love and encouragement and for giving me time to complete this book. I thank my son, Arthur, for his support and for playing table tennis during the winter evenings as the final manuscript took shape. I continue to be inspired by my Great Uncle Bill (William Ferrar) whose many mathematics books provide the motivation for me to share my ideas and experience. I give a special note to my cats, Cleo and Zeldaa, for keeping me company, lying on my desk while I typed.

Jonathan Ferrar

I would like to thank my wonderful wife Sara and my children, Alexander and Isabella, for giving me time to write this book on the frequent rainy weekends that come with living in the South East of England. I'd also like to thank my mother (Ann) and father (Richard), who both instilled in me a strong work ethic. Finally, I'd also like to thank the wider people analytics community – their passion, energy and willingness to share make our field an exciting and rewarding place to be.

David Green

The core model, Insight222 Nine Dimensions for Excellence in People Analytics®, is a registered trademark of Insight222 Limited.

The following models in this book are the intellectual property and copyright of Jonathan Ferrar, David Green and Insight222 Limited:

- DRIVE: Five Ages of People Analytics
- Focus-Impact-Value Model
- Seven Types of Stakeholders
- The Four Responsibilities of People Analytics

The following models are the intellectual property and the copyright of Insight222 Limited:

- Insight222 Operating Model for People Analytics
- People Analytics Value Chain
- Nine Skills for the Future HR Professional

The following models were used with permission from and are the copyright of Nigel Guenole, Jonathan Ferrar and Sheri Feinzig:

- Eight Step Model for Purposeful Analytics
- Seven Forces of Demand
- Complexity-Impact Matrix
- Six Skills for Success

These models are reproduced from and first mentioned in *The Power of People: Learn how successful organizations use workforce analytics to improve business performance* (Pearson, 2017).

PART ONE
The case for people analytics

Introduction

People analytics is not about HR. People analytics is about the business. It is about delivering commercial value, value to employees and the workforce, and value to managers and executives so they can make people-related decisions based on facts. At its best, it delivers impact to the board of directors, investors and broader society too.

Delivering people analytics requires solid foundations, intelligent use of resources and a passion for business value. Sequential maturity models are no longer valid – any business can use people analytics to immediately deliver value if they focus on a number of dimensions in parallel.

People analytics as a discipline is expanding in importance in HR and across the business world, generally. There are more people with analytical skills in HR than ever before, and the depth of expertise is growing annually according to LinkedIn (2020). Senior leaders recognize that a data-driven approach to their people function is now more important than ever. Human resources leaders who invest in people analytics are finding new ways to help their companies compete in the marketplace.

The following chapter captures these messages in detail and makes a case for business leaders to invest in people analytics.

Reference

LinkedIn (2020) Global Talent Trends 2020 [Report] Available from: https://business.linkedin.com/talent-solutions/recruiting-tips/global-talent-trends-2020 [Last accessed 7 February 2021]

The business value of people analytics

People analytics contributes hundreds of millions of dollars to the top and bottom lines of organizations.

At IBM, former CEO Ginni Rometty stated that the company saved 'nearly $300 million in retention cost in its predictive attrition program' (Rosenbaum, 2019). Using people analytics, it identified those people most at risk of leaving and prescribed actions in advance to help managers make the right decisions.

Google saved approximately $400 million by reducing new hires' onboarding time from nine months to six months (McAleer, 2018). It created email nudges to help new hires succeed in their roles by regularly highlighting the behaviours of top performers (Bock, 2019).

It's not just technology companies that are benefitting from people analytics; organizations of all kinds are reaping the financial reward of this work. For example, shoe retailer Clarks found that a single percentage point in employee engagement is worth an additional 0.4 per cent of improved business performance (Levenson and Pillans, 2017). Put in the context of Clarks' 2019 Annual Report (C&J Clark Limited, 2019), this calculates as almost £60 million per percentage point of employee engagement.

And the opportunity is much greater.

In a 2019 study, Accenture concluded that US $3.1 trillion of untapped future revenue growth lay in people data – specifically, the responsible use of that data combined with the employee trust garnered – for the 6,000 largest publicly listed global companies in its research sample (Shook, Knickrehm and Sage-Gavin, 2019). This is an average of $500 million per company that can be generated from people analytics.

Various other studies have found that companies with advanced capabilities in people analytics tend to have higher performance across a range of financial metrics. These include 30 per cent higher stock prices over three years (Bersin by Deloitte, 2013), 79 per cent higher return on equity (Sierra-Cedar, 2014), 96 per cent higher revenues over three years (Chakrabarti, 2017) and 56 per cent higher profit margins (Martin, 2018) than their counterparts.

These are all powerful reasons for the growing enthusiasm for creating excellence in people analytics.

What is people analytics?

The definition of people analytics has been published on numerous occasions. At its core, people analytics is:

> The analysis of employee and workforce data to reveal insights and provide recommendations to improve business outcomes.

Figure 0.1 People analytics consists of multiple activities and outcomes

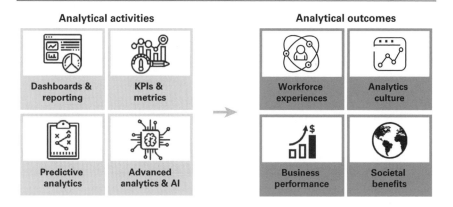

As Figure 0.1 shows, the definition of people analytics we use in this book consists of a collection of activities:

- Dashboards and reporting – sharing information and insights from people data in reports and dashboards often in a formal, standardized and repeatable fashion.

- Key performance indicators (KPIs) and metrics – measuring the most important metrics for the enterprise and those of value to C-suite executives, boards and investors.

- Predictive analytics – using statistical techniques and other mathematical analysis techniques to predict, forecast and plan scenarios for the future.

- Advanced analytics and artificial intelligence (AI) – applying very advanced techniques and technology to provide insights and recommendations, using, for example, machine learning, AI, deep learning and cognitive computing.

And outcomes:

- Workforce experiences – such as employee experiences, the democratization of data to managers, insights delivered to executives and overall workforce performance improvement. Workforce experiences also includes the advanced outcomes provided by analytics that improve the human-centred experience of work. These outcomes are discussed further in Chapter 7 (Workforce Experiences) and the Epilogue.

- Analytics culture – including building awareness of people analytics in HR, developing analytical skills for HR professionals and scaling people analytics to all managers in a company. See Chapter 9 (Culture) for more detail.

- Business performance – composed of financial impact, managing risk and compliance, market share growth, and informing and influencing the business strategy. These are all discussed in Chapter 8 (Business Outcomes). 'Business performance' also includes topics such as the CEO skills conundrum and investor demands, which are described in the Epilogue.

- Societal value – typically more advanced outcomes of people analytics, such as inclusion, equality and gender pay. These are discussed in the Epilogue.

In general, leading people analytics teams deliver significant value to the enterprise by focusing on business challenges, engaging with business executive stakeholders to sponsor significant work and working with colleagues across the business.

The most advanced people analytics teams have a business-first approach – they work with business executives as well as HR executives. They focus on the most strategically and operationally important people topics in the business. They quantify their work output and generate a return on investment that leaves business executives wanting more. They provide insights into customer relationships and retention, financial profitability, productivity, collaboration, innovation, sales performance and employee development.

These leading teams make a difference to the experiences of the people in their workforce, build a culture of people analytics across the enterprise and focus on more complex societal topics. They productize the best solutions, scale them across the company and then embed them into business operations. This enables leaders and managers to have insights at their fingertips to improve their operations and business performance. In essence, they focus on all of the outcomes highlighted in Figure 0.1.

DRIVE: Five Ages of People Analytics

There are many articles on the progress of people analytics through the ages. The topic has been covered well by Guenole, Ferrar and Feinzig (2017) and in the *Forbes* 2015 article, 'The geeks arrive in HR: people analytics is here' (Bersin, 2015).

Our analysis and research lead us to believe there are five 'ages' in total to describe the history and future of modern people analytics. We call these DRIVE: Five Ages of People Analytics (see Figure 0.2).

Figure 0.2   DRIVE: Five Ages of People Analytics

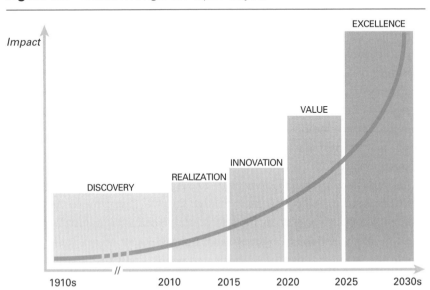

We will consider the first four of these Ages in detail in this chapter. The Age of Excellence will be introduced in the Epilogue.

The Age of Discovery: 1910s–2010

The Age of Discovery

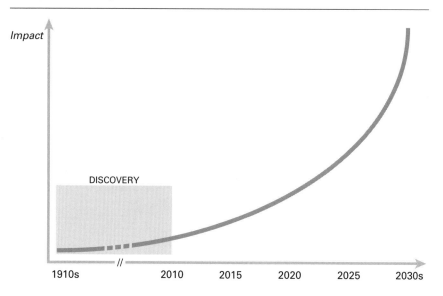

The rising use of people analytics has been gradual. Indeed, the origins can be traced back over a hundred years ago to Frederick Taylor's book, *The Principles of Scientific Management* in 1911. Taylor's ideas sought to optimize tasks, drive efficiency and maximize productivity through measuring everything employees did. A notable Taylorist of that era is Ford Motor Company, which famously used scientific analysis to automate processes in the car manufacturing plant and, therefore, provide efficiencies and increase production speed.

Another significant development in The Age of Discovery, which would eventually lead to the people analytics we know today, came in the 1940s when, in the post-war era, organizations established mass industrialization. The role of the industrial organizational psychologist arose. Today, these people are an integral part of sophisticated people analytics.

Fast-forward to the 1980s and 1990s, which saw an expansion of the human resources department from a sole focus on administration to recruitment, development, reward and performance management. This created a need to measure processes and the efficiency by which people were hired, deployed and developed across the workforce. One influential text on this topic was *The HR Scorecard: Linking people, strategy and performance* (Becker, Ulrich and Huselid, 2001), which introduced a measurement system to illustrate how HR can impact business performance.

By the first decade of the 21st century, people were being recruited into formal HR analytics or employee engagement functions. The onset of the internet and the ability to collect quantitative and qualitative data in large volumes changed the desire and ability to measure more than just the human resources processes. These early teams in large multinational organizations often consisted of only a few people, delivering work such as annual employee engagement surveys. Overall, people analytics functions of The Age of Discovery were administrative 'white-glove' functions, tackling data collection, statistics, reporting and business diagnosis, typically for a handful of senior executives and only occasionally undertaking analyses on complex business topics at the behest of the CEO.

The Age of Realization: 2010–2015

The Age of Realization

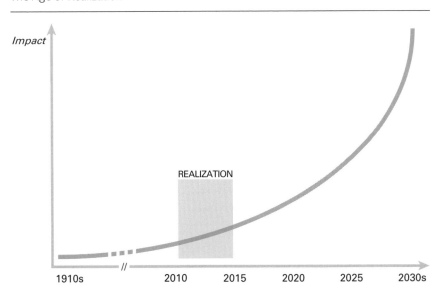

It was the 2008 global financial crisis that changed everything for the field of people analytics. The advent of Big Data and the use of analytics by business functions such as marketing, combined with a desire to measure and monitor everything with an adequate level of efficiency and effectiveness, led to the realization that analytics was critical. Teams that delivered insights to senior business executives allowed those organizations to flourish in the post-global financial crisis era. The Age of Realization was epitomized by the development of maturity models and the emergence of leading practices in big technology companies, in particular.

Large teams established in companies like Google, Microsoft and IBM could use their external product teams' expertise to translate this into a similar experience for their employees. These teams grew fast and focused on often complex predictive analytics projects. With senior executives' sponsorship, they could then scale these solutions, harness their technology prowess and deliver significant value.

This surge in the growth of people analytics sparked by the global financial crisis was eloquently captured in the *Harvard Business Review* cover article 'Competing on talent analytics' (Davenport, Harris and Shapiro, 2010). This article had a notable influence on almost every people analytics practitioner at the time. It articulates how organizations such as Google, Starbucks and AT&T were 'increasingly adopting sophisticated methods of analysing employee data to enhance their competitive advantage'. The paper highlighted how Best Buy[1] calculated the dollar value of employee engagement. It was one of the earliest published examples of using people data to deliver commercial value.

By the mid-2010s, people analytics teams had emerged in many multinational organizations. These teams were mainly 'service teams' managing a large number of requests from senior HR business partners and in some cases, senior executives and board directors. Work included everything from reporting, dashboard and data requests to very complex advanced analytics programs. In some cases, substantial financial value was created by understanding the drivers of employee attrition, customer retention, leadership behaviours and diversity. The most advanced teams were using various people and other business data from sources inside and outside the company.

In the early 2010s, Google took people analytics mainstream with its Project Oxygen (Garvin, 2013), which scientifically communicated the commonly held belief of the attributes of managers, communicated in 'Google language' for Google as a company. It changed how business executives saw the value of human resources processes and how analytics could predict the capabilities and behaviours needed to achieve competitive advantage. Project Oxygen took the generic understanding of people used in the previous decades to a specific, scientific, value-oriented insight for Google itself and published it in mainstream media, capturing the attention of executives worldwide. It followed it up with Project Aristotle (Duhigg, 2016), a brilliant study that looked at how to build the perfect team – with accuracy. Google's journey in analytics was memorialized by its then Senior Vice President of People Operations, Laszlo Bock, in his 2015 book, *Work Rules! Insights from inside Google that will transform how you live and lead.*

While some firms such as Google were doing outstanding work, most people analytics teams remained stuck in a reporting role. A leading practitioner, Thomas Rasmussen, and leading management thinker, Dave Ulrich, wrote about this in a 2015 paper, 'Learning from practice: how HR analytics avoids being a management fad'. Of the recommendations highlighted, two stand out: 'Start with the business problem' and 'Train HR professionals to have an analytical mindset'.

The paper also issues a warning: 'HR analytics in its current form will continue to fail to add real value to companies'.

More specialized approaches to people analytics began to appear, and practitioners started to document their work to help the field. For example, Ben Waber examined how sensors provide fresh insights into understanding how people work and collaborate in his book, *People Analytics: How social sensing technology will transform business and what it tells us about the future of work* (2013). Publications appeared to help people with the technical aspects of people analytics, such as Martin R Edwards and Kirsten Edwards' *Predictive HR Analytics: Mastering the HR metric* (2019), which provided a step-by-step guide to carrying out analyses using the statistical package SPSS.

The rise of people analytics up to this point had been influenced by maturity models. They were increasingly prevalent in the early and middle years of the 2010s. In general, maturity models can be helpful in the early stages of the journey of any business transformation. They have been used extensively by consulting organizations to develop clear criteria and measure progress.

Readers working in the people analytics space will recognize the Talent Analytics Maturity Model (Bersin by Deloitte, 2013 and Chakrabarti, 2017). This and many others evolved, typically consisting of four levels of maturity: operational reporting, advanced reporting, advanced analytics and predictive/prescriptive analytics. Models published in recent years also include a fifth level, focused on AI and cognitive computing technologies.

However, maturity models have several deficiencies when talking about what the people analytics field requires in the 2020s. Most critically, that building capability in people analytics 'must be' linear.

This is unhelpful and now counterproductive.

Adopting a linear approach to people analytics will not create impact quickly enough for business leaders in today's world. Indicating that a company cannot conduct predictive analytics until it has established its reporting metrics and dashboards is fundamentally wrong. In practice, these of course can occur at the same time, in parallel. This is because people analytics teams are expected to deliver value quickly across its entire remit. All forms of people analytics are likely to be required concurrently when the focus is (as it should be) on solving business problems. This is why the definition shown above includes a variety of activities and outcomes. They can occur simultaneously.

Maturity is fine, but excellence is better.

The Age of Innovation: 2015–2020

The Age of Innovation

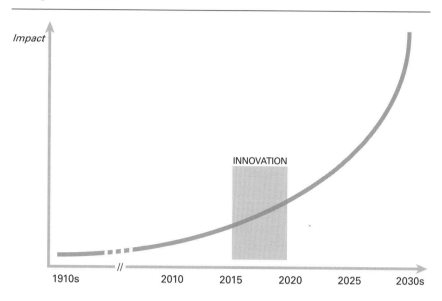

The mid-2010s marked a change in trajectory for the people analytics field. The primary driver was executive expectation: the chief human resources officer (CHRO) was increasingly being asked by the chief executive officer (CEO) to modernize their workforce in response to market demands.

The Age of Innovation was characterized by new models, new uses of technology, specialization, an increase in the number of practitioners entering the people analytics profession and new approaches to creating business value.

New models for using people analytics to advance business performance appeared more frequently. One such model is Alec Levenson's call for HR analytics and the business to be brought together (Levenson, 2015).

Another example that has gained traction in many companies is the idea of running people analytics like a business, detailed in *The Power of People: Learn how successful organizations use workforce analytics to improve business performance* (Guenole, Ferrar and Feinzig, 2017). In the course of the detailed research of over 50 large multinational organizations, it became apparent that the companies with thriving people analytics functions were the ones that started with the business problem and not the data. The authors found that leading companies had a strong operating model for people analytics and were actively engaged in building a data-driven culture across the HR function.

The focus on business value and running people analytics like a business has only intensified. Examples of impactful people analytics, helpfully curated and published in annual collections, contain resources for the curious and provide a fascinating insight into the evolution of the field (Green, 2017, 2018, 2019a, 2020a and 2021).

New technology emerged to gather and analyse Big Data from new sources such as social media and networks. Such technologies and the business cases for their use have started to become popular. Early pioneers in this space include Michael Arena, whose book, *Adaptive Space: How GM and other companies are positively disrupting themselves and transforming into agile organizations* (2018) explores how networks between people and organizations deliver significant value.

Other specializations, particularly around skills, began to emerge. One of the most important was the use of storytelling to bring data to life – in other words, moving data from science to business, and from research to action. The most powerful book on this topic was *Storytelling with Data: A data visualization guide for business professionals* by Cole Nussbaumer Knaflic (2018). She, along with other specialists, now teaches these techniques to HR practitioners and analysts, boosting the analytical capability of the entire human resources profession.

The Age of Innovation saw people analytics shift from being a supplementary function within HR to a core component of people strategy of the business overall. It has helped create business-aligned human resources organizations across the globe. This was highlighted in the 2017 report by Corporate Research Forum, Strategic Workforce Analytics (Levenson and Pillans, 2017), which revealed that 69 per cent of organizations with 10,000 employees or more had a people analytics team. By the close of the decade, people analytics was appearing in organizations of all sizes, industries and geographies.

Concurrently, there has been a swell of talent entering the field to feed this rapid rise in demand. According to research by LinkedIn in 2018, there was a three-fold increase between 2013 and 2018 in the number of HR professionals in North America who list 'analytics skills' in their LinkedIn profiles (LinkedIn Talent Solutions, 2018c).

This phenomenon is not restricted to North America, either. The regions of Asia-Pacific (APAC) and Europe, Middle East and Africa (EMEA) told similar stories, with a 70 per cent increase over the same period (2013–18) in APAC and a 61 per cent increase in EMEA between 2017 and 2018 (LinkedIn Talent Solutions, 2018a, b). These increases are a combination of human resources professionals acquiring the skills to do analytics and an influx of data science and analytics professionals into HR from other areas of the business such as finance, marketing and operations.

The business impact of all of this is reflected in the 2019 Accenture study highlighted previously: 91 per cent of 1,400 C-level business leaders it surveyed across 13 major companies recognized that new technologies and sources of workplace data could be used to unlock value that is 'trapped' in the enterprise. The study also reported that 62 per cent of these organizations were already using new sources of workforce data to a large or significant extent (Shook, Knickrehm and Sage-Gavin, 2019).

Further evidence of the surge in people analytics came to light in Deloitte's Global Human Capital Trends Report 2018, which identified 'People Data' as the joint most important trend as rated by over 11,000 respondents. To those who had been in the people analytics field for over five years (like us), this recognition felt like a landmark moment.

With the benefit of hindsight, perhaps we shouldn't be surprised. An increasing number of case studies emphasizing the business value derived from people analytics appeared in major publications.

One very clear example that emphasized the essence of business value from people analytics came from a company outside the technology space: global data company Nielsen, which discovered that for every 1 per cent of employee attrition, it could avoid $5 million in business costs.[2] The analysis also revealed other insights (such as internal mobility as the key driver of retention), but it was the direct link between a people insight and a financial metric that saw business executives connect with and get excited about people analytics. Nielsen combined statistics with strong communication to stakeholders and clear storytelling around both business value and benefits to the employees.

A further innovative example of how analytics is quantifying value comes from Unilever. Their chief human resources officer outlined that for every $1.00 the company invests in employee well-being, it provides a return of $2.50 (Green, 2019b).

Both the Nielsen and Unilever examples underline the capability that people data can deliver to both the business and employee. And it is this that leads us to The Age of Value.

The Age of Value: 2020–2025

The Age of Value

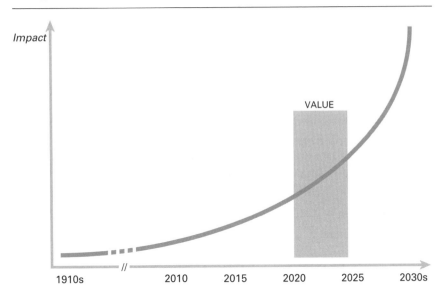

Just as business leaders and chief human resources officers now widely recognize the value that people analytics can provide, so do human resources professionals themselves. Research conducted in 2019 found that 82 per cent of HR practitioners believed people analytics drives business value shown in Figure 0.3 (Styr, 2020).

The World Economic Forum (2019) published its report, HR 4.0: Shaping people strategies in the Fourth Industrial Revolution, which identified six imperatives for the HR function of the future. All six are underpinned by people data and analytics. These observations were supported by LinkedIn, in

Figure 0.3   Question: Do you believe that people analytics drives business value?

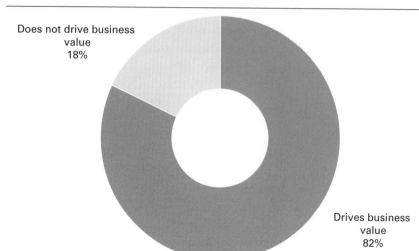

Does not drive business
value
18%

Drives business
value
82%

its Global Talent Trends 2020 Report, which ranked 'People Analytics' as one of the four most important trends in the future of recruiting and human resources.

Another indicator of the explosion of people analytics can be seen in the proliferation of conferences on the topic: from just 24 conferences taking place in 2016, to 150 scheduled for 2020 including prestigious events such as the Wharton People Analytics Conference, People Analytics and the Future of Work and UNLEASH. This is a 500 per cent increase in demand in just 48 months – without even mentioning the growth of digital learning and training (Green, 2016 and 2020b).

The HR technology market also surged, where the number of people analytics technology vendors has dramatically increased, as detailed in a 2020 report from RedThread Research (Garr and Mehrotra, 2020). Major acquisitions indicate the enormous valuations that people data firms carry. Indeed, LinkedIn's acquisition by Microsoft in 2016 for $26.2 billion was the first of many in this space (Microsoft News Center, 2016).

As 2019 turned into 2020, the field of people analytics, to paraphrase Harold MacMillan, Prime Minister of the United Kingdom from 1957 to 1963, had 'never had it so good'.

2020 was a pivotal year in people analytics. With the triple crises of the global COVID-19 pandemic, racial inequality and financial uncertainty, people analytics had to step up. They were required to provide data and information to C-suite executives in rapid response to the global pandemic in topics such as remote working, infection, absenteeism and mental well-being. This pushed the function of people analytics to new levels of urgency and accuracy for daily operational decisions and longer-term strategic scenario planning.

As such, there was an indication that people analytics – as a function within organizations - was investing in both people and technology to address these increased demands. A study by Insight222 Research in 2020 revealed that 93 per cent of HR functions would increase or maintain the size of their people analytics function even amid the financial uncertainty created by the global pandemic (Figure 0.4a). Furthermore, 97 per cent would increase or maintain their technology investment in people analytics (Figure 0.4b) (Ferrar, Styr and Ktena, 2020).

Supported by the data and insights provided by people analytics, the role of the chief human resources officer became ever-more critical in 2020. 'In a pandemic, a Chief People Officer can make or break a company', began an article in *The Economist* comparing the criticality of the role to that played by the chief financial officer (CFO) during the global financial crisis. The article profiles three CHROs (from IBM, Amazon and Electronic Arts) and the role they played to help their respective organizations through the crisis and their ability to provide data-driven insights that enabled their organizations to take action (The Economist, 2020).

Figure 0.4a   Question: Relative to the rest of HR, over the next 18–24 months, is the people analytics team in your company expected overall to increase or decrease? (n = 60)

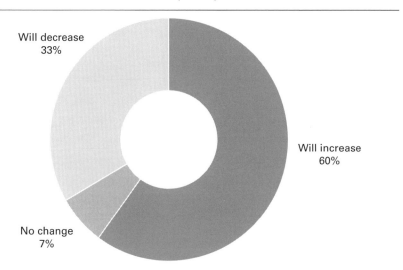

Figure 0.4b   Question: Regarding your investment in technology supporting people analytics, is your investment over the next 18–24 months likely to increase? (n=60)

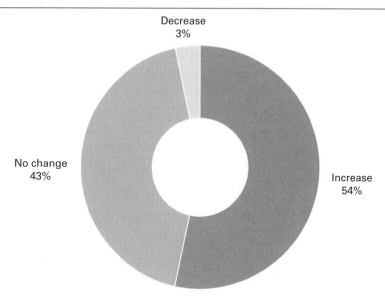

Decrease
3%

No change
43%

Increase
54%

Furthermore, this era is defined by people analytics, delivering value directly to the business. The Age of Value is characterized by four requirements or 'pillars':

i   more **trust** between stakeholder groups especially executives and leaders;

ii   more **inclusion** in the work environment, rather than focusing on 'just' the topic of diversity;

iii a greater **purpose** to a 'higher calling';

iv   a greater sense of **equality**.

These are shaped by eight megatrends (Figure 0.5):

1   rapid technological advances;

2   raised intensity of competition;

3   increased demand for skills;

4   consumer-like employee expectations;

5   exponential growth in people data;

6   shifting labour demographics;

7   new work models;

8   changing regulatory environment.

Figure 0.5   The Age of Value is characterized by trust, inclusion, purpose and
equality, with eight megatrends influencing demand and activity

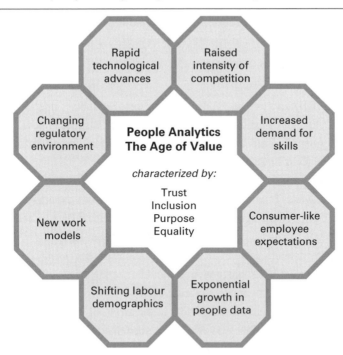

There is a widespread view that many, if not all, of these megatrends have
been accelerated further by the pandemic. For example, in a 2020 *Forbes*
article, Heather McGowan asserted: 'where we once saw the future of work
unfolding over years, we now believe that with coronavirus as an accelerant,
everything we've predicted about the future of work will unfold in months'
(McGowan, 2020).

Throughout all our research, we searched for companies that demonstrated a sense of understanding of The Age of Value. We looked for those
that focused on the most pressing business issues and delivered material
value. We considered those that had a focus on the four 'pillars' and eight
megatrends outlined above too. One of those companies is National Australia
Bank, and its story emphasizes the shape of people analytics in The Age of
Value.

 **CASE STUDY**

People analytics in practice: National Australia Bank

There are two words in people analytics – 'people' and 'analytics'. National Australia Bank[3] is one of the best examples of these two working together in harmony.

In a 2020 *iTnews* article, Thomas Rasmussen, Executive General Manager, Employee Experience, Digital & Analytics, discusses how National Australia Bank uses people analytics to unlock the power of 40,000 staff (Crozier, 2020).

Recognized as one of the world's leading practitioners in the field of people analytics, Thomas developed his people analytics expertise while building the functions at A.P. Møller – Maersk[4] and Royal Dutch Shell[5] before taking up the reins at National Australia Bank in 2017. He consistently delivers value to all the organizations he works with, guided by one principle: 'All people analytics should drive business value as long as the psychology of people is realized'.

Thomas always puts business value at the forefront. He believes that people analytics best delivers value when positioned in HR to leverage the psychology of people and that technology is an enabler to scale solutions across the enterprise.

'Start with something the business cares deeply about,' Thomas advises. 'If you involve them throughout, they will use analytics intelligently to make decisions.'

The best example of a business-driven people analytics project that Thomas initiated during his first year at the bank was to understand the people drivers of business performance in the retail bank.

Sally Smith, Head of People Insights and Research at National Australia Bank, who led the project, reminisces: 'It all started when a senior business leader approached us with a hypothesis they wanted to investigate with data.'

The senior business leader believed that good leadership, high employee engagement and the right team all working together drives higher customer satisfaction at the local bank branch level.

The people analytics team quickly discovered that this belief was widely shared among other key stakeholders. 'We sensed a real desire in the business to test this hypothesis with data,' Sally explains. 'Would the data substantiate this, and if so, what would be the key drivers of customer satisfaction?'

People data alone was not going to help understand this business situation; the people analytics team needed to work with the bank's other analytics experts. Partnering with their colleagues in other enterprise analytics teams, the team merged customer Net Promoter Score, real estate and market segmentation data and financial data, and in doing so joined together commercial data with people data (Figure 0.6).

Data privacy was carefully considered. The team worked closely with the bank's Data Privacy Officer, and anonymity was preserved throughout the analysis with all data held at the aggregate level only.

Figure 0.6   Examples of typical data sources for a customer, engagement, financial analysis

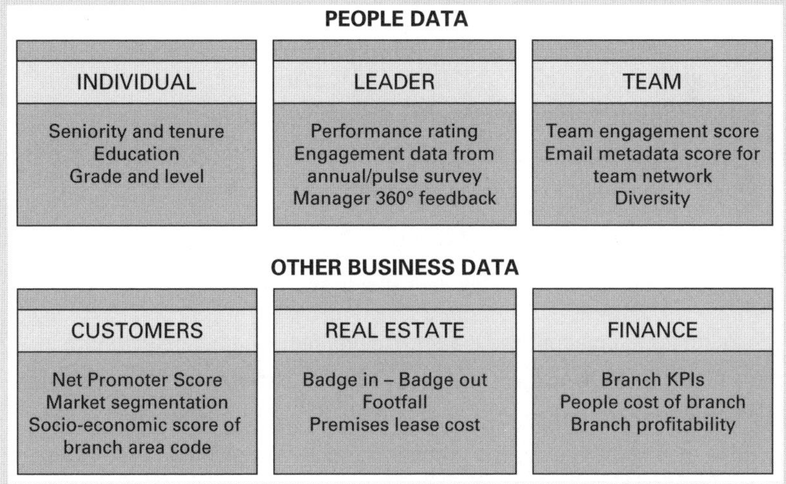

PEOPLE DATA

INDIVIDUAL	LEADER	TEAM
Seniority and tenure Education Grade and level	Performance rating Engagement data from annual/pulse survey Manager 360° feedback	Team engagement score Email metadata score for team network Diversity

OTHER BUSINESS DATA

CUSTOMERS	REAL ESTATE	FINANCE
Net Promoter Score Market segmentation Socio-economic score of branch area code	Badge in – Badge out Footfall Premises lease cost	Branch KPIs People cost of branch Branch profitability

SOURCE Reproduced with kind permission of National Australia Bank, 7 May 2020

While Thomas had only been at the bank for a little more than a year, the team were able to undertake the analysis with seven years of longitudinal data. This applied to both the people data and the commercial data sources in most cases. This meant the team had a very rich dataset with which to perform the statistical analysis and linkage to Net Promoter Score.

In line with his philosophy of how to conduct a successful project, Thomas recalls that the people analytics team worked closely with the business sponsors throughout the analysis:

'From a change perspective, having sponsors engaged right from the start enabled the work to progress quickly. Leaders were consulted in an iterative fashion with results so that subsequent hypotheses could be tested.'

By the end of the journey, the project sponsors and other business stakeholders were motivated by the analysis and invested in the project – there was now real impetus for action.

The key finding of the project was the relationship between certain people factors and customer satisfaction. This was the first time that people factors had been measured and statistically proven to affect customer satisfaction. The three most significant people factors identified were:

1 **Employee engagement**: As Thomas reveals: 'In branches with the highest employee engagement, the customer satisfaction is twice as high.' The detailed analysis found that a leader rated highly by their team drives higher engagement than a leader that was rated poorly by their team. The good leaders drive employee engagement, which in turn drives customer satisfaction.

2 **Average tenure in role**: The bank found that tenure in role was a far more accurate barometer of capability than competencies. As the proportion of the team with at least two years tenure in role increased then the customer experience improved.

3 **Safety:** Customer satisfaction improved as the number of reported incidents, accidents and sick days in a branch decreased.

'We found that accomplished leaders driving high engagement, tenure in role and a safe working environment are key ingredients for high customer satisfaction,' says Thomas.

'To some extent, the analysis proved executive intuition. However, the beauty of the analysis was that we had evidence-based proof for the actual factors that affect customer satisfaction and therefore business performance.' Thomas reflects: 'It made it tangible. We gave leaders the actual data and insights. They loved it. It made them realize what we could do and how they could use people analytics to improve their branch performance.'

The bank's findings were in line with external academic research, which finds that people factors are responsible for 20–25 per cent of customer satisfaction.

The people analytics team also demonstrated the direction of causality over time, finding that if a good leader is replaced by a bad leader as rated by their team, employee engagement starts to drop. Average tenure in role then starts to fall as employees leave: who wants to work for a bad leader? The number of reported incidents, accidents and sick days also increase as employee well-being is given less attention. This creates a negative spiral where customer satisfaction is impacted and NPS scores begin to diminish.

The opposite is true also. The data showed that in instances where a great leader is appointed to a branch, the people factors mentioned all shift in the right direction and this leads to the customer satisfaction scores improving, too.

The fact that the analysis had longitudinal data enabled the team to demonstrate the direction of causality.

As invariably is the case with people analytics, the team also identified one unexpected insight in their analysis: branches led by female leaders had a higher customer satisfaction score on average than those led by male leaders. An unexpected finding like this leads people analytics experts to conduct further analyses to identify underlying causes such as 'What is it about our female leaders that gives the bank these results?'

The results of the analysis led to a change in the bank's approach to reward, linking branch performance with employee engagement. Moreover, the three key people factors identified were given more prominence, weighting and focus as well as being used as forward-looking metrics to give early indicators to branch performance. Branch leaders like this because the indicators are evidence-based predictors of success.

The project emphasizes the benefit of a cross-functional approach to analytics aligned to a common business challenge. It also demonstrates Thomas's beliefs around business value, scaling analytics and the role that human resources (HR) plays in an evidence-based world.

The business value of people analytics

'If you want to be successful with people analytics,' says Thomas, 'make sure there is an outcome that business executives really care about.'

Throughout his career, Thomas learnt to work closely with business executives, which helped him develop his understanding of each company's internal and external dynamics. He believes that becoming knowledgeable about your business and its environment – both internal and external – is a critical element that makes for a respected people analytics leader. This strengthened Thomas's business acumen and made him a credible partner.

Additionally, Thomas learnt that embedding solutions in the business through effective change management was essential for people analytics. 'Don't underestimate the importance of change management in actioning the insights and driving measurable value. The business leader is the most important part of the change management activity.'

This business-led philosophy and cross-functional collaborative approach is something that Thomas believes truly adds value across the value chain and provides the opportunity to break down traditional silos.

Scaling analytics using technology

Thomas firmly believes that the technology component is critical to scaling people analytics.

'Instead of initiatives that only impact a few hundred people at a time, technology will enable people analytics to provide a positive impact for the bank's 40,000-strong workforce. That's what I think is truly exciting about technology,' says Thomas. 'And that [scale] actually also then gives us data that we can feed back into the process.'

Furthermore, National Australia Bank has merged people analytics with employee experience and digital HR technology (Figure 0.7) to create a powerhouse that delivers evidence-based management and the consumerization of the employee relationship.

Figure 0.7   People analytics at National Australia Bank

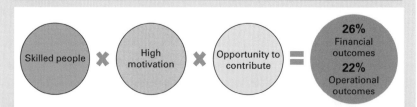

SOURCE Reproduced with kind permission of National Australia Bank, 7 May 2020

'The analytics will tell you how you are doing and what works. The employee experience will help you tweak it, make it intuitive, make sure people use it and that it is adopted by the business. The digital component enables you to scale it.'

With this approach, Thomas has expanded his responsibility to include employee experience, HR technology and people analytics. This is the right direction for excellence in people analytics.

The role of HR in an evidence-based world

As the field of people analytics has developed, conflicting opinions have emerged as to whether the function should be based in HR or under a company-wide function such as strategy or enterprise analytics.

This is a topic that Thomas addressed in his seminal paper, co-authored with Dave Ulrich in 2015, on how HR avoids being a management fad.

At the time, Thomas and Dave advocated 'taking HR analytics out of HR,' further explaining that: 'Analytics typically only yields truly new insights when multiple fields and perspectives are combined, so any functional denomination prior to "analytics" is really just a sign that it has not matured enough yet to just be a natural part of "analytics".'

Thomas's position on where people analytics should be based in the organization has shifted based on his experience at National Australia Bank. The Chief Data Officer Glenda Crisp's approach provides a template for others to follow.

The bank operates a hub and spoke model through an Enterprise Analytics Data Council, which fosters collaboration, provides access to centrally located technical expertise and drives learning and career opportunities for all analytics professionals across the bank.

The 'hub' is the central enterprise analytics team, providing strong governance, collaboration across different analytical teams and a prioritization framework to ensure that the bank's analytics teams focus on the most important topics across the group.

'As systems and processes become more digitized data becomes the lifeblood of the organization, and it is important to ensure good guidelines and framework are established and clear,' Glenda said in an article published on ZDNet.com (Barbaschow, 2019).

The 'spokes' are the individual specialist analytics teams, which are generally organizationally aligned to each function. The belief is that the expertise of each function is important to guide the analytics. Therefore, it is more effective for people analytics to be close to human resource professionals who can help guide the 'people' part of people analytics to ensure the psychology of humans is brought to the fore in the data science.

Additionally, a programme has been developed to upskill all of the bank's employees in the use of data and analytics as well as the ethics involved. In Barbaschow's aforementioned 2019 article, The Data Guild is referred to as a forum that focuses on 'educating the bank's workforce on the importance of good data governance, data quality, and ethics.'

The success of the bank's approach has led to Thomas changing his mind on whether people analytics should be based in or outside HR.

'To do good customer analytics, you need to understand customers, spend time in a branch and know the bank's products. The same applies for people analytics,' explains Thomas. 'You need to understand the psychology of people and how they behave. This means you can't fully centralize analytics as it risks becoming too distant.'

'People analytics needs to be located in HR but have access to technical expertise from a central analytics team.'

Summary: the case for people analytics

Activities and outcomes like those described in the case study above are discussed throughout this book.

People analytics is no longer a 'nice to have' for companies but an absolute must-have for any chief executive officer or chief human resources officer if they want to positively impact all of the stakeholders across the enterprise.

The Age of Excellence

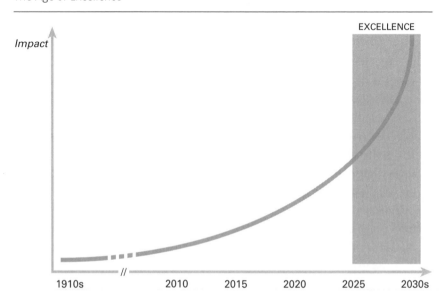

The Nine Dimensions discussed in the remainder of this book, if conducted well, will improve the value that can be derived from people analytics – and in turn, deliver 'Excellence'.

Creating value – at scale, among the HR profession, worldwide in multiple countries and organizations – will transition us to The Age of Excellence.

References

Arena, M J (2018) *Adaptive Space: How GM and other companies are positively disrupting themselves and transforming into agile organizations*, McGraw-Hill, New York, NY

Barbaschow, A (2019) NAB doubles down on value of data and analytics with new in-house guilds [Online] ZDNet, 11 July. Available from: https://www.zdnet.com/article/nab-doubles-down-on-value-of-data-and-analytics-with-new-in-house-guilds/ (archived at https://perma.cc/D35R-YJAW) [Last accessed 7 February 2021]

Becker, B, Ulrich, D and Huselid, M A (2001) *The HR Scorecard: Linking people, strategy and performance*, Harvard Business School Press, Brighton, MA

Bersin by Deloitte (2013) High-Impact Talent Analytics: building a world-class measurement and analytics function [Report] SHRM. Available from: https://www.shrm.org/ResourcesAndTools/hr-topics/technology/Documents/hita100113sg.pdf (archived at https://perma.cc/6VDY-E5HK) [Last accessed 7 February 2021]

Bersin, J (2015) The geeks arrive in HR: people analytics is here, *Forbes*, 1 February. Available from: https://www.forbes.com/sites/joshbersin/2015/02/01/geeks-arrive-in-hr-people-analytics-is-here/?sh=6c2ce2fe73b4 (archived at https://perma.cc/VN5H-4L7D) [Last accessed 7 February 2021]

Bock, L (2015) *Work Rules! Insights from inside Google that will transform how you live and lead*, John Murray Press, London

Bock, L (2019) You learn best when you learn less, *Harvard Business Review*, 17 June. Available from: https://hbr.org/2019/06/you-learn-best-when-you-learn-less (archived at https://perma.cc/UL37-GXCN) [Last accessed 7 February 2021]

C&J Clark Limited (2019) Annual Report and Financial Statements for the year ended 2 February 2019. Available from: https://find-and-update.company-information.service.gov.uk/company/03314066/filing-history?page=1 (archived at https://perma.cc/2T7X-UKMR) [Last accessed 12 March 2021]

Chakrabarti, M (2017) High-Impact People Analytics Industry [Report] Bersin by Deloitte, Oakland, CA

Crozier, R (2020) NAB uses 'people analytics' to unlock power of 40k staff, *iTnews*, 10 March. Available from: https://www.itnews.com.au/news/nab-uses-people-analytics-to-unlock-power-of-40k-staff-539112 (archived at https://perma.cc/VC82-4QA8) [Last accessed 7 February 2021]

Davenport, T H, Harris, J and Shapiro, J (2010) Competing on talent analytics, *Harvard Business Review*, 88 (10), pp 52–8 (October)

Deloitte (2018) Global human capital trends report [Report] Deloitte Development LLC. Available from: https://www2.deloitte.com/us/en/insights/focus/human-capital-trends/2018.html (archived at https://perma.cc/48NG-ARHS) [Last accessed 7 February 2021]

Duhigg, C (2016) What Google learned from its quest to build the perfect team, *The New York Times Magazine*, 25 February. Available from: https://www.nytimes.com/2016/02/28/magazine/what-google-learned-from-its-quest-to-build-the-perfect-team.html (archived at https://perma.cc/Z4KD-GQY8) [Last accessed 7 February 2021]

Edwards, M R and Edwards, K (2019) *Predictive HR Analytics: Mastering the HR metric*, 2nd edn, Kogan Page, London

Garr, S and Mehrotra, P (2020) People Analytics Technology Vendors: What you need to know [Report] RedThread Research, 3 December. Available from: https://redthreadresearch.com/pat-the-vendors/ (archived at https://perma.cc/27PL-M2G2) [Last accessed 7 February 2021]

Garvin, D A (2013) How Google sold its engineers on management, *Harvard Business Review* (December). Available from: https://hbr.org/2013/12/how-google-sold-its-engineers-on-management (archived at https://perma.cc/PSE4-JXXR) [Last accessed 7 February 2021]

Green, D (2016) 24 Conferences on people analytics to attend in 2016/17 [Blog] LinkedIn, 20 July. Available from: https://www.linkedin.com/pulse/22-conferences-people-analytics-attend-201617-david-green/ (archived at https://perma.cc/VJN9-8HWZ) [Last accessed 7 February 2021]

Green, D (2017) The 30 best HR analytics articles of 2016 [Blog] LinkedIn, 23 January. Available from: https://www.linkedin.com/pulse/30-best-hr-analytics-articles-2016-david-green (archived at https://perma.cc/6CDJ-DC3V) [Last accessed 7 February 2021]

Green, D (2018) Top 40 HR & people analytics articles of 2017 [Blog] LinkedIn, 15 January. Available from: https://www.linkedin.com/pulse/top-40-hr-people-analytics-articles-2017-david-green (archived at https://perma.cc/F2PN-3RQV) [Last accessed 7 February 2021]

Green, D (2019a) Top 40 HR & people analytics articles of 2018 [Blog] LinkedIn, 7 January. Available from: https://www.linkedin.com/pulse/top-40-hr-people-analytics-articles-2018-david-green (archived at https://perma.cc/RK6F-SU5G) [Last accessed 7 February 2021]

Green, D (2019b) Using HR analytics and technology to drive business value at Unilever [Podcast] myHRfuture, 8 October. Available from: https://www.myhrfuture.com/digital-hr-leaders-podcast/2019/10/8/using-hr-analytics-and-technology-to-drive-business-value-at-unilever (archived at https://perma.cc/68K7-QGW7) [Last accessed 7 February 2021]

Green, D (2020a) The best HR and people analytics articles of 2019 [Blog] LinkedIn, 13 January. Available from: https://www.linkedin.com/pulse/best-hr-people-analytics-articles-2019-david-green (archived at https://perma.cc/UY75-5KKA) [Last accessed 7 February 2021]

Green, D (2020b) 150+ Conferences to attend in 2020 on HR tech, people analytics, employee experience and the future of work [Blog] myHRfuture. 30 December. Available from: https://www.myhrfuture.com/blog/2019/12/30/150-conferences-to-attend-in-2020-on-hr-tech-people-analytics-employee-experience-and-the-future-of-work (archived at https://perma.cc/MD8U-URVM) [Last accessed 7 February 2021]

Green, D (2021) The best HR and people analytics articles of 2020 [Blog] LinkedIn, 7 January. Available from: https://www.linkedin.com/pulse/best-hr-people-analytics-articles-2020-david-green (archived at https://perma.cc/2ACW-HYXC) [Last accessed 7 February 2021]

Guenole, N, Ferrar, J and Feinzig, S (2017) *The Power of People: Learn how successful organizations use workforce analytics to improve business performance*, Pearson, London

Ferrar, J, Styr, C and Ktena, A (2020) Delivering Value at Scale: A new operating model for people analytics [Report] Insight222 Research, 24 November 2020. Available from: https://www.insight222.com/people-analytics-operating-model-research (archived at https://perma.cc/J53L-DU95) [Last accessed 7 February 2021]

Levenson, A (2015) *Strategic Analytics: Advancing strategy execution and organizational effectiveness*, Berrett-Koehler Publishers, Oakland, CA

Levenson, A and Pillans, G (2017) Strategic Workforce Analytics [Report] Corporate Research Forum, 11 March. Available from: https://www.crforum.co.uk/research-and-resources/research-report-strategic-workforce-analytics/ (archived at https://perma.cc/4A4F-G297) [Last accessed 7 February 2021]

LinkedIn Talent Solutions (2018a) The Rise of Analytics in HR: An era of talent intelligence, Asia-Pacific [Report] Available at: https://business.linkedin.com/content/dam/me/business/en-us/talent-solutions/cx/2018/pdf/full-report.pdf (archived at https://perma.cc/VHG2-Z6FE) [Last accessed 7 February 2021]

LinkedIn Talent Solutions (2018b) The Rise of Analytics in HR: The era of talent intelligence is here, EMEA [Report] Available at: https://business.linkedin.com/content/dam/me/business/en-us/talent-solutions/talent-intelligence/workforce/pdfs/Final_EMEA_Rise-of-Analytics-Report.pdf (archived at https://perma.cc/CCY8-48S7) [Last accessed 29 January 2021]

LinkedIn Talent Solutions (2018c) The Rise of Analytics in HR: The era of talent intelligence is here, North America [Report] Available at: https://business.linkedin.com/content/dam/me/business/en-us/talent-solutions/talent-intelligence/workforce/pdfs/Final_v4_NAMER_Rise-of-Analytics-Report.pdf (archived at https://perma.cc/UG8W-FY48) [Last accessed 7 February 2021]

Martin, L (2018) The Age of People Analytics: Survey on characteristics, value achieved, and leading practices of advanced organizations [Report] Visier. Available from: https://hello.visier.com/age-of-people-analytics-research-report. html (archived at https://perma.cc/HK5Q-6ZKZ) [Last accessed 7 February 2021]

McAleer, K (2018) Humu is using machine learning to create a happier workplace, Berkeley Sutardja Center for Entrepreneurship & Technology, 20 November. Available from: https://scet.berkeley.edu/humu-is-using-machine-learning-to-make-a-happier-workplace/ (archived at https://perma.cc/476Y-24QE) [Last accessed 7 February 2021]

McGowan, H E (2020) How the coronavirus pandemic is accelerating the future of work, *Forbes*, 23 March. Available from: https://www.forbes.com/sites/heather mcgowan/2020/03/23/the-coronavirus-pandemic-accelerates-the-future-of-work-and-provides-opportunity/ (archived at https://perma.cc/UG3J-7CVE) [Last accessed 7 February 2021]

Microsoft News Center (2016) Microsoft to acquire LinkedIn [Blog] Microsoft, 13 June. Available from: https://news.microsoft.com/2016/06/13/microsoft-to-acquire-linkedin/ (archived at https://perma.cc/MH2H-7MR7) [Last accessed 24 April 2021]

Nussbaumer Knaflic, C (2018) *Storytelling with Data: A data visualization guide for business professionals,* Wiley, New York, NY

Rasmussen, T and Ulrich, D (2015) Learning from practice: how HR analytics avoids being a management fad, *Organizational Dynamics*, **44** (3), pp 236–42 (May)

Rosenbaum, E (2019) IBM artificial intelligence can predict with 95% accuracy which workers are about to quit their jobs, CNBC, 3 April. Available from: https://www.cnbc.com/2019/04/03/ibm-ai-can-predict-with-95-percent-accuracy-which-employees-will-quit.html (archived at https://perma.cc/PL4Q-5NDM) [Last accessed 7 February 2021]

Shook, E, Knickrehm, M and Sage-Gavin, E (2019) Decoding Organizational DNA: Trust, data and unlocking value in the digital workplace [Report] Accenture. Available from: https://www.accenture.com/gb-en/insights/future-workforce/workforce-data-organizational-dna (archived at https://perma.cc/X77G-Y66R) [Last accessed 7 February 2021]

Sierra-Cedar (2014) Sierra-Cedar HR Systems Survey. Available from: http://humanresourcereports.info/resourcefiles/9bbfd85f-d9b7-479c-b104-81c0f46eb47a_Sierra-Cedar_2014-2015_HRSystemsSurveyWhitePaper.pdf (archived at https://perma.cc/BD6K-7DQ5) [Last accessed 7 February 2021]

Styr, C (2020) How to build a data-driven culture in HR [Blog] myHRfuture, 24 July. Available from: https://www.myhrfuture.com/blog/2018/10/31/how-do-you-build-a-data-driven-culture-in-hr (archived at https://perma.cc/82HQ-FYHU) [Last accessed 7 February 2021]

Taylor, F (1911) *The Principles of Scientific Management*, Harper & Brothers, New York. Available from: http://strategy.sjsu.edu/www.stable/pdf/Taylor,%20F.%20 W.%20(1911).%20New%20York,%20Harper%20&%20Brothers.pdf (archived at https://perma.cc/FSU7-BYRM) [Last accessed 7 February 2021]

The Economist (2020) The coronavirus crisis thrusts corporate HR chiefs into the spotlight, *The Economist*, 24 March. Available from: https://www.economist. com/business/2020/03/24/the-coronavirus-crisis-thrusts-corporate-hr-chiefs-into-the-spotlight (archived at https://perma.cc/AL99-4WYD) [Last accessed 7 February 2021]

Waber, B (2013) *People Analytics: How social sensing technology will transform business and what it tells us about the Future of Work*, FT Press, London, UK

World Economic Forum (2019) HR 4.0: Shaping people strategies in the Fourth Industrial Revolution [Report]. Available from: https://www.weforum.org/ reports/hr4-0-shaping-people-strategies-in-the-fourth-industrial-revolution (archived at https://perma.cc/289J-5SCE) [Last accessed 7 February 2021]

Notes

1 Best Buy Co, Inc is a US multinational consumer electronics retailer headquartered in Richfield, Minnesota.

2 The Nielsen case study is outlined on pp 59–64 in Guenole, Ferrar and Feinzig (2017).

3 Headquartered in Melbourne, National Australia Bank is one of the largest banks in the world, serving over 9,000,000 customers across more than 900 locations in Australia, New Zealand and around the world.

4 A.P. Møller – Maersk, also known as Maersk, is a Danish integrated container logistics company and boasts a team of 76,000 operating in 130 countries (see https://www.maersk.com/about (archived at https://perma.cc/344V-HW8F), last accessed 31 January 2021).

5 Royal Dutch Shell – or Shell as it is better known – is a 'supermajor' group of energy and petrochemical companies headquartered in the Netherlands. Made up of 82,000 employees across the globe, Shell is regularly listed as one of the top three biggest companies in the world (see https://www.shell.com/about-us. html (archived at https://perma.cc/7X3N-QXBG), last accessed 31 January 2021).

PART TWO
Nine Dimensions for Excellence in People Analytics

Governance 01

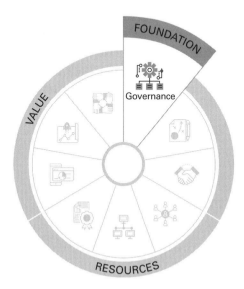

In this chapter, we examine the solid foundation that allows for robust structures, high-class standards and engaged people to keep the people analytics function accountable to their mission.

DISCOVER...

- why the corporate strategy is the foundation for people analytics;
- the importance of creating a brand and mission;
- how to create stewardship, accountability and enablement.

WITH INSIGHTS FROM...

- Novartis International A.G., on aligning people analytics to the business strategy;
- Trimble, Inc., on creating a brand for people analytics that enhances credibility;
- Lloyds Banking Group, on establishing ethical standards for people analytics.

Overview

> ## GOVERNANCE
>
> Governance, as one of the Nine Dimensions, refers to the mechanisms, processes and procedures by which people analytics 'operates'. It underpins all analytics and ensures the right people provide direction for work, that the structure and stewardship for managing data and projects are implemented and applicable, and that risks are managed appropriately.

People analytics requires sound governance to apply principles of accountability, responsibility, transparency and collaboration. It is grounded in the following areas: aligning people analytics with corporate strategy, providing a mission and brand for the people analytics function, creating stewardship, accountability and enablement and finally, having a strong operating model. The first three of these are the subject of this chapter.

The latter is discussed in Chapter 4 (Skills), where the operating model is reviewed in detail in the context of how the team is best organized. We also outline the operating model in the context of the People Analytics Value Chain in Chapter 8 (Business Outcomes).

Sadly, the topic of governance for people analytics is generally met with a lack of enthusiasm, or even scepticism. It is unusual to find human resources executives or people analytics professionals who actually want to spend time and money on establishing strong governance for people analytics. Indeed, we regularly hear comments such as 'We don't need more steering committees!' and 'Are you sure that we need to spend time on governance? We know who to go to when we need them!' Our research taught us that the difficulty with this stance is that by the time people analytics teams need to engage the right people, it is too late.

In our experience, few human resources executives want to spend money on good governance for people analytics. As we will see in Chapter 6 (Data), executives will often procure a core HR platform for millions of dollars, willingly, in the belief that this solves all analytics issues. But the task of extracting investment in sensible, agile and dynamic governance, even though it's a fraction of the cost, is more of a challenge.

Governance is invariably the difference between good work and great work. It can also define one's reputation; the difference between being regarded as credible – or not. This is why governance is a foundational element of all successful businesses. And, governance as a topic has been embedded in businesses for centuries. Four recent definitions of corporate governance are:

> Corporate governance is the collection of mechanisms, processes and relations by which corporations are controlled and operated. (Shailer, 2004)

> Governance structures and principles identify the distribution of rights and responsibilities among different participants in the corporation and include the rules and procedures for making decisions in corporate affairs. (Lin, 2011)

> Corporate governance is the system that allocates duties and authority among a company's stockholders, board of directors and management. Recognized principles help guide the advancement of corporate governance as well as the ability of US public corporations to compete in the global marketplace, create jobs and generate economic growth. (SHRM, 2016)

> Good corporate governance is about effectively supervising the management of a company to uphold the company's integrity, achieve more open and rigorous procedures and ensure legal compliance. Ultimately it should also promote good relations with stakeholders, including shareholders and employees. (CIPD, 2020)

Refined in the context of our experience and the Nine Dimensions, we recommend that governance for people analytics is best defined as:

> The mechanisms, processes and procedures by which a company operates and manages risk for people analytics.

Governance underpins all analytics, ensuring good standards and roles. It provides the right people for the right work, the structure and stewardship for managing data, and the management of associated risks are clearly and properly conducted.

Without governance, analytics work loses focus and the risk of conducting unnecessary work with generating substandard value increases. In worst-case scenarios, poor governance increases the risk of negative publicity and an increased chance of reputational damage. In the very worst-case scenarios, it could lead to fines, such as those levied of up to 4 per cent of company global annual revenues for lack of compliance to GDPR regulations[1] (IT Governance Privacy Team, 2020), such as in the case of H&M, which was fined €35.3 million over employee surveillance (BBC News, 2020).

Figure 1.1   Why implement governance for people analytics?

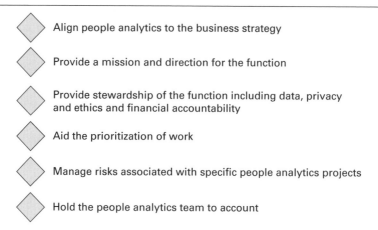

Align people analytics to the business strategy

Provide a mission and direction for the function

Provide stewardship of the function including data, privacy and ethics and financial accountability

Aid the prioritization of work

Manage risks associated with specific people analytics projects

Hold the people analytics team to account

We have observed that decisions made without effective governance can centre around the HIPPO principle[2] or the 'one who shouts the loudest'. Without criteria-based prioritization, the team could be working on Pet Projects or Trivial Endeavours (see Chapter 2, Methodology) or have wildly varying levels of sponsorship for different opinions, and hypotheses change due to stakeholders changing their mind.

Throughout the rest of this chapter, we will discuss three types of governance for people analytics:

- aligning people analytics with corporate strategy;
- providing a mission and brand for the function;
- creating stewardship, accountability and enablement.

Aligning people analytics with corporate strategy

In the research for this book, we heard many of the following phrases from people analytics leaders. They indicate that the leaders lacked focus and direction:

i   The HR leadership team doesn't agree on priorities for people analytics.

ii   Which 'Quick Win' project should I work on?

iii I would like to add a new member to my team, but I don't know which country to recruit them in.

iv I would like to influence the roles and responsibilities of the 'data reporting team' but they don't report to me.

v How can I secure more investment for analytics?

vi How can I prove the value for analytics?

When discussing these topics more deeply, it was clear that these questions were hiding the underlying problems of lack of clarity on the mission, conflicting or overlapping priorities and a feeling of inadequacy.

When working with certain teams, we found that several actions implemented well could reverse this situation. Each action was actually relatively simple to implement, but the topics had been discarded for too long. In these companies, we found that human resources leaders were often so busy 'doing' that they were not 'thinking' – when it came to people analytics.

Actions recommended to companies of this nature are to:

- meet stakeholders to understand the business challenges and most important topics (see Chapter 3, Stakeholder Management);
- align the people analytics mission to the corporate strategy;
- be realistic about what can be achieved;
- establish effective prioritization (see Chapter 2, Methodology).

One example of this in practice is described in the case study below, Start with strategy: Novartis. The new people analytics leader started with one clear objective: aligning everything the team does with the corporate strategy. The key message is: *Good things will happen when you align people analytics work with corporate strategy.*

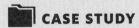

CASE STUDY

Start with strategy: Novartis

Since becoming Chief Executive Officer in 2018, Dr Vasant 'Vas' Narasimhan has led a strategic and cultural transformation at Novartis[3] to build a leading medicines company globally powered by advanced therapy platforms and data science.

One of Vas's first moves in the organization was to refocus the corporate strategy on five priorities (see Figure 1.2).

Figure 1.2   The five priorities of Novartis's strategy

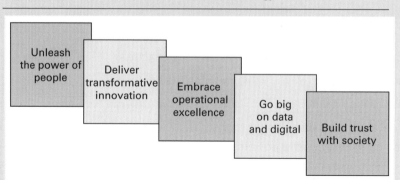

SOURCE Novartis (2021), reproduced with kind permission of Novartis, April 2021

We first met the Novartis People & Organization (P&O) team in November 2018. The first thing that struck us was that the team never used the term 'HR' – it was, still is, and likely always will be, 'P&O'. It's as if Novartis has taken the old proverb 'The beginning of wisdom is to call things by their proper name'[4] to heart: there is such a strong culture of 'doing things' that even the organization's language is aligned to its work. With this specific use of language in mind, we were keen to understand what the words of the fourth priority, 'Go big on data and digital,' would mean. How does people analytics 'go big' quickly?

We were struck by the way that Chief People & Organization Officer Steven Baert was focused on creating an analytical mindset to drive organizational change in areas such as culture and performance.

This was emphasized upon meeting Tripti Jha, Chief Talent and People Solutions Officer, in early 2019. Tripti explained to us how the 'go big on data and digital' priority was being brought to life in the P&O organization. 'People analytics needs to generate insights that augment the quality of P&O decisions and outcomes. The first step on my journey is to appoint an ambitious people analytics leader who brings in the right mindset towards analytics and understands the organizational context well. I am confident that will happen by Spring.' And it did happen: Ashish Pant was appointed as Global Head of People Analytics in April 2019.

Ashish quickly got going. He started with a small team of five people and focused the first two months on mapping out a three-phase plan covering 2019–2022 (see Figure 1.3) that would establish processes and analytics complementary to Vas's five priorities for Novartis shown above.

Figure 1.3   Novartis's people analytics three-phase plan, 2019–2022

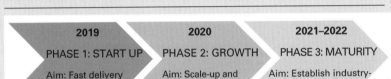

2019	2020	2021–2022
PHASE 1: START UP	PHASE 2: GROWTH	PHASE 3: MATURITY
Aim: Fast delivery of solutions	Aim: Scale-up and delivery	Aim: Establish industry-leading practice

SOURCE Reproduced with kind permission of Novartis, April 2021

In November of 2019, the end of Phase 1, we realized how much planning Ashish had put in. We met him at an event in the Netherlands, and during the evening got an insight into his character and activity. It was on a chilly boat on the Amsterdam canals that we understood Ashish's passion for people analytics. 'Novartis's data is fragmented across HR,' he said between mouthfuls of *rijsttafel*. 'In HR, we are harmonizing the ownership of people data within the people analytics team, while we develop an integrated data strategy. The next step is to tightly tie the data strategy stream into the analytical solution design.' We were struck by how clear the plans were, and how tightly the P&O strategy was aligned to the business.

By the middle of 2020 (Phase 2), it was clear that Novartis's people analytics plan had multiple strands to it, all tied to the overall strategy. While he was working on building an integrated P&O data strategy, Ashish spent time enabling P&O to use data with a series of training modules. In parallel, enterprise analytics solutions in learning, rewards and talent management organizational development (conceptualized in Phase 1) were developed and rolled out in the organization, forming the core of Novartis's People Analytics Centre of Excellence (CoE).

As we write this case study, Ashish is nearing the end of Phase 2. He is keen to reflect and share his learnings from the journey so far.
As shown in Figure 1.4, since the beginning of the three-phase plan, Ashish's team has grown more than five times in size. 'Building an incredible team of data and analytics experts and business partners who really believe in using people data to solve the company's challenges has been the most important part of the last 18 months. We could never fully unlock the business value of people data without them.'

Interestingly, Ashish notes that his roster of teammates is composed of data science and HR skills. 'I personally find that data experts who are

Figure 1.4 Novartis's people analytics team growth

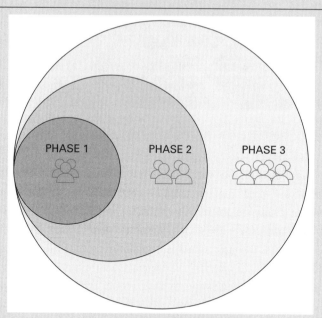

SOURCE Reproduced with kind permission of Novartis, April 2021

taught about HR can have a strong impact in people analytics work, sometimes much more than hiring HR experts and teaching them about statistics and fostering an understanding of what people analytics is trying to achieve.'

At the beginning of 2021, Novartis has started to embark on Phase 3 of the people analytics journey (see Figure 1.3). Ashish sees the team shifting focus to scale-up and growth, aiming to achieve full scale, capability and capacity wise. Internally, the team built and began implementing the P&O data strategy we had discussed on the boat. In the wider business, the focus is on delivering CoE solutions for challenges such as pay equity, learning, culture measurement and scaling them throughout the 100,000+ workforce. Ashish anticipates this will enable the team to grow further in the coming years, making people analytics and data significant parts of the P&O organization, and one of the largest people analytics functions in the world.

The question is, will it deliver impact? Ashish is thoughtful and reflective about this. 'An important goal in 2020 was supporting the development of an analytical mindset within P&O and helping them to value aggregated people data while ensuring individual data privacy. The true goal is delivering value through productizing the solutions – and that is impossible unless we get the culture of P&O right.' Therefore, one of Ashish's focuses in Phase 3 is to build the P&O community of users who are able to think through the underlying business problems and how data can be used to solve them.

Productizing people analytics – and making them useful – for the business means that the analytics team can consult with business stakeholders directly about their people challenges and diagnose the problems that they have in a language those functions all understand. That language is data – underpinned, again, by the fourth Priority (Figure 1.2) in the corporate strategy. Going forward, this will enable Novartis to link P&O with the rest of the organizational objectives as it hurtles along its growth trajectory.

'We are looking to build local customer models that will see the products we developed in 2020 embedded seamlessly into the business. But that needs local support!' Additionally, Ashish explains, that needs the rapid development of proofs of concept (PoCs) to foster buy-in. 'The final piece of the puzzle is to finish rolling out our data strategy. Then we will be in a position to link people data with all other data from around the company. And that is the moment that people analytics will truly be aligned across the entire Novartis business.'

Reflecting on the last two years and our conversations with Steven, Tripti and Ashish, we have consistently been struck by the clarity of vision, alignment to business strategy and methodical approach that Novartis has applied to ensure that operational activity is embedded in the five priorities.

It's one of the more profound examples of where corporate strategy is explicitly integrated into the people analytics function that we have seen in the field: rapidly expanding the people analytics team with a focus on productization and value. The Novartis P&O team really will 'go big on data and digital'.

TOP TIP

Go big or go home!

Providing a mission and brand for the function

One trend we have observed in leading people analytics teams of all sizes and industries is the general business practice of developing a vision statement, a mission statement and a brand for people analytics.

Writing a vision or mission statement has been covered in detail in *The Power of People: Learn how successful organizations use workforce analytics to improve business performance* (Guenole, Ferrar and Feinzig, 2017), so we will not discuss it here in detail. One point is worth paraphrasing: There is no magic formula for writing vision and mission statements, but they should be well informed by stakeholders' views about what is important.

When defining the purpose for the team, it is worth considering the following four items:

Ambition: Clarify the ambition of people analytics with a statement or short document. In essence, this defines the purpose and desire of the team.

Principles: Write short, simple principles to guide the team. This is discussed below in the case study, Credibility begins with a clear brand: Trimble, which includes examples of principles used by the people analytics leader.

Mission: Develop a short statement describing what the people analytics function is going to deliver. For example, as described below, Suku Mariappan outlines that the mission for people analytics at Trimble, Inc. 'must be that at every moment you should solve a business problem – to help the business become better'.

Brand: Produce a defining symbol, icon or logo that distinguishes the function and defines its presence. It will make the people analytics team become more visible and known to the various stakeholders and audiences.

These topics will emerge throughout this book, in different ways and under unique circumstances. But one thing that differentiates leading people analytics teams from others is that they have some – or all – of these items listed above.

We will now move to the case study, Credibility begins with a clear brand: Trimble. The key message is: *Infuse all people analytics activities with high-quality, reliable outputs and a focus on business challenges. That will define your brand and mission for people analytics.*

CASE STUDY

Credibility begins with a clear brand: Trimble

Sukumaran (Suku) Mariappan is the Vice President, Global HR Technology and People Analytics at Trimble, Inc.[5] Since its establishment in 2016, people analytics at Trimble has developed a strong brand within the company – so much so that it has its own logo, which is used as a quality mark denoting that work it produces has been reviewed and validated by Trimble People Analytics.

The brand is underpinned by three guiding principles:

1 Focus on answering questions and solving important business problems rather than metrics, reports and dashboards.

2 Be clear and transparent about data weaknesses and assumptions.

3 Data and insights shared too soon with the wrong people or carelessly can damage trust.

Suku has a clear theory: sticking to these three principles increases the credibility of people analytics. And when credibility is high, insights are implemented and deliver higher business impact.

Several factors support Suku's approach: A chief human resources officer (CHRO) that is committed to analytics, a strong and reliable brand, and the agreement to focus on business problems.

An essential first step was to gain the support of this approach from his manager, Senior Vice President and CHRO, Mike Scarpa. 'This is how we want to operate HR as a function,' says Mike. 'When I talk to my peers or the board [of directors], it is important to provide evidence, so that decision making is easier. If data suggests certainty and is credible, then we will make better decisions. "In data, we trust" to quote an old phrase.'[6]

Suku agrees: 'The vision and commitment of the CHRO to data-driven HR continues to be critical for the long-term success of people analytics.'

The second step involved creating a strong brand for people analytics. This brand was established to deliver insights that have a high level of reliability around business problems that really matter. 'First and foremost, we developed a brand based on credible analysis,' Suku reflects. 'There was no particular moment when we felt we had "arrived". It was more a continual journey of building the brand based on small steps of providing credible facts and insights.'

The brand became so synonymous with quality and reliability that Suku developed a logo (see Figure 1.5) for Trimble People Analytics, which evolved over time. Mike confirms: 'Part of a brand is the visualization of it by using a logo.'

Figure 1.5   Logo for People Analytics at Trimble, Inc.

SOURCE Reproduced with kind permission of Trimble, Inc., August 2020

This logo is a 'stamp of approval' on any people analytics work delivered to stakeholders. Where the logo appears, the recipient knows that the work is credible, of high quality and trustworthy. The power of branding!

Mike confirms: 'Whenever stakeholders see people analyses or insights that have not been stamped with the logo, the people analytics team is asked to validate the findings and insights. Even with our finance team; we have team members coming to us to validate data and insights.'

Finally, the people analytics team focuses on problems that matter. Initially, it focused on Quick Wins such as, 'why are people leaving the company?' As time has gone by and momentum gathered, they focused on more complex topics like how performance management improves business performance.

The focus is always on topics with a business impact.

And the priority is to always apply the right analysis – even if it is a simple analysis over a more complex one – to produce a high-quality output. As Suku explains, 'You will have a greater chance of success by doing an average or simple statistical analysis on the right business problem, than using advanced analytics on the wrong problem.'

With the brand established and credibility improving incrementally with every successful deliverable, Suku and his team have continued to improve upon and gain greater recognition for their work. Throughout 2017, the people analytics group emerged as a reliable team, and by 2018 they were being recognized internally for their faster pace and high credibility.

It was in this period that they started working on the impact of performance management on business outcomes.

Like many organizations, Trimble moved away from its traditional approach to performance management. As Mike describes, 'We blew it up!' However, unlike many organizations, Trimble used people analytics to validate the move to the new practices and continues to use data to help managers improve individual and team performance.

Initially, Trimble introduced 'T-Time' in 2017. 'T-Time' is the Trimble expression for the quarterly discussions between manager and employee using different themes each time, as shown in Figure 1.6.

Figure 1.6 T-Time quarterly meeting topics at Trimble, Inc.

SOURCE Reproduced with kind permission of Trimble, Inc., August 2020

In late 2017, Suku and his team began to show impressive insights. Looking at the effect of T-Time on attrition and engagement, the team found that where employees had zero or one T-Time per year, attrition either increased or was similar to that in years prior. However, when employees had at least two T-Times per year, attrition improved to the point that it was virtually zero when an employee had all four T-Times in an annual cycle.

Managers commented that there was a correlation between T-Time and attrition, though not necessarily a causative relationship. The people analytics team analysed additional information drawn from the recently introduced quarterly Pulse Survey – another process that had changed from the traditional annual engagement survey. Since the Pulse Survey asked questions specifically about T-Time – and since employee engagement was widely accepted as a causal link to business performance – Suku now had a way to properly link T-Time to business results.

By 2019, Trimble's people analytics team had demonstrated that attrition consistently declines for employees who have more regular quarterly T-Times – five times less attrition than compared with employees with zero T-Times. Full participation in T-Times created a 300 per cent increase in employee Net Promoter Score (eNPS). The impact was so profound that Kim Chaumillon, Vice President, Global Talent Management, recalled its profound impact at DisruptHR (2019): 'The engagement and attrition evidence was so compelling that for the first time in my career I had business executives promoting HR programmes.'

These results have altered the behaviour of managers and the expectations of employees. Effective employee engagement helped improve retention and thereby helped drive improving business results too. Suku is very proud of the impact he and the team have had.

Mike is also delighted with the work – and with Suku. 'He is a rockstar! The person you have in the people analytics role is critical; they need to have a natural curiosity, love data and understand the business. You need high-quality work. And the mission of people analytics must be that at every moment you should solve a business problem – to help the business become better.'

TOP TIP

Build the brand for people analytics internally.

Creating stewardship, accountability and enablement

We have discussed linking the team's work to the corporate strategy and defining the mission and brand. These will include using methods such as stakeholder engagement and prioritization described in detail in Chapter 2 (Methodology) and Chapter 3 (Stakeholder Management).

Once this is done, it is time to 'roll your sleeves up' and establish practices that will allow for repeatable, dynamic and agile governance. In short, who will help at an executive level to keep the function 'travelling in the right direction'? To do this, there are six types of governance that can be used. Five of these allow oversight on:

- ethics and privacy, as it relates to people data and analytics;
- the financial model to determine the return on investment (ROI) of analytics projects;
- the stewardship of people data;
- the prioritization of analytics work and projects;
- the operating model for success of the people analytics team.

The sixth type of governance body is called the 'board of people analytics'. This can be seen as an overall steering group that can meet in an agile – or formal – capacity to provide direction and enablement for the people analytics function. It could be combined with any of the other five topics listed above. Indeed, the board of people analytics could serve to combine all activities and governance responsibilities into one group of people.

In terms of these six types of governance, we discuss data stewardship in detail in Chapter 6 (Data) and the prioritization of projects in Chapter 2

Figure 1.7   The six types of governance

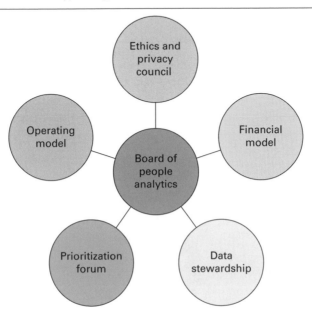

(Methodology). Additionally, we discuss the topic of the operating model as a People Analytics Value Chain in Chapter 8 (Business Outcomes) and as a structure for managing the people analytics team in Chapter 4 (Skills). This chapter considers the remaining three types of governance: the board of people analytics, financial model, and ethics and privacy.

Board of people analytics

Overseeing the governance model and structure for the people analytics function, the board of people analytics enables its mission, goals and work. The board is not intended to replace the formal management structure of the organization, which is required for performance management and day-to-day guidance and coaching.

Instead, acting similarly to a board of directors, the board of people analytics is responsible for aiding the strategy and work of people analytics. It should also take a holistic view across the entire function and ensure that the people analytics team can deliver value across the organization.

An efficient board of people analytics engages and accounts for the business's purpose, vision, mission, risk and accountability.

The board is composed of several people, ideally including a mix of business executives, functional executives and HR leaders. A suggested structure is shown in Figure 1.8. We recommend that the people analytics leader should be the chairperson and facilitator of this group.

Figure 1.8   The board of people analytics

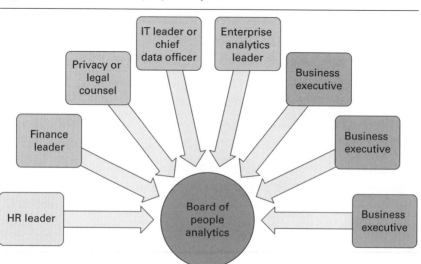

Financial model

The capacity to measure business value is essential to great governance. While it's not imperative to have a formal 'council' for this element, there should be an agreed partnership between finance and the people analytics team.

This partnership aims to establish an understanding and a method for measuring business value to determine an outcome and return on investment (ROI) for each people analytics project. For more on the topic of working with finance see Chapter 8 (Business Outcomes).

Ethics and privacy council

Responsible for maintaining high standards for privacy, compliance and ethics, the ethics and privacy council manages aspects of data privacy, and the ethical and moral aspects of the types of projects included in the people analytics function's focus.

Good governance also takes a company's values into account, with ethics and privacy concerns jeopardizing 81 per cent of people analytics projects (Green, 2018). Additionally, robust structures with trust at the core ensure work achieves maximum engagement and impact across the entire organization and, in general, improves business posture (Petersen, 2020).

Figure 1.9 shows a typical composition of an ethics and privacy council. While it sounds very formal, the actual council may operate on a very flexible and agile basis. One of the cornerstones of an ethics and privacy council is providing guidelines to the organization about the wise and ethical use of people data. This is particularly important because of the principle of 'fair exchange of value' discussed in Chapter 3 (Stakeholder Management).

As was discussed in a 2020 article in *Harvard Business Review*, it's not enough to hope that ethics are at the forefront when companies are considering people analytics work. It's important to build employee trust in the use of people data and tackle ethics and privacy head on, being open and transparent with how data is used (Chamorro-Premuzic and Bailie, 2020).

An ethics charter is one such mechanism for mitigating these risks around the use of people data. During the research for this book, we found that less than a quarter of companies have an ethics charter or equivalent mechanism for people analytics. Those that do, usually possess successful people analytics teams, create value for the business and provide benefits back to the employees as a fair exchange of value.

Figure 1.9 The ethics and privacy council

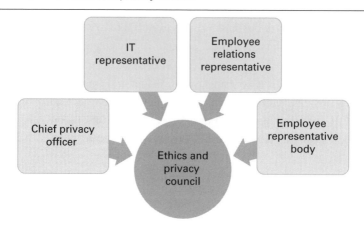

The following case study, Ethics, ethics, ethics: Lloyds Banking Group, describes how one company implemented an ethics charter and addressed other related topics. The key message is: *People analytics is nothing without embedded ethical practices!*

CASE STUDY

Ethics, ethics, ethics: Lloyds Banking Group

'Ethics is a way of operating' states Andy Papworth, Director of People Insight and Cost Management at Lloyds Banking Group (Lloyds)[7]. 'It's a philosophy and speaks volumes about the organization. We view it as more than compliance, more than the law.'

The last decade has been a tough one for the financial services industry, not just to recover from the 2008 financial crisis and mis-selling of PPI insurance products (Treanor, 2016), but also to achieve stability.

Under the leadership of António Horta-Osório (Chief Executive Officer since 2011), Lloyds has responded strongly to the financial crisis and the journey is well documented (Dunkley and Jenkins, 2017). Since the crisis, the government had sold the last of its shares in the bank, returning Lloyds to full private ownership. Additionally, Lloyds responded to PPI by paying compensation early and before other UK lenders.

The bank's propensity to tackle complex financial situations quickly sets the underlying framework for how seriously ethics forms a part of Lloyds's culture today. Within this strong culture, Andy and his Head of Strategic Workforce Planning and People Analytics, Justine Thompson, are entrusted with implementing ethical practices in people analytics. Andy has enjoyed a long career in numerous operational and executive roles across the bank, which has given him a clear appreciation of how seriously his employer takes ethical practices and conduct.

'We didn't want to make ethics for people analytics a "tick box" exercise,' Andy and Justine told us over coffee in their London headquarters. Inspired by the work of other organizations in constructing an ethical backbone for people analytics, the team at Lloyds, under their leadership, developed an approach for the bank. 'We reviewed the bank's Code of Responsibility[8] to understand what Lloyds considers important. This was an essential step. It was then critical that we test the ethical practices of all people analytics and cost management work, so we involved colleagues in developing the framework and principles.'

Recognizing the important role human resources business partners (HRBPs) play in people analytics, they were asked for their thoughts and experiences in managing people data using a range of focus groups, 1:1 interviews and discussion forums. Collecting all this information from dozens of HRBPs who deal with colleagues and managers every day meant that the team quickly developed an understanding of what was important and what wasn't.

Justine explains, 'We identified champions across our HRBP population who could test ideas in an iterative way. By doing this, the champions created trust among our HR colleagues who in turn became our ambassadors and "clients" for people analytics work.'

As the development of the people analytics ethics charter took shape, the team continued to keep it simple – this was not going to be a complex document or set of processes. They wanted the ethics charter to become a working document. An example of one element of this, the principles, is shown in Figure 1.10.

The ethics charter was designed to help the people analytics team use people-related data in a way that would make colleagues feel safe and protected and consequently help reveal insights in the business. Consequently, the ethics charter continuously improves people practices, enhances colleague experiences and at the same time brings business value to the company.

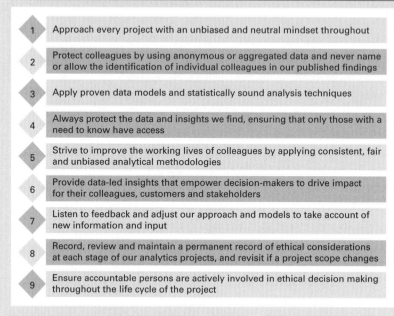

Figure 1.10   Guiding principles for the ethics charter of people analytics in Lloyds Banking Group

1. Approach every project with an unbiased and neutral mindset throughout

2. Protect colleagues by using anonymous or aggregated data and never name or allow the identification of individual colleagues in our published findings

3. Apply proven data models and statistically sound analysis techniques

4. Always protect the data and insights we find, ensuring that only those with a need to know have access

5. Strive to improve the working lives of colleagues by applying consistent, fair and unbiased analytical methodologies

6. Provide data-led insights that empower decision-makers to drive impact for their colleagues, customers and stakeholders

7. Listen to feedback and adjust our approach and models to take account of new information and input

8. Record, review and maintain a permanent record of ethical considerations at each stage of our analytics projects, and revisit if a project scope changes

9. Ensure accountable persons are actively involved in ethical decision making throughout the life cycle of the project

SOURCE Adapted from and reproduced with kind permission of Lloyds Banking Group, July 2020

An important step in the process was to secure the sponsorship, for example, with the CHRO and wider HR community. The team knew that getting sponsorship would enable them to elevate the topic to the right level of the organization. It believed that ethical use of people data should pervade through the entire company. This starts with senior sponsors endorsing the approach and ensuring it is consistent with Lloyds's overall approach to ethical topics.

The final piece of the jigsaw involved working with a third-party organization to provide an independent assessment of the work. The bank has worked with the Centre for Responsible Business at Birmingham University[9] on a number of topics for many years – another indication of how Lloyds takes its approach to ethical practices seriously. With this expertise and relationship, the team felt that getting advice from an academic third party would ensure the work would become even more robust.

After approximately six months, the ethics charter was finally launched. Justine reflects: 'Having a charter allowed us to engage our HR professionals and managers across the bank and all of our colleagues. We were open about how we use their data and what the benefits are for everyone.'

A year on, both Andy and Justine agree on the defining moment for the ethics charter: 'Our CHRO contacted us one day to ask us about compliance and people data. The Financial Conduct Authority had referenced the topic.' It was a salient moment for the team to test the strength of this element of their people analytics governance.

'Within minutes, we had sent all of the work – our entire ethics charter. We got a very quick response: "no further questions". That made us proud. To get that level of acceptance was an important milestone.'

Andy, Justine and their team now have the impetus to move to the next level of people analytics. They are confident that their work will always have ethics at its core and benefit colleagues across the bank.

TOP TIP

Involve stakeholders in developing an ethics charter.

Summary

Governance provides the mechanisms, processes and procedures by which a company operates and manages risk for people analytics. The following key steps set the direction for people analytics:

- Align the work of people analytics with the corporate strategy.
- Work with stakeholders to produce a memorable vision statement that clarifies the purpose and ambition of people analytics in the organization.
- Develop a mission statement that defines the function's objectives, guides the team and provides clarity on the outcomes it will deliver.
- Think like a marketeer and build a brand that provides visibility for people analytics across the business – be known to your stakeholders.
- Form a 'board of people analytics' to provide direction and enablement for the people analytics function.
- Make ethics a priority through the development of an ethics charter that provides transparency, and governs the wise and ethical use of people data.

References

BBC News (2020) H&M fined for breaking GDPR over employee surveillance [News] BBC News, Technology, 5 October. Available from: https://www.bbc.co.uk/news/technology-54418936 (archived at https://perma.cc/7TTV-6PYV) [Last accessed 7 February 2021]

Chamorro-Premuzic, T and Bailie, I (2020) Tech is transforming people analytics. Is that a good thing? *Harvard Business Review*, 21 October. Available from: https://hbr.org/2020/10/tech-is-transforming-people-analytics-is-that-a-good-thing (archived at https://perma.cc/5MYX-YJ3B) [Last accessed 27 April 2021]

CIPD (2020) Corporate governance: an introduction [Factsheet] Available from: https://www.cipd.co.uk/knowledge/strategy/governance/factsheet (archived at https://perma.cc/9Q46-KS7B) [Last accessed 7 February 2021]

DisruptHR (2019) Kim Chaumillon, Vice President, Global Talent Management, Trimble Inc, presents the T-Time story at a DisruptHR event in San Francisco [Video]. Available from: https://vimeo.com/369991767 (archived at https://perma.cc/FY4X-48U2) [Last accessed 7 February 2021]

Dunkley, E and Jenkins, P (2017) How Lloyds came back from the brink, *Financial Times*, 17 May. Available from: https://www.ft.com/content/34e57e76-3a87-11e7-821a-6027b8a20f23 (archived at https://perma.cc/FX52-LRXV) [Last accessed 7 February 2021]

Green, D (2018) Ethics & people analytics [Blog] myHRfuture, 19 March. Available from: https://www.myhrfuture.com/blog/2018/3/19/ethics-people-analytics (archived at https://perma.cc/K83Q-JZWB) [Last accessed 7 February 2021]

Guenole, N, Ferrar, J and Feinzig, S (2017) *The Power of People: Learn how successful organizations use workforce analytics to improve business performance*, Pearson, London

IT Governance Privacy Team (2020) *EU General Data Protection Regulation (GDPR): An implementation and compliance guide*, 4th edn, ITGP, Ely, Cambs

Lin, T C W (2011) The corporate governance of iconic executives, 87 *Notre Dame Law Review* 351. Available from: http://ssrn.com/abstract=2040922 (archived at https://perma.cc/L4QD-BSX6) [Last accessed 7 February 2021]

Novartis (2021) Our strategy. Available from: https://www.novartis.com/our-company/our-strategy (archived at https://perma.cc/W66F-NMHZ) [Last accessed 11 March 2021]

Petersen, D (2020) 6 Steps to ethically sound people analytics [Blog] myHRfuture, 20 October. Available from: https://www.myhrfuture.com/blog/2018/11/19/six-steps-to-ethically-sound-people-analytics (archived at https://perma.cc/7N3Q-3LYQ) [Last accessed 7 February 2021]

Shailer, G (2004) *An Introduction to Corporate Governance in Australia*, Pearson Education Australia, Sydney

SHRM (2016) Introduction to the Human Resources Discipline of Ethics and Corporate Social Responsibility and Sustainability [Report], February. Available from: https://www.shrm.org/resourcesandtools/tools-and-samples/toolkits/pages/introfethicsandsustainability.aspx (archived at https://perma.cc/4C5T-TD3N) [Last accessed 7 February 2021]

Treanor, J (2016) PPI claims: all you need to know about the mis-selling scandal, *Guardian*, 2 August 2016. Available from: https://www.theguardian.com/business/2016/aug/02/ppi-claims-all-you-need-to-know-about-the-mis-selling-scandal (archived at https://perma.cc/KKL4-57S2) [Last accessed 7 February 2021]

Notes

1   The EU GDPR sets a maximum fine of €20 million (about £18 million) or 4 per cent of annual global turnover – whichever is greater – for infringements (see https://www.itgovernance.co.uk/dpa-and-gdpr-penalties (archived at https://perma.cc/4ND5-THWC), last accessed 15 January 2021).

2   The HIPPO principle is the principle whereby work is assigned based on the Highest Paid Person's Opinion.

3   Novartis International A.G. is a Swiss multinational pharmaceutical company based in Basel, Switzerland. It is one of the largest pharmaceutical companies in the world, by both market capitalization and sales (see https://www.novartis.com/our-company (archived at https://perma.cc/U894-5CV5), last accessed 25 March 2021).

4   Commonly attributed to the Chinese philosopher, Confucius.

5   Trimble, Inc. (NASDAQ: TRMB) is a global provider of commercial technology solutions that enable professionals and field mobile workers to transform their work processes across a range of industries, including construction, geospatial, agriculture and transportation. Headquartered in Sunnyvale, California, Trimble is powered by more than 11,000 employees in over 35 countries (see https://www.trimble.com/corporate/about_at_glance.aspx, last accessed 11 March 2021).

6   Adapted from the quote 'In God we trust, all others must bring data' (W Edwards Deming).

7   Lloyds Banking Group was established in 2009 when Lloyds TSB acquired HBOS. With a history dating back to the 17th century, today the bank has 65,000 employees (see https://www.lloydsbankinggroup.com/who-we-are.html (archived at https://perma.cc/N9X9-J8BX), last accessed 11 March 2021).

8 Lloyds Bank Code of Responsibility (see https://www.lloydsbankinggroup.com/assets/pdfs/who-we-are/responsible-business/downloads/group-codes-and-policies/2019-code-of-responsibility.pdf (archived at https://perma.cc/64QP-R72A), last accessed 3 June 2020).

9 Lloyds Banking Group Centre for Responsible Business (see https://www.birmingham.ac.uk/research/responsible-business/index.aspx (archived at https://perma.cc/2F9E-TQU4), last accessed 6 February 2021).

Methodology 02

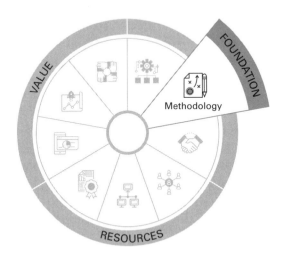

In this chapter, we discuss the practices and methodologies available for repeatable, impactful people analytics including criteria-based prioritization, the Focus-Impact-Value Model and working with sponsors.

DISCOVER...

- ways in which prioritization enables business-focused analytics;
- why an analytical methodology based on Focus-Impact-Value is always the right approach;
- how to work with sponsors to improve the likelihood of success.

WITH INSIGHTS FROM...

- Merck & Co., Inc., on how to be agile in a pandemic;
- American Eagle Outfitters®, on developing a people analytics manifesto;
- Swarovski AG, on delivering top-line growth with the right sponsor.

Overview

METHODOLOGY

Methodology, as one of the Nine Dimensions, focuses on the processes and frameworks that should be established for repeatable and dynamic people analytics. These include the way in which the prioritization of work occurs and the use of effective and transparent criteria, plus the involvement of sponsors and how to provide focus to the team while creating impact and delivering value.

Sound methodologies, designed and implemented correctly, ensure that people analytics work is undertaken effectively and will deliver value to both the business and its workforce, dynamically and sustainably. Of all the Nine Dimensions, this is one that a lot of companies speak to us about.

People analytics involves three significant investments: expertise in the form of people (experts, analysts, stakeholders and sponsors); finances in the shape of money to procure and harness people, data and technology, and the trust dividend of all workers (employees, managers and executives). Without these three, the impact and progress of people analytics in the organization will likely not realize its full potential and value.

There are numerous processes, decision-making tools, protocols and procedures that shape a people analytics project or function. Though this chapter examines a small selection of them, it is worth noting that all great methodologies are focused, impactful and deliver value.

The most successful methodologies for people analytics have three components: effective prioritization, defined processes and committed sponsors. We will consider each of these in turn.

Effective prioritization

Renowned contemporary management expert, Simon Sinek, states in his book *Start With Why* (2011): 'People don't buy what you do; they buy why you do it. And what you do simply proves what you believe.'

The same applies to people analytics. Executives, managers and employees are not interested in 'what' is done (which statistical techniques are chosen, what technology is used, etc). They care about 'why' the work is being done and how it will benefit them or the organization (why is the company investing time and money in this?). People care about the purpose and the outcome.

When it comes to successful people analytics, we believe that the purpose, or 'why', is intrinsically linked to value for the business.

The question of 'what is the business value?' in any organization often has a surprisingly simple set of answers when people can act on them. As such, the first task when undertaking people analytics work is to *ask the right questions* of stakeholders. We address this further in Chapter 3 (Stakeholder Management).

Following this, it is essential to prioritize the various requests for work. Being able to prioritize the work effectively will allow stakeholders, including employees themselves, to gain confidence that the people analytics team focuses on the topics that matter most to the organization. However, to be able to conduct effective prioritization, people analytics teams should understand the business in depth: what is its purpose, what does it make, what does it sell, how is it measured, what is its focus, what are its responsibilities to employees, shareholders and communities, etc? It is therefore important to listen to all stakeholders and understand the business.

Determine the business priorities

Equipped with an understanding of the business, it's time to determine what work and projects the people analytics team should focus on. But who is best placed to decide this?

Ask business leaders for their top three priorities

During our discussions with people analytics leaders, we found a number who ask business leaders, 'Which of these challenges is our top priority?' Even in the smallest companies, it is extremely rare that one leader's priority is the same as another's. Without at least one well-informed and balanced decision-maker, projects will inevitably fail to add value to at least one major stakeholder. As one people analytics leader in a large electronics firm said to us: 'We are in danger of just doing the work of the person that shouts the loudest'. This is not effective prioritization.

Therefore, better than asking for the 'top priority', ask leaders to express their top three priorities for the business as they see them over the next 12–24 months; this will allow leaders to talk generally and in line with the business strategies, and for the people analytics consultant to get a good broad view of the most important opportunities for analysis.

Focus on business topics that deliver value, not those du jour

Leaders' opinions matter. However, be aware of 'favourite topics' du jour – a human resources leader or business executive with a favourite project or topic can be troublesome for people analytics leaders.

Working with the chief human resources officer (CHRO) to understand the business challenges driving the C-suite is key. Understand 'why' each business leader is interested in particular topics. Determine what they are expecting, their hypotheses, and what they are trying to uncover and drive as a result.

Additionally, when a project du jour appears – often concealed as a 'quick favour' request by a senior leader, people analytics teams should filter the quick data requests from the real business questions. It is the former that will help the leader today. But it is the latter that will help the business leader in the long term.

It is important to understand the difference between the two types of requests – and the drain on resources. Effective questioning and discussion will help distinguish between them, which is another reason why we recommend having dedicated people analytics consultants (see Chapter 4, Skills).

Ask a broad range of leaders. Don't rely on one influential stakeholder

We will discuss working with stakeholders in detail in Chapter 3 (Stakeholder Management), but in short, we recommend taking input from many different stakeholders across the business.

However, in many organizations we have worked with, we have found that a significant proportion of people analytics work is commissioned by influential individual stakeholders, without others being involved. This is especially typical of organizations with smaller people analytics teams where senior leaders tend to develop relationships with individual analysts.

On the surface, the single individual business leader has their work request completed, and the people analytics team is busy and feels valued in supporting someone who is requesting their services. All is good, right? Wrong!

This is a tricky situation for several reasons. In longer-term projects, having a single influential leader who frequently dominates the agenda without other input, can mean that the project gets distracted. Also, the work undertaken might be part of a larger important initiative. Therefore, such additional work from the dominating leader can significantly reduce momentum and traction. In our experience, these projects fail to add much value to the business – and can be draining to work on.

Consider this example: in a global financial services organization, a very influential head of reward and compensation commissioned a people analytics project on employee compensation. The work took six months and consumed analysts entirely for that period. When the analysis was finished, this leader did not like the insights or recommendations. They decided to cancel the project. There were no other leaders involved. The project was not discussed with other leaders, and there was no cross-functional discussion about the work. Six months' work was wasted.

Set up a dynamic prioritization forum to discuss priorities

Comprising representatives from different functions, a prioritization forum can be very helpful. At its core, it is a small group of people who collectively can provide a balanced view of the options available to people analytics.

We recommend a small team as follows:

- a human resources executive to provide input on people priorities across the enterprise;
- a business representative that is senior enough to have an enterprise view of what is important;
- a finance executive to provide a perspective on the financial value of recommended work.

The project prioritization forum is responsible for:

- agreeing criteria for prioritization;
- selecting 'Quick Wins' and 'Big Bets' projects against these criteria (see the Complexity-Impact Matrix later in this chapter);
- reviewing progress of selected people analytics projects;
- reconfirming routinely, and therefore dynamically, that the projects and work selected will continue – and considering new requests and ideas.

Figure 2.1   The project prioritization forum

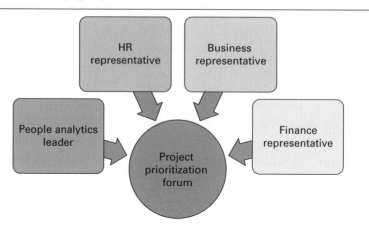

Figure 2.2   The Complexity-Impact Matrix

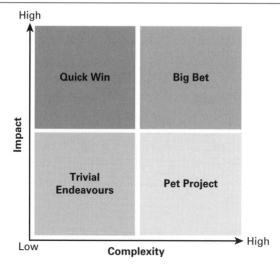

SOURCE Guenole, Ferrar and Feinzig (2017)

The people analytics leader's responsibility is to guide the prioritization forum, encouraging participants to share, discuss and determine the value and requirement for each initiative.

Please note that, as mentioned in Chapter 1 (Governance), this prioritization forum can be combined with any of the other governance forums.

Use a robust framework: the Complexity-Impact Matrix

Companies use many tools to guide the order of work to be done. The Complexity-Impact Matrix is one such tool we recommend. It is discussed in detail in *The Power of People: Learn how successful organizations use workforce analytics to improve business performance* (Guenole, Ferrar and Feinzig, 2017). The model is designed to assess projects according to their relative impact and complexity.

Impact Depicted on the y-axis, 'impact' shows the magnitude of value-driven factors relative to a people analytics initiative. Three main criteria for assessing impact are:

- alignment to the business strategies;
- financial value;
- benefits to the workforce.

Complexity Displayed on the horizontal x-axis, 'complexity' shows the difficulty of the activity and resources required to deliver a people analytics project. The individual criteria for assessing complexity include:

- availability, accessibility and quality of data;
- availability of required technology;
- availability and expertise of resources;
- organization politics;
- whether there are one or more business sponsors for the project;
- likelihood and ease of productizing and implementing the analytics solution into the business.

When projects are assessed using these criteria, each project can be located on the matrix as either a Quick Win, Big Bet, Trivial Endeavour or Pet Project.

Quick Win: People analytics is not always complex – Quick Win projects are ideal for delivering high impact and represent the lowest relative level of complexity. These projects often have engaged sponsors and deliver value with limited investment. Other industry experts agree that these are often the best projects to seek and complete (Marritt, 2018).

Big Bet: These projects are usually highly complex, often multi-year projects, but they also offer the greatest value to the organization. They usually require a significant investment of time and money and will require significant sponsorship. Every leading people analytics team has at least one Big Bet in their portfolio, gaining support and attention at the most significant levels of the company.

Trivial Endeavours: Our experience has shown that people analytics teams with limited investment or interest from senior executives will have many Trivial Endeavours in their portfolio. They often absorb a lot of the people analytics team's collective energy and time and rarely deliver significant business value. Typical Trivial Endeavours include data requests, reporting, creating dashboards and projects sponsored by people with limited influence.

Pet Project: These are the least valuable projects. Pet Projects absorb a lot of time due to their complexity, yet yield limited, if any, value due to the lack of impact they will have, even if they are completed well.

Developing a well-honed approach to prioritizing work – such as that described above in the Complexity-Impact Matrix (Figure 2.2) – ensures that, in times of crisis such as the onset of a global pandemic, the people analytics team can pivot and meet the new and many requirements from the business. The case study below, Prioritization in a pandemic: Merck & Co., Inc., provides a powerful example of this flexibility in practice. The team's key message is: *People analytics requires structure and flexibility, simultaneously.*

 CASE STUDY

Prioritization in a pandemic: Merck & Co., Inc.

It's great to have structured prioritization for projects (such as those outlined in this chapter). But what happens when the business is operating in circumstances such as a global pandemic or other major crisis? People analytics needs to be able to respond quickly.

The Workforce Analytics team at US pharmaceutical company, Merck & Co., Inc.,[1] knows how to support the business in times of crisis. Jeremy Shapiro is the Executive Director of Workforce Analytics, and one of the most highly regarded and influential leaders in the people analytics field. Jeremy's career at Merck & Co., Inc., Morgan Stanley and the Omnicom Group makes him an experienced business leader and an accomplished HR executive.

Jeremy's approach to prioritizing in people analytics work is centred around three principles: living the company's values and priorities, empathizing with employees' needs and understanding the business strategy.

Jeremy reflected on how his team successfully navigated the COVID-19 pandemic and associated economic disruptions over a video call in the second half of 2020.

'Patients rely on companies like us, and during a global pandemic, this need was magnified. Even though Workforce Analytics isn't on the front line, we knew that we could help and jumped into action. Senior leaders prioritized three things: the health and safety of our employees, continuity of the supply chain and continue normal operations.'

These three priorities provided the guidelines for how the team focused its efforts and what work would be done first. For the Workforce Analytics team, this translated into a 'stacked' method for prioritizing work.[2] This involved ordering work according to its relevance to the business strategy, and urgency and importance to the company as a whole. In times of crisis, the interpretation of what work is most important must be narrow and clear. The need for lengthy prioritization discussions is diminished when everyone is clear on what must be done.

'I asked the team to imagine that leaders are speaking directly to them as individuals and describing their needs.' This practice enabled the team to put itself in business leaders' shoes without the need to go back and ask for clarification, interpretation and direction.

Jeremy, as a leader, also has a personal value of empathy. He feels the team can have meaningful discussions and reflections on the business strategy and leaders' needs if team members are open with each other and communicate freely. 'Underlining their humanity and the humanity of our colleagues and patients makes prioritization with empathy possible.'

The team quickly adapted to pandemic-related business priorities. The guidance from the business and Jeremy meant that people intuitively knew where to focus their time and resources. Leaders needed specific types of data and updates about their people, but since everyone in the company was moving at speed, there was no time to pause and formally establish requirements.

'We used our understanding of the business, plus empathy to get in front of requests,' Jeremy explains. 'It was not perfect, but we were able to operate with a bit less reactivity, even at the peak of the pandemic. Given that we all had to adjust to a different working environment ourselves, every little bit helped.'

In this crisis-driven approach to prioritization, Jeremy and his team acted instinctively to deliver value. One of the ways they did this was to create an agile team of HR, facilities, operations and cybersecurity talent. Together, they created a real-time dashboard of the status of the workforce and its impact on company facilities. The team partnered with internal medical staff and epidemiologists to create the same types of data visualizations medical professionals in the field used to manage their pandemic response.

Finally, the team launched a series of timely surveys and employee listening analyses to understand the impact of the crisis on employees, and assess actions to manage health and safety and maintain supply chains and normal operations. This data also alerted the team to numerous smaller requests for insights to help individual leaders and managers. All of these initiatives were considered successes in the business and made a difference to patients, employees and the company.

During the COVID-19 pandemic, the team used this approach to solve significant business problems before they were even communicated to HR business partners: 'We knew from our company values that our patients come first. We also knew that our CEO had previously spoken about employee health and safety. Finally, we knew as human beings and news-watchers how COVID-19 was affecting the workplace, especially manufacturing.'

Because the team had a sound understanding of the business and employees' needs, it anticipated requests and quickly took action: incorporating external data into its reporting with input from the company's scientific experts, the team produced accurate executive-level dashboards to improve business intelligence and decision making. The initiative was a considerable success in the business and made a difference to patients, employees and the company.

The Workforce Analytics team's prioritization in times of crisis emphasizes an intuitive understanding of business questions, confidence to select topics and respond quickly, in real time (see right-hand side of Figure 2.3).

Figure 2.3 The approach to prioritizing work in a crisis at Merck & Co., Inc.

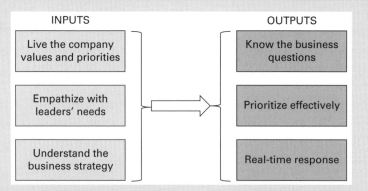

SOURCE Reproduced with kind permission of Merck & Co., Inc., January 2021

While the inputs are the same in times of crisis and non-crisis, the levels of intuition and confidence take on new importance. This is what makes people analytics succeed in crisis and is a particular skill of the leader.

'Responding to many requests before they are communicated comes more naturally, now,' Jeremy reflects. 'Merck & Co., Inc. is dedicated to saving and improving lives. Our business runs on this value, as does the workforce analytics team.'

> **TOP TIP**
>
> Know the business strategy inside-out to build intuition and confidence, since they will be needed in times of crisis.

Defined processes

People analytics teams globally find stable, efficient and clean processes for undertaking work to overcome obstacles and ensure outcomes are delivered efficiently and collaboratively. There are numerous models for undertaking good analytics projects such as the following two, which were developed by people analytics experts.

The analytics value chain

One methodology used by many is the analytics value chain. It was outlined by Google's people analytics team as early as 2011 (Dekas, 2011) and is available on Google's re:Work website (2021). Academics that are prominent in the people analytics field such as Dr Sjoerd van den Heuvel have also frequently highlighted the usefulness of this approach (van den Heuvel and Bondarouk, 2017).

The basis of this approach is to move away from opinions driving action, to using data, metrics and analyses to validate those opinions, beliefs and hypotheses first. Once insights are revealed these can be used to support the decision making required to take action (see Figure 2.4).

Figure 2.4   Value chain methodology

SOURCE Adapted from Dekas (2011) and van den Heuvel and Bondarouk (2017)

Figure 2.5   Eight Step Model for Purposeful Analytics

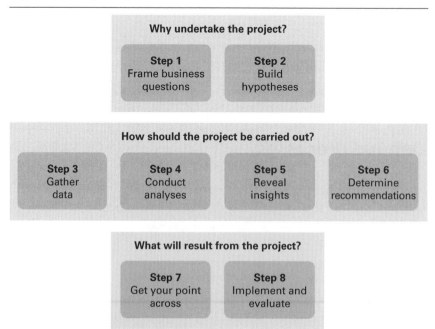

SOURCE Guenole, Ferrar and Feinzig (2017)

The Eight Step Model

The Eight Step Model for Purposeful Analytics is another example of an effective model for designing and delivering people analytics projects at every level (Guenole, Ferrar and Feinzig, 2017). It is shaped by three key questions:

1 Why undertake the project?

2 How should the project be carried out?

3 What will result from the project?

This model highlights and complements the starting point of all effective people analytics work: start by framing the business question. This approach is supported by other people in this field (Levenson and Pillans, 2017), and by methodologies followed by the people analytics teams at companies such as McKinsey (McNulty, 2018) and LinkedIn (McClaren, 2020).

The Focus-Impact-Value Model

The people analytics team's work requires focus to make it successful in creating impact and delivering value. The model described in Figure 2.6 has a simple, if effective, approach and follows the questions outlined at the start of this book (see Preface: a word from the authors):

- **What should I focus on?** Practitioners who focus on business challenges linked to the company's people strategy are more successful in their endeavours.

- **How can I improve my impact?** Organizations that build solid foundations and don't dive into solving technology and data issues create more impact on a long-term basis.

- **How can I create more value?** Leaders that prioritize their work with the end goal in mind deliver more value for the business and the employees themselves.

Figure 2.6 Focus-Impact-Value Model

FOCUS   IMPACT   VALUE

Focus

Using the prioritization criteria described earlier in this chapter, each project and every element of work undertaken in people analytics is delivered with purpose and value. Focusing on each project requires certain core elements:

- **Define the project's scope:** This requires establishing boundaries around the business units included, the countries and/or the geographical entities, cities and locations that will be analysed, group of employees or other factors that limit and bind the study to a defined group of people.

- **Clarify the project sponsor:** One of the most important elements is to secure a business sponsor (see later in this chapter).

- **Outline the overall resources available:** Define the budget required and the time frames needed. If it is necessary to split the project into phases, then define clear objectives and a time frame for each phase.

Impact

This refers to the expected outcome of the work for the consumers – or recipient – of the work. The four key audiences of people analytics work are described in Chapter 7 (Workforce Experiences) and summarized here as: the employee, the workforce, the manager and the executive.

It is key that a methodical approach is taken to consider each group and understand the answer to the question 'what would happen if...?' This technique aims to anticipate the likely outcome of the analytics work and its impact on each audience.

For example, let's look at a project focused on network analysis of sales professionals. In this scenario, we will consider that the business is trying to understand if certain internal and external relationship network profiles improve individuals' sales performance.

Now let's consider the 'what if...?' question based on a hypothetical outcome: What if the best sales professionals have a balanced profile of internal and external networks?

By asking this question (and potentially other questions), we can start to answer from the perspective of the stakeholder groups:

- Would we change the recruitment process to accommodate testing for balanced networks?

- Would we change the training programme for sales professionals to develop the ability to build new networks?

- Would we implement these changes if there is a cost attached to the change programme?
- Would we change our systems to measure the networks of sales professionals, so that these networks can be used as a predictor of success?

The key to 'Impact' is to anticipate likely outcomes and not enter into analytics blindly.

Value

In the context of setting up projects or work for success, value is defined as the financial value, risk mitigation or engagement of customers, clients or workers as a result of the people analytics project.

The aim with 'Value' is to assess potential value at the end of the project should the hypothesis be proven or disproven. This will determine:

- if the work is important to undertake;
- if a sponsor is required;
- if stakeholders will release budget for skills, data or technology for the work;
- if there is likely to be significant impact on any of the stakeholder groups.

Focusing on the analytics work or project up front, defining its scope, understanding the likely impact on all Seven Types of Stakeholders described in Chapter 3 (Stakeholder Management) and defining the high-level financial value, risk mitigation, or engagement for customers or employees and workers provides a solid platform for deciding whether or not to proceed with work.

For the work that proceeds, the next step is to gain sponsorship for the most important people analytics work and projects.

A good example of adopting a rigorous methodology for people analytics is seen in the following case study, Set yourself up for great work: American Eagle Outfitters®. This case considers the processes, stakeholders and manifesto needed to ensure success. The key message is: *Setting up a small team requires a few essential ingredients.*

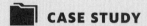

CASE STUDY

Set yourself up for great work: American Eagle Outfitters®

At the time of discussing this case study in 2020, American Eagle Outfitters® (AEO)[3] used analytics in a sophisticated manner for customer and sales data and had done so for many years. AEO knew it was time to do the same for people data. Cory Ingram, People Analytics Leader, was the person to help them do it, along with the small but capable people analytics team at AEO.

The AEO people analytics team has achieved much since it was established in 2017. It has transformed from a 'reporting' team to an 'outside-in' business-driven function and can now leverage active and passive data to tackle business questions. It has done all of this with endless enthusiasm for the retail industry, never losing sight of the end result.

'It's a personal philosophy I developed from observations at AEO,' Cory reflects. 'In a retail business, people, customer and sales data are symbiotic, and they all meet together in one place: the cash register. If we want to solve business problems, we have to link it to customers and sales.'

Cory was recruited into his first people analytics role in 2018. His background in HR, consulting and actuarial science provided him with a strong HR skill set and a passion for data, but he needed to get up to speed with people analytics, fast. 'It was like being at school again,' Cory recalls. 'I read many books, listened to podcasts, joined peer communities and attended the top conferences.' This period of discovery prepared Cory well for his first people analytics leadership role in 2019.

Equipped with a natural enthusiasm and extensive knowledge of the latest developments in the field, Cory and his manager, Senior Vice President of Total Rewards, Jessica Catanese, worked together to secure the ingredients they needed to get started: 'Jessica has deep networks at AEO,' Cory explains. 'We were able to leverage that to open doors to the right stakeholders knowing that this would help us prioritize effectively.' Jessica also has a clear understanding of the strategic HR agenda, reporting directly to the CHRO, which was crucial in setting the agenda for analytics across HR.

The AEO people analytics team had all the essential components needed to succeed (see Figure 2.7). These included Jessica's knowledge of the

Figure 2.7 Ingredients needed to set a small team up for greatness at American Eagle Outfitters®

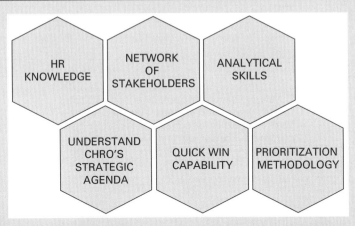

SOURCE Reproduced with kind permission of American Eagle Outfitters®, December 2020

corporation, access to stakeholders and clear understanding of the strategic agenda. Additionally, the team benefitted from Cory's analytical skills, HR knowledge and his mindset to deliver value with a small team.

Using AEO's existing proclivity for data-driven insights in customer experience and sales as a case for using people data, the pair quickly established a rapport with senior stakeholders around people analytics, building on the initial foundation set by Cory's predecessor. As needs were clarified with stakeholders, the team realized two final components were required to reach the next level: prioritization of work and additional resources. The people analytics function would not reach its full potential working on individual projects alone; Cory would have to research and set up a method for prioritizing work from the needs collected across the entire business and more resources would be needed to deliver Quick Win projects (see Figure 2.2) to the company.

These final two components were implemented in early 2020. With support from a new analyst, the team was able to tackle descriptive analytics and address more ad hoc requests, building credibility incrementally. Cory could now look for opportunities to show the impact of people analytics on the business: 'The team didn't have a way to show the value we could deliver. We didn't really have a formal foundation in place or any good road map to show our HR business partners or external business partners where we were going and what that vision looked like.' More groundwork was needed.

Figure 2.8 The why, how and what of people analytics – an extract from the People Analytics Manifesto at American Eagle Outfitters®

WHY
- Elevate, accelerate and empower our associates
- Create a legacy and an impact on our people
- Make lives easier for our associates, allowing them to inspire and lead our customers and the general world
- Create value for AEO through our people data

HOW
- Inspire data seekers by helping make data-driven decisions
- Hire, develop and retain the best talent with data-driven insights
- Democratize data, insights and results
- Meet at the cash register to connect customer and sales analytics with people analytics

WHAT
- User-friendly and interactive deliverables that provide insights and drive/measure action
- Advanced analytics around all major moments of the associates' journey
- Self-service reports, dashboards and insights
- Analytic projects tied directly to business goals/strategy and HR goals/strategy

SOURCE Reproduced with kind permission of American Eagle Outfitters®, December 2020

In September 2019, Cory began writing AEO's People Analytics Manifesto, setting out the framework for the 'why, how, and what' of people analytics at the company (Figure 2.8). The structure of the Manifesto is based on the Insight222 Nine Dimensions for Excellence in People Analytics® model, adapted by Cory for AEO's culture and dynamics. It is an impressive document, clearly defining work from foundational elements to outcomes. It includes a business-focused section that describes how people across AEO can and should work with the people analytics team including sections on 'What questions should a leader ask at the beginning of interactions with people analytics?' and 'What questions will the people analytics team ask you as a stakeholder?'

Twelve months into its development, the Manifesto exists as a 40-page document, with an accompanying presentation and plans for educational videos for stakeholders to collaborate effectively with the team. Next, says Cory, is a formal discovery process with end users. 'Every time we get requests, we try to understand how the work will align with the Manifesto. We think about the business problem first and let that determine where we focus our time and drive results. We ask: Who is the final end-user? What is its bigger impact on our people and the business?'

'In companies where people analytics is relatively new, I don't think that many end users really know the questions they can and should ask,' Cory reflects. 'People don't automatically know what people analytics is and what it can do – so the team has to help enable that vision.'

This approach made a big difference in 2020 as business priorities changed rapidly. With its foundations in place and end users aware of how people analytics supports work and employees, the team was able to jump into action and help the business and the workforce at incredible speed.

'When we looked at a major business initiative and pillar – inclusivity and diversity in the workplace – we knew people analytics could provide relevant leadership insights and recommendations. We anticipated the types of questions that leaders would ask and responded proactively.'

Within days of publishing the insights internally, the team was asked to join a meeting with the executive leadership team (ELT). The people analytics team presented to the ELT three times on this topic between March and September 2020. In addition, Cory and his team conducted individual meetings with each ELT member to gather their specific input and further build a partnership for the future. 'The ELT has begun to embrace people analytics strategically. They have realized we can deliver insights and metrics quickly so that decisions can be made in line with the speed of business.'

The team entered a new phase. 'Responding to core business challenges with input from senior stakeholders meant we didn't have to pound the pavement any more,' Cory remembers, proudly. 'Senior business leaders were requesting our presence in leadership meetings to provide insights on key topics and some of our work started going directly to the CEO and board of directors.'

'When I joined AEO in 2018, "People Analytics" was seen as just a data and reporting function,' Cory muses. 'I am delighted that the foundational elements, the Manifesto, the skilled team, and the insights and recommendations delivered are having an impact across AEO. The people analytics function is now embedded in the business and has an incredibly bright future.'

TOP TIP

Build a 'Why? – How? – What?' manifesto for the people analytics team.

Committed sponsors

There are seven types of stakeholders (see Chapter 3 – Stakeholder Management). Of these, one is particularly vital to projects: sponsors.

The project sponsor is the person providing support for the project through their personal commitment, helping with financial aspects and personal endorsements. Having a project sponsor ensures that the project will be *recognized*, and any outcomes will likely be *implemented* to create business *value*. They support the activity and the project itself, including its purpose, direction, objective and outcomes, and encourage the people analytics leader and their team.

Finding great sponsors

Look for great sponsors that:

- have a business problem that they want to be solved;
- are involved in the work and the business area;
- are passionate about the work of the project;
- have the authority to make things happen.

In finding sponsors, don't be afraid to simply approach executives directly. If the request will enhance their business, most people will be delighted to support work that will help them and their business be more successful. When asked, many successful people analytics professionals have stated that they have secured sponsors easily just by framing their question succinctly and by talking with the sponsor about why they are the best person.

Securing a sponsor's commitment

Terms of reference create a 'contract' with the sponsor. This will enable their commitment to be secured and in return, allow them to gain commitment from the people analytics team. It will also demonstrate that the team is 'serious' in its endeavours. It provides clarity and commitment. While it is not necessary to create a formal document, it is certainly recommended that the commitments are documented in writing – in an email.

The analytics team should commit to: conducting the work, adhering to time frames, contacting the sponsor if there are problems, and helping the sponsor understand the insights, recommendations and actions needed.

The sponsor should commit to: authorizing the work, scheduling time for reviews, removing roadblocks, providing direction, communicating actions and implementing recommendations.

An extremely powerful example of the business value generated by identifying and securing an enthusiastic sponsor follows in the case study, The right sponsor: Swarovski. The team's key message is: *Finding the right sponsor pays dividends.*

 CASE STUDY

The right sponsor: Swarovski

'Our vision is that data and analytics inform all people decisions,' Oliver Kasper, Head of Corporate People Analytics, Digital HR & Portfolio Strategy at Swarovski,[4] said in a meeting of his new and enthusiastic team in July 2018. It was the middle of summer, and the team of three had just concluded a statistical analysis of attrition in one of Swarovski's biggest business units. The project had been initiated mainly by an HR leader who had noticed retention, which was already a challenge, was decreasing even further. The leader asked the team to 'take a look'. The business unit in question was a key market, substantial in size, and so Oliver's team focused on this with urgency.

The report was of very high quality. When it was complete, it consisted of a 53-page statistical analysis in R.[5] They analysed 173 different people data elements looking for relationships as to why sales consultants had shorter tenure than expected. The work was superlative and statistically robust. But the clear business impact was not defined at that time. The team wondered: 'What was the impact on top- and bottom-line business results?'

Swarovski is a business with impact on thousands of customers around the world. Swarovski adds sparkle to everyday life with high-quality products and services that exceed their customers' desires. When Daniel Swarovski founded Swarovski in 1895, his vision was to create a diamond for everyone.

In recognition of this history, Oliver and his team considered why the retention project might be important. Couching its people analysis in the context of the wider business, the team realized it could link the retention of people directly to business metrics, such as the conversion of customers to sales in their stores.

The people analytics team identified three steps to take:

- Refocus the report on business value – in particular, retail sales.

- Elevate the project beyond pure statistics.

- Secure a passionate and business-minded sponsor to translate and upsell their project outside of HR.

Oliver and his team presented the retention study insights and recommendations to the business unit's head of retail and the global HR leadership team. These recommendations outlined changes to the way incentives were rewarded when staff went beyond the probationary period, and amendments to training courses for new staff would benefit employees and the business. With the buy-in of the business and the HR function, it became a smooth process to implement the recommended changes.

But the people analytics team needed more – for the team's insights to have the desired business impact, it needed to enlist more global stakeholders outside of HR who cared about their work.

A bold spirit, Oliver directly sought out Swarovski's global head of retail, to learn where the findings of this work were most needed.

Keen to discuss ways to improve the business, the global head of retail saw the team's credible work and their ability to communicate actions. He also noted that Oliver's proposal addressed an area of management that he was passionate about: the interaction between customers and staff, and the impact of good store management.

Oliver and the team had secured their sponsor.

Within one month, the project evolved from 'predictive retention' to 'how do stores convert more customers' or 'How to drive better sales with people analytics'. Rejuvenated with a fresh business objective, the people analytics project evolved into a strategic initiative.

Oliver and his team, together with the retail management team, identified six people factors affecting the conversion rate of visitors to their stores to become customers who purchased Swarovski jewellery and crystal.

These were:

- employee retention;
- staffing and scheduling;
- the store manager's leadership characteristics;

Figure 2.9 Conversion rate analysis in Swarovski

SOURCE Reproduced with kind permission of Swarovski, August 2020

- sales consultants' behaviour, attributes and skills;
- employees being trained to the correct level at the right time;
- team composition in mid- to larger-size stores.

The training analysis, for example, revealed that learning and development had a positive relationship with staff retention, and that certain training courses were more effective than others at improving business performance.

As a result of these findings, Swarovski redesigned training offerings with a performance-based approach – focused on those courses that most affected sales performance.

Another study highlighted the impact of certain personality traits on business performance; so, Swarovski started a pilot with neuroscience-based games and artificial intelligence algorithms to select the best talent, together with a vendor. The company also planned to put in place a new assessment of store managers, identifying gaps and implementing development actions.

Senior executives in Swarovski became very interested in people analytics. Every aspect of the analysis was assessed to see if it had a positive business benefit.

Eight months on from the initial discussion of the 53-page report, Oliver and his team had learnt several significant lessons: analytics is more impactful with a strong methodology, a robust and clear purpose and a business sponsor.

The people analytics team quickly assimilated the learnings from this project and applied them to the rest of its subsequent work. It created an entire road map of work in people analytics, which has since become a regular agenda topic at Swarovski's most senior executive retail team meeting.

People analytics projects are discussed, evaluated and refined with the global head of retail on a monthly basis. The people analytics team is also regularly invited to present findings and discuss business improvement programmes as part of the global retail management team offsite meetings. Additionally, several projects based on the six people factors for store conversion have begun in a number of locations worldwide.

'The impact of our work is that the team moved from "push" to "pull",' Oliver recalls. 'Business leaders come to us proactively to solve their challenges. The demand for people analytics work significantly exceeds our capacity.'

'The important steps are to identify the most business-critical topics in your company that relate to people and engage a sponsor who you work with from the start. For Swarovski, as soon as I enlisted a senior business sponsor, the project rapidly increased in importance, and the benefits to the retail business improved dramatically.'

TOP TIP

Successful analytics needs a senior business sponsor.

Summary

Effective prioritization, well-defined processes and committed sponsors are three key components of successful people analytics. Leading teams follow these recommendations with regard to methodology:

- Ask the question: 'what is the business value?' before embarking on any people analytics work.
- Identify potential work by engaging with stakeholders, clearly defining business questions and developing strong hypotheses.
- Set up a project prioritization forum comprising the people analytics leader and representatives from HR, finance and the business that reviews priorities, enables progress and provides guidance.
- Select projects using a robust framework (such as the Complexity-Impact Matrix) that prioritizes high-impact 'Quick Win' and 'Big Bet' work and eschews low-impact 'Trivial Endeavours' and 'Pet Project' work.
- Create impact by focusing on solving business challenges and prioritizing work with the end goal in mind deliver more value.
- Identify a sponsor for every piece of significant work: one who has a clear business problem they want to solve as well as the willingness and authority to implement recommendations.

References

Dekas, K (2011) People analytics: using data to drive HR strategy and action [Video]. Available from: https://www.youtube.com/watch?v=l6ISTjupi5g (archived at https://perma.cc/8P3K-ZTNV) [Last accessed 21 March 2021]

Guenole, N, Ferrar, J and Feinzig, S (2017) *The Power of People: Learn how successful organizations use workforce analytics to improve business performance*, Pearson, London

Levenson, A and Pillans, G (2017) Strategic Workforce Analytics [Report] Corporate Research Forum, 11 March. Available from: https://www.crforum.co.uk/research-and-resources/research-report-strategic-workforce-analytics/ (archived at https://perma.cc/L55K-JVMG) [Last accessed 7 February 2021]

Marritt, A (2018) Sometimes the best solutions aren't the most sophisticated [Blog] OrganizationView, 15 April. Available from: https://www.organizationview.com/insights-articles/2018/5/25/sometimes-the-best-solutions-arent-the-most-sophisticated (archived at https://perma.cc/N9CS-AFNZ) [Last accessed 7 February 2021]

McLaren, S (2020) How the IMPACT Framework Can Help You Solve Your Company's Toughest Business Problems [Report] LinkedIn Talent Solutions, 24 February. Available from: https://business.linkedin.com/talent-solutions/blog/talent-analytics/2020/use-impact-framework-to-solve-companys-toughest-problems (archived at https://perma.cc/2GNU-9FUE) [Last accessed 7 February 2021]

McNulty, K (2018) Constructing your analytics team around the analytics value lifecycle [Blog] LinkedIn, 28 December. Available from: https://www.linkedin.com/pulse/constructing-your-analytics-team-around-value-keith-mcnulty/ (archived at https://perma.cc/4KN7-CTLF) [Last accessed 7 February 2021]

Re:Work (2021) People analytics guide: adopt an analytics mindset. Available from: https://rework.withgoogle.com/guides/analytics-adopt-an-analytics-mindset/steps/understand-the-analytics-value-chain/ (archived at https://perma.cc/86MG-HYTH) [Last accessed 21 March 2021]

Sinek, S (2011) *Start With Why: How great leaders inspire everyone to take action*, Penguin, London

van den Heuvel, S and Bondarouk, T (2017) The rise (and fall?) of HR analytics: a study into the future application, value, structure, and system support, *Journal of Organizational Effectiveness: People and Performance*, **4** (2). Available from: https://www.researchgate.net/publication/317119630_The_rise_and_fall_of_HR_analytics_A_study_into_the_future_application_value_structure_and_system_support (archived at https://perma.cc/9Y8A-ER39) [Last accessed 21 March 2021]

Notes

1 Merck & Co., Inc., known as MSD outside of the US and Canada, is an American multinational pharmaceutical company, incorporated in New Jersey in 1891. It is one of the largest pharmaceutical companies in the world, and had more than 70,000 employees as of 2019 (see https://www.merck.com/company-overview/history/ (archived at https://perma.cc/G84E-BFPQ), last accessed 7 February 2021).

2 As defined by Steve Fenton (see https://www.stevefenton.co.uk/2017/03/work-prioritisation-vs-stack-ranking/ (archived at https://perma.cc/G5B9-27TU), last accessed 7 February 2021).

3 American Eagle Outfitters® (NYSE: AEO) is a leading global speciality retailer offering high-quality, on-trend clothing, accessories and personal care products at affordable prices under its American Eagle® and Aerie® brands. Founded in 1977, AEO employed 46,000 people in 2019 (see https://www.aeo-inc.com/ (archived at https://perma.cc/HS5F-C9BN), last accessed 7 February 2021).

4 Swarovski AG is a €2.7 billion business with over 27,000 employees and approximately 3,000 stores globally (see https://www.swarovski.com/en_GB-GB/s-brand/Swarovski-Brand/ (archived at https://perma.cc/F2RJ-ENVN), last accessed 7 February 2021).

5 R is a free statistical computing and graphics programming language and software environment, supported by the R Foundation for Statistical Computing (see https://www.r-project.org/about.html (archived at https://perma.cc/D24E-HNSF), last accessed 7 February 2021).

Stakeholder Management

In this chapter, we discuss the types of stakeholders that can provide direction, inspiration and enablement for people analytics and how best to engage with them in a structured and purposeful way.

DISCOVER...

- the Seven Types of Stakeholders for people analytics;
- how to create a stakeholder map and engagement plan for success;
- tips for managing stakeholders.

WITH INSIGHTS FROM...

- Johnson & Johnson, on developing great stakeholders at the very top;
- The Viessmann Group, on the value of an analytical CHRO;
- Syngenta A.G., on the importance of having a stakeholder engagement plan.

Overview

STAKEHOLDER MANAGEMENT

Stakeholder Management, as one of the Nine Dimensions, discusses the different types of stakeholders that people analytics teams will interact with to create impact and deliver value. In particular, it focuses on building a purposeful stakeholder map, how to engage and conduct effective meetings, and what to do in the long term to build effective and sustainable relationships across all stakeholders.

During our research and our conversations with clients, companies who want to build or transform their people analytics function usually suggest they should start by building an operating model, 'sorting out' their data or buying some new technology. We disagree. Instead, we recommend that the first step – irrespective of how well established the function is – is for the people analytics team to engage with stakeholders.

Meeting with stakeholders is the most important activity in people analytics, particularly during a transformation. It allows clarity around the mission, an understanding of current business challenges and sets the direction for the entire function and its work. It is only after meeting stakeholders and understanding their needs that decisions should be made around topics such as skills, operating model, data and technology. Approaching stakeholders is discussed in several case studies throughout the book, including a highly detailed description in the case study Transformation in practice: Allstate, in Part Three (The next steps for people analytics).

People analytics delivers the most value when it is fully embedded in the operations of a company. The chances of achieving seamless integration are entirely dependent on how well stakeholders are engaged: the more focus placed on stakeholders, the more likely an organization will be successful in people analytics activities.

The best people analytics leaders understand the importance of prioritizing stakeholder management. Piyush Mathur explained his approach to engaging stakeholders on joining Johnson & Johnson (J&J) as Global Head of

Workforce Analytics in an episode of the Digital HR Leaders podcast in 2020: 'The best way to understand how you can unlock value for that function [people analytics] is to go and meet the business leaders and HR leaders. In my first 90 days, I met 60-plus business and HR leaders, and I was fortunate enough to meet our CEO and some of his direct reports and really tried to understand where is it that we can add value as a function.' Piyush and his approach are further outlined in the case study below, Stakeholder Management at the top: Johnson & Johnson, in which he aligns the team to the most important priorities, and sets them up to deliver value to the business and J&J's employees.

Stakeholder management is critical across all aspects of people analytics, but especially when it comes to establishing the ambition and business projects, defining robust ethical practices, gathering, analysing and securing data, and implementing recommendations. Effectively collaborating with stakeholders should mean that work will generate value for the organization and the workforce at all levels.

The key is identifying the right stakeholders to engage. We will discuss a technique for mapping stakeholders later in this chapter. First, let's consider the Seven Types of Stakeholders who interact with people analytics teams (see Figure 3.1).

Each of these seven stakeholder types adds value in specific parts of people analytics. For some, the team depends on them for achieving successful outcomes to projects. Others will provide direction. Others still will be essential in providing the very data that is needed to be analysed. However, all seven types of stakeholders are important if people analytics is to achieve its potential.

We will now explore each type of stakeholder.

Figure 3.1 Seven Types of Stakeholders

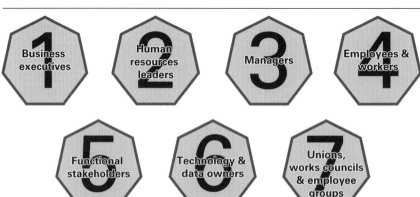

Stakeholder 1: Business executives

The first category of stakeholders is business executives. This category of stakeholder includes members of the board of directors, operating committee, C-suite and senior leaders responsible for a division, region or business line. They typically have direct responsibility for areas of the business such as sales and commercial, product development, research and manufacturing.

Working with these leaders means that projects and work will impact upon the right business challenges. These will make the business more efficient, productive and competitive in the future. Business executive stakeholders typically look for insights on the workforce that will improve business profitability, revenue growth, competitiveness and risk. Therefore, engaging with these stakeholders directly to discuss their challenges and how 'people aspects' might improve their business is a sensible action to take. Conversations with senior business leaders allow an understanding of the value and business tone for all types of analytics.

Business executives are also key to enabling the implementation of solutions. They can unlock valuable new data, too; for example, a sales executive can provide data about territories, customers and sales.

Below, we learn in the case study, Stakeholder Management at the top: Johnson & Johnson, how one newly appointed people analytics leader gained access to very senior business stakeholders. The key message is: *Doing stakeholder management correctly from the beginning enhances your probability of success in everything you do.*

 CASE STUDY

Stakeholder Management at the top: Johnson & Johnson

Johnson & Johnson (J&J)[1] is one of the most recognizable names on the planet, especially if you have children and have used its baby products. Its workforce totals approximately 135,000 employees globally and its revenue across three sectors (pharmaceuticals, medical devices and consumer) topped US $82 billion in 2019 (Johnson & Johnson, 2020).

The team at Johnson & Johnson believes good health is the foundation of vibrant lives, thriving communities and forward progress. That's why for more than 130 years, it has aimed to keep people well at every age and every stage of life. Today, as the world's largest and most broadly based health care company, J&J is committed to using its reach and size for good. It strives to improve access and affordability, create healthier communities, and put a healthy mind, body and environment within reach of everyone, everywhere. Today, J&J's Workforce Analytics team meets that challenge for the benefit and well-being of J&J employees.

In a company with clear values that are stipulated in a credo statement,[2] relationship building and stakeholder management are likely part of the culture. Upon joining J&J as Global Head of Talent Management (Enterprise Functions) and Workforce Analytics in 2017, Piyush Mathur found exactly this and, to his surprise, Piyush's desire to meet senior stakeholders quickly was welcomed with open arms. However, Piyush didn't do this just because of the culture – he did it because he felt it was essential to the success of people analytics.

Piyush was joining a workforce analytics function that was already four years old and had made great progress and developed expertise in running enterprise annual engagement surveys, implementing strategic scorecards and was starting to conduct research studies. Piyush reflected on how he could add value to a team with so much expertise and the fact that his former organization had a workforce only one-third of the size he found at J&J.

Piyush had a lot of experience managing senior stakeholders in his previous organization since he had been a member of the executive committee and reported to its CEO as a commercial leader. He was curious to understand how that experience would add value at J&J. As a new executive at J&J, this meant building a strong internal network. He researched everything he could about the company, its executives and his new Workforce Analytics team. By the time he joined the company, Piyush had the beginnings of an understanding about the business's people, history, strategy, values and structure. More importantly, he had already drawn up a list of people he wanted to meet.

In his first week, Piyush worked on getting to know his workforce analytics colleagues and understanding from them how they were already working with the business. His first objective was to understand J&J's business priorities and how people analytics could support them. Piyush spent his first 90 days meeting 60 senior business and HR leaders – including the CEO and all of his direct reports.

Piyush derived three key understandings of people analytics at J&J from his meetings with these leaders: first, there was an opportunity to better connect the data being collected to insights; second, there was scope to further integrate the team's strategy with that of the business; and finally, stakeholders recognized the value of the team mostly from its annual workforce survey.

The interviews also revealed opportunities for further prioritization and segregation of work across his new team. Upon talking to his team in detail during his first few days at J&J, Piyush was able to form an understanding of its composition and the skill sets and interests available. Reflecting on these findings together with those from the stakeholder meetings, it was clear to Piyush that a new team structure would help accelerate business impact and unlock the potential of the Workforce Analytics team. He established four groups of speciality: Advisory Services, Modeling & Insights, Organizational Enablement & Workforce Planning and a Survey Center of Excellence.

The keystone of this structure was the Advisory Services group. Piyush gave it a core responsibility of stakeholder management. As a group made up of people with backgrounds typically in commercial insights or business unit HR (BUHR), the Advisory Services team were perfectly positioned to enter into business-related discussions with the HR executive committee and the CHRO's direct reports. Piyush asked the team to insert themselves into the network, map out the key stakeholders and become embedded in those people's teams, attending their leadership meetings and getting a clear understanding of each stakeholder's priorities.

The directive was that Advisory Services would capture all the needs of the HR executive committee and business leaders, and then relate anything beyond a 15-minute database query to the data, statistics and IO psychology experts in the Modeling & Insights team. Piyush wanted Advisory Services entirely focused on the business, and not doing all the analytics themselves.

Finally, Piyush implemented a new ethos for stakeholder management for workforce analytics. He set up the philosophy that 'insight without outcome is overhead' and enabling it with four distinct steps and a structured approach to enhance stakeholder management. Where before engagement with stakeholders had been ad hoc, Piyush wanted Advisory Services to focus on structured steps to enhance stakeholder management (Figure 3.2).

Step One was to prioritize for impact. This was essential as the team had a limited amount of resources and, helmed by business-minded Piyush, an obligation to keep an enterprise-wide perspective on work.

A robust stakeholder map (see Figure 3.5) enabled the team to navigate J&J's complex network and work out the wider impact of projects. In 2018, Advisory Services identified 12 key stakeholders as an executive committee

Figure 3.2   J&J's Advisory Services 'treasure map' to great stakeholder management

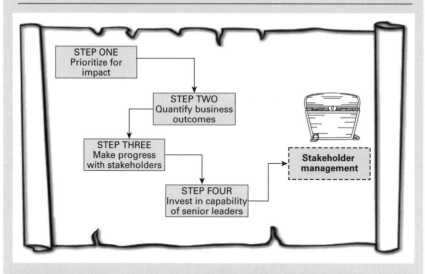

SOURCE   Reproduced with kind permission of Johnson & Johnson, February 2021

for people analytics. It gathered each stakeholder's priorities for the year ahead. The team then collectively reviewed each priority and drew up a list of cross-sector and enterprise-wide projects. These would be the projects the Workforce Analytics team would commit to working on for 70 per cent of its time over the next 12 months. The team's remaining 30 per cent capacity and resources were reserved for any other requests, which would be selected based on their potential business impact.

The approach made for some difficult conversations, but having a contract and commitment for projects that would address the business's needs made it smoother: knowing what projects were definitely going to be completed, believing that the team would be there to support them if needed, and understanding that there was a limited capacity for work because the team were focused on the wider business, were the key messages. The contract protected Workforce Analytics, too. Whenever some sectors wanted the team to do more or a different piece of analytics work, Piyush and Advisory Services would step in to negotiate: if we do this, you will have to trade-off with some of the previously committed work. This demonstrates how a consulting mindset is at the heart of stakeholder management.

The team could now move to Step Two: quantifying business outcomes in a relevant, evidence-based way underlined the need for prioritization and stakeholder cooperation. It also gave significant weight to the conversation when Advisory Services had to explain why it chose to work on one project over another.

At first, Advisory Services attempted to estimate the business outcome of work up front. This approach continues to work regularly, but in the case of significant projects, the team reached out to colleagues in other business units such as finance for help. For example, when Workforce Analytics wanted to assess the value of a retention project in China before starting work, teaming up with finance meant it could produce a quantifiable estimate of the impact of attrition on the business. Wielding return on investment and measures of potential impact, the team could quickly justify why it chose the most valuable work to any stakeholder. And this quickly gained credibility and buy-in for people analytics throughout the business.

Step Three was to progress these relationships. Advisory Services needed to consistently monitor and maintain contact with stakeholders, so it established a colour-coded RAG[3] chart to track stakeholder relationships in real time. This was the ideal way to focus the team's attention and effort as it allowed people to easily identify stakeholders who need help. Piyush also organized quarterly meetings with the 12-person executive committee to keep the conversation going on ongoing projects, pending initiatives and new ideas.

Step Four of the new stakeholder management ethos was to build capability with senior leaders. Over 18 months, with sponsorship from the CHRO, Piyush engaged with the C-suite and their direct reports to develop basic people analytics capability and created value to their business through fact-based people decisions.

With great stakeholder management at the highest level of the company, the Workforce Analytics team continues to provide real value to the business with people analytics. Piyush explains, 'the COVID-19 pandemic provided a true test of the strength of the new stakeholder management ethos. Like all businesses, we needed to respond extremely quickly. Because we were already hand-in-glove with key stakeholders, I found that it made a huge difference in not only listening to our employee sentiment on a weekly basis but also responding to their needs in almost real time.'

TOP TIP

Follow the stakeholder map to unlock the treasure trove of people analytics.

Stakeholder 2: HR leaders

Essential to any people analytics work is engaging with human resources executives, especially the chief human resources officer (CHRO) and their direct team. This group can place the heaviest demand on the people analytics team, and understanding their work and objectives is key.

Regarding the work itself, having senior human resources leaders committed is an asset in every element of people analytics. When investment is required, they can provide advice on preparing a business case. Senior leaders may even have budget available. When appropriate communication is required, they can be a supporter and advocate. They can guide work and provide change management advice when implementing solutions.

The CHRO themselves should also be a powerful supporter of the people analytics team. At the very least, they will be a significant customer; at most, they could be a boss and investor. Aside from a reporting relationship, the CHRO will also provide great insight into the corporate and organizational culture and the important (or not) role that people analytics will play in the business.

As a member of the C-suite, the CHRO can provide access to senior business leaders and information about other significant business, which might affect or accelerate key people analytics work. Finally, an engaged CHRO will support the implementation of outcomes.

One example of a senior human resources leader that makes a difference is described in the case study, The analytical CHRO: The Viessmann Group. That leader, Steffen Buch, is particularly thoughtful about using data and insights to solve complex problems, with the key message: *An analytical mindset is the future of HR.*

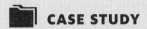

CASE STUDY

The analytical CHRO: The Viessmann Group

An analytical mindset is now a prerequisite for success in HR. Steffen Buch first had clear thoughts on this in 2015: 'I wanted to get away from that "gut feeling" approach you often see in HR, where people say, "I think we should do something," but not have the empirical evidence to back it up.' Steffen took his first step towards developing an analytics-driven HR function later that year, beginning with collecting essential data and identifying KPIs. But his ideal scenario was to lead an HR organization with analytics at its core.

Steffen joined The Viessmann Group[4] as the Senior Vice President of HR activities in 2017. Steffen felt initially that the HR department provided administrative support for the rest of the company more than anything else. 'I wanted to change the game, and change it very fast. For me, people analytics is a perfect example where HR can make a difference even with limited resources.' Being business-minded, Steffen was also highly motivated to help the business succeed in the marketplace and believed that people analytics could be the differentiator.

When it came time to establish a people analytics department, Steffen was looking for three primary competencies: an understanding of analytics; business acumen; and an understanding of psychology. Steffen recruited Mark-Christian Schmidt to join him at Viessmann as Head of People Analytics saying, 'Although he was working in a completely different job at the time, Mark-Christian demonstrated all three of these competencies.'

The two leaders met to discuss how people analytics could 'change the game' at Viessmann. If they were going to establish a data-driven people culture across the company, the question they had to answer first was: how can HR work both top-down and bottom-up? 'If you imagine the business like a river with lots of small streams running into and off it,' says Steffen, 'we wanted to put HR at the very heart of the place where those streams meet. We wanted to focus on the business, and deliver to employees, using analytics to affect the whole river.'

Steffen and Mark-Christian began thinking about the bottom-up approach: how they could have an impact on employees. With the relevant data, they found that almost 50 per cent of Viessmann employees who left the company identified a lack of professional and personal development as a significant driving factor in their decision to leave. Considering that individual development improves satisfaction and attracts high potential talent, the leaders knew that personal and career development would have a big impact on the employees' motivation to build long careers at the company.

At the same time, Co-CEO and fourth-generation founder of The Viessmann Group Max Viessmann was defining a new strategy for the company. Upon discussing this with Steffen, he asked the question, how do I know if I have got the right talent to deliver against this strategy? The question and the conversations that followed helped Steffen realize that employee development and career progression was also a top-down topic. He had found the confluence of the river (Figure 3.3).

Figure 3.3 Viessmann wanted to put HR at the confluence of people data

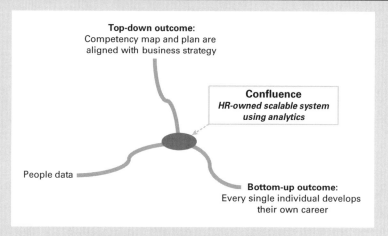

SOURCE Reproduced with kind permission of The Viessmann Group, November 2020

Steffen and Mark realized they could use people analytics to establish a scalable system that would address the development, skills and strategic challenges from both directions. The 'game-changer' would be an analytically driven competency model that HR would develop, and employees would own. If the work was going to produce a useful product, it would require a complex analytical project to define the components. Steffen remembers the moment he realized this clearly: 'The supervisory board believed that HR should be the function that should define which competencies were needed to deliver the strategy and help employees and grow in parallel with this.'

Reflecting more, Steffen recalls: 'How would I know what competencies you need in a Heat Pumps Development area? I'm not an engineer! But I can't ask the engineers themselves, also, because they don't necessarily know what is in the future, either.' Steffen realized he needed an analytical system that crowd-sourced information from existing employees, executives and managers, plus external research into the future of their work.

The people analytics team also combined data from progression planning, past performance, strategy and current skill sets to map out Viessmann's first competency model. The cross-functional co-created product emphasized HR's place at the confluence of the river, and it was useful to everyone: employees loved it because it helped them see the future, managers needed this data to have good conversations with employees, and executives wanted to see how career development would help deliver the strategic goals.

The platform was known internally as 'ViGrow'. ViGrow pulls data from 'job cards' that detail individuals' roles, salary, training record and feedback. By 2020, over 4,000 job cards had been completed, accounting for more than one-third of the total number of roles at Viessmann. ViGrow was becoming the established system for a skills-based mentoring programme, personalized training and a new format for performance review.

The breadth of data within ViGrow provided an overview of development, cost, skills gap and strategic direction for the business goals. Steffen believes that ViGrow is the analytical system that he had been looking for to bring HR into a data-driven world while benefitting both employees and the business.

Steffen also realized that being analytically driven means you have to manage communication and stakeholders well, throughout. 'Change management and implementation don't happen in a vacuum,' Steffen adds. 'So, we spent 50 per cent of our time doing the people analytics development, and the other 50 per cent on stakeholder management and communications. Gathering feedback and sharing our ideas – which only sparked more ideas, such as when we would suggest use cases for ViGrow – only made the platform stronger and more useful both top-down and bottom-up.'

A rigorous campaign of presentations, town halls and global roadshows (Figure 3.4) meant that employees around the world could engage with and contribute to the development of ViGrow. Covering multiple counties as far apart as China, Turkey and the US, Steffen gathered insights and engaged almost 25 per cent of employees in a three-month period.

As well as the ongoing conversation with Max, Steffen worked to secure senior executive buy-in from across the business. Involving them iteratively and incrementally meant that Steffen could develop prototypes and modules that would immediately demonstrate HR's intention to solve strategic problems.

Figure 3.4   Elements of the ViGrow communications strategy at Viessmann

SOURCE Reproduced with kind permission of The Viessmann Group, November 2020

Job cards and career profiles are at the core of employee development and, at the aggregate level, executive decision making. ViGrow is a supercharged, outcomes-driven, HR-owned platform built on simplified processes that benefits both individual employees and the business.

But more important than the product is the belief that Steffen had in building an HR culture built around top-down and bottom-up priorities rooted in analytics. It is often said that having chief human resources officer buy-in is important – but what is even more important is having them involved in driving analytics.

> **TOP TIP**
>
> Be bold, think analytically, engage stakeholders – the rest is 'easy'!

Stakeholder 3: Managers

The 'manager' category of stakeholder can be considered through three lenses: as a manager, as an employee and as a consumer. The former is discussed here, the second is discussed in the next subsection and the third is discussed in detail in Chapter 7 (Workforce Experiences).

All managers across an organization are increasingly interested in using people analytics to help them manage their teams, improve individual and team performance, and provide them with insights about themselves. It makes sense, then, that managers are generally interested in the outcomes of people analytics work. These stakeholders need access to data, want more insights to help them manage their people and regularly look for ways to more expertly guide individual employees to achieve more and perform better in their organizations.

It is almost impossible to engage all managers and gather entirely comprehensive input for people analytics projects. It is therefore an option to gather a group of managers as a 'manager representative group' that can become a body of people with whom the people analytics team can gain input, insights and feedback. An alternative is to collect feedback using employee listening techniques or text analysis (see Chapter 6, Data).

Stakeholder 4: Employees and workers

The role of the workforce as a stakeholder is very important. Ultimately, it is the workforce that is affected directly by people analytics work. There are three considerations: employees as providers of data, the employee ethics as it relates to people analytics, and employees as a consumer. The third of these will be discussed in Chapter 7 (Workforce Experiences).

Now, consider the employee as a source of data. People analytics is only possible with good quality data; the more, the better. We have discussed the growing amount of unstructured data and the fact that technologies exist to gather, manage and analyse this. With this opportunity, it is important to think of employees as the source of this data. The data itself is discussed in Chapter 6 (Data), but the topic of most interest with employees is the notion of 'fair exchange of value'.[5] If employees see benefit, then it is likely that they will contribute data.

This moves us to the topic of ethics and privacy. We have discussed this in more detail in Chapter 1 (Governance) and in the case study, Ethics, ethics, ethics: Lloyds Banking Group. The key is to involve employees in the development of ethical practices for people analytics. In that way, they will be more likely to participate in data-gathering situations, whether active[6] or passive.[7] This is what Accenture described in their 2019 study as the 'trust dividend'[8] (Shook, Knickrehm and Sage-Gavin, 2019).

Managing all the company's workforce with so much diversity is complex. Leading people analytics functions use a combination of focus groups, formal 'employee representative groups', active data gathering using surveys and text analysis and, increasingly, passive data gathering from company collaboration systems.

Stakeholder 5: Functional stakeholders

Collaborating with members of operational or functional departments such as marketing, finance, legal, real estate and IT can be invaluable as these functional stakeholders have expertise in their particular areas. Effective partnerships will always make the work of people analytics better.

Functional stakeholders should be engaged for various reasons: enabling projects to be scoped and understood for business impact, progressing projects that encounter problems, and providing support in specific areas such as creating an ethics charter (in the case of legal) or an investment case or ROI model (in the case of finance).

These stakeholders, in particular, can be a source of data sharing as described in Chapter 6 (Data). We believe in the principle of 'shared data is power', and this is a principle that is best held collectively with colleagues in other functions.

Ensuring HR as a function doesn't remain solely focused on HR topics greatly enhances people analytics work and leads to more impactful outputs. To do this, working with these functional stakeholders is essential.

Stakeholder 6: Technology and data owners

New ideas will open up when meeting this category of stakeholder. Technology and data owners such as IT, enterprise analytics teams and contracted vendors can ensure there is access to and understanding of technology and data across the organization.

Technology and data owners are integral to strategies for capturing and storing people data. Listen closely to their advice and they may even improve the efficiency and outcomes of the people analytics function by recommending ways to automate analytical solutions and help procure new tools and technologies.

Our advice is to be as open as possible to new technology and new data sources. These can elevate people analytics to new levels, as outlined in Chapter 5 (Technology) and Chapter 6 (Data). Having the enterprise or dedicated IT and analytics teams close by, metaphorically speaking, will enable the people analytics team to respond quickly to requests when needed, and long-term keep close to trends in the technology marketplace.

Stakeholder 7: Unions, works councils and employee groups

Occasionally, people analytics must involve unions, works councils and formal employment bodies for regulatory or legal reasons. Even when this isn't the case, it is worth involving these stakeholders as they can offer valid recommendations for making analytics projects more suitable and assist with employee communications once work is completed.

They can be especially supportive in helping gather opinion from the workforce as a collective stakeholder, as discussed above. Unions, works councils and employee groups can also be useful in a sticky situation, managing difficult topics and complicated aspects up front and providing invaluable support when operating in multiple countries, through their understanding of local cultures and regulations.

Building a stakeholder plan

Stakeholder mapping is a methodology to help determine which stakeholders are most important to meet. Completed well, a stakeholder map provides direction on the frequency of meeting stakeholders, the reasons for meeting each person and the topics to cover.

The process for stakeholder mapping essentially has two steps:

Listing stakeholders Beginning with an organizational analysis, list all of the stakeholders within the organization that will be useful to enable people analytics to deliver business value. Focus on each of the Seven Types of Stakeholders mentioned above. Be bold and don't be selective. This step is about listing individual people, or at a minimum the roles of those people that are important, even if the names aren't known.

If there are stakeholders omitted, or there is a whole category among the Seven Types of Stakeholders that is empty, or if there is any doubt about which category a stakeholder falls into, show the list to a colleague or human resources leader for help. Alternatively, complete this exercise as a team: it will be a collective people analytics stakeholder map in this case.

Figure 3.5 The stakeholder map

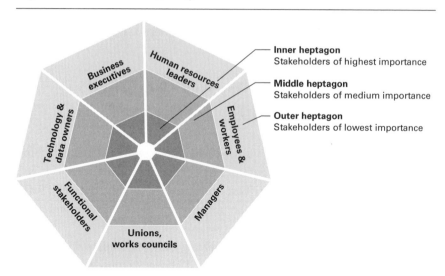

Prioritizing for importance   The second step is to prioritize the list. For this, we use the 'bullseye' approach. Think of the target as a series of concentric circles or heptagons – this is the 'map' (see Figure 3.5).

With a 'map' in hand, discuss and decide on the importance for each of the identified stakeholders: what is their importance for enabling people analytics to create more impact and deliver more value? Then place them on the map, with the most important in the middle and least important on the outer edge. If using a heptagon map, it is possible to see immediately if any categories are missing or if there are too many stakeholders in one category.

The map becomes a visual representation of the stakeholders that should be approached, and the order in which they should be engaged. It will become a dynamic document to assist with creating value from people analytics.

At the end of this activity, there will be a complete stakeholder map identifying all of the stakeholders required, listed by their importance to people analytics, or a specific people analytics project. This will be a helpful aid for developing an understanding of business priorities based on what the stakeholders talk about, which is discussed in Chapter 2 (Methodology).

Once a stakeholder map is complete, the process of meeting people can begin. Stakeholder meetings present the ideal opportunity to establish the business's priorities, HR's priorities, current people analytics work and measures of success. These meetings are also an opportunity for educating leaders about the potential and actual business benefits of people analytics.

Before arranging any stakeholder meetings with business executives, it's important to find out more about the person including their business goals, work history in the company and prior to the company, if recently appointed.

Meeting stakeholders of any type can be a very exciting and rewarding experience. One very strong example of this is shown in the case study, Business stakeholders are critical for success: Syngenta. The key message is: *Listening to your business stakeholders sets you up for success.*

 CASE STUDY

Business stakeholders are critical for success: Syngenta

It was a cold, damp day in December 2018 in England and it was almost the shortest day of the year. The sun was barely creeping through the clouds, and we were thankful that it was not raining. It was a memorable day because we were talking with Madhura Chakrabarti via videoconference about her new role in Syngenta.[9] Madhura was speaking from Basel, Switzerland, where she had been living for only a month. She was in the early stages of her new role as Global Head of People Analytics.

We were in discussion about developing her mission and goals for people analytics. As an ex-consultant and research scientist, Madhura had years of experience in gathering information to enable the formation of a business strategy.

'How many business stakeholders have you met as part of your first 30 days?'

Her answer surprised us. Madhura had focused her early discussions on gathering input from across the human resources function and had met with many of the HR business partners and Centre of Excellence (CoE) leaders. Her discussions were providing her with lots of information. However, we couldn't help feeling that she was missing a valuable component of her data gathering as she hadn't met a single business stakeholder at that point.

We talked about the need to gather insights from a broad spectrum of stakeholders and especially business leaders. Madhura became very reflective.

Our next conversation was in January 2019. This was a memorable day, too, joining this video conference as the sun was shining through the window. Madhura was again dialling in from her Syngenta offices in Basel.

'I have met about 15 senior business executives in the last 30 days,' she exclaims. 'I am excited by the depth of conversation with these business executives. It has changed my perspective. Talking to HR leaders gave me a great window into our company, and now listening to the profit and loss owners has given me another, different, perspective.'

By now, Madhura was two-thirds of the way into her first 100 days[10] and her people analytics strategy was being shaped with a broad set of insights from across a whole spectrum of business, functional, IT and HR professionals and leaders.

'Talking with senior business executives helped me understand Syngenta to a much greater level,' Madhura explains. 'They told me stories about their business. One executive talked about our business in South America. They explained that the business is helping local farmers as well as working with the municipal government on effective training programmes. They remarked on how difficult it is to find or develop the rare talent that understands crop science and that can also work with local governments. It was inspiring to get to the details of where people make a difference in the world. It helped me understand how Syngenta changes lives and helps farmers and businesses flourish.'

Additionally, Madhura talks about passion: 'The passion of a business executive is different from that of an HR or other functional leader. They see the business differently. I came away from conversations incredibly motivated to help them, and it shapes how I'm thinking.'

Madhura summarized the conversations into four topics which are focused on business outcomes (see Figure 3.6). 'The strategy almost wrote itself,' she exclaims.

Approaching the end of the 100 days in February 2019, Madhura sought to solidify the people analytics strategy. She met with the HR leadership team (HRLT) to secure buy-in for the strategy and the priority topics. The team were very excited to invest in the people analytics function because Madhura outlined topics that the business executives wanted and topics that the HRLT agreed with.

Madhura engaged the HR leadership team in real-time polling in order to prioritize the topics. Not only did she gain support for the people analytics strategy, she also demonstrated the power of real-time analytics to define

Figure 3.6 Topics for people analytics, following stakeholder discussions with business executives at Syngenta

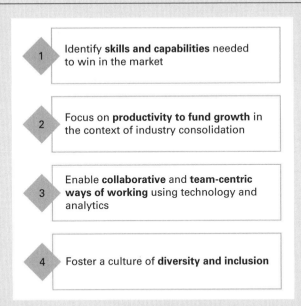

1 — Identify **skills and capabilities** needed to win in the market

2 — Focus on **productivity to fund growth** in the context of industry consolidation

3 — Enable **collaborative** and **team-centric ways of working** using technology and analytics

4 — Foster a culture of **diversity and inclusion**

SOURCE Reproduced with kind permission of Syngenta, April 2020

priorities. Even if it was a small group, this real-time polling showed how gathering data and involving people in the solution was an effective way to create action.

By March of that year, Madhura had a 'business-first' people analytics strategy with the full buy-in of HR leadership. 'In the end, I met with approximately 70 professionals and executives during my first 100 days. These all helped shape my strategy, especially the 15 business executives who gave me the most important insights into the business operations of Syngenta.'

Looking back on her first 100 days, Madhura reflects and shares her learning.

'I had worked in people analytics for years, understanding the marketplace, working with vendors and clients in a range of industries,' she reflects, pausing to consider her previous life. 'The skill I had learnt most in the first three months in Syngenta was the skill to "listen".'

'I learnt how to listen and not react. I learnt how to ask insightful open questions and then absorb the stories. Only then could I extract the themes. Listening is the greatest skill.'

At Syngenta, Madhura found that what she learnt from talking to HR leaders and practitioners was incredibly helpful too. 'Of course, you cannot just talk and listen to business leaders because I need to influence the HR agenda to affect change. So, talking to HR business partners and CoE leaders was incredibly important. It was the mix of conversations with different stakeholders that really helped me in the first few months.'

Asked how to summarize her first 100 days, Madhura is clearly in a thoughtful mood as she ponders this question. Finally, she answers: 'Listen, diagnose, play your "I am new" card to ask as many questions as possible, bring in external insights, create your strategy, be flexible to change, and be

> **TOP TIP**
>
> Listening to business stakeholders shapes the work of people analytics to focus on business outcomes.

Summary

Working effectively with stakeholders is the most important activity in people analytics and sets the direction for the function and its work. Take a considered approach to stakeholder management with the following:

- Meet with stakeholders and get a clear understanding of their needs, as the first step of evolving or transforming a people analytics function.

- Interact with all Seven Types of Stakeholders.

- Build a purposeful stakeholder map by listing all the relevant people in the company to rank them on a high, medium and low priority basis.

- Find out about stakeholders, their work and any preferred style, before meeting them.

- Ask good questions and remember that listening to a broad range of business stakeholders shapes the work of people analytics and helps create the relationships needed for long-term success.

References

Digital HR Leaders (2020) How J&J uses people analytics to drive business outcomes, with Piyush Mathur [Podcast] myHRfuture, 10 March. Available from: https://www.myhrfuture.com/digital-hr-leaders-podcast/2020/3/10/how-johnson-and-johnson-uses-people-analytics-to-drive-business-outcomes (archived at https://perma.cc/F2WZ-T9GC) [Last accessed 7 February 2021]

Johnson & Johnson (2020) 2019 Annual Report [Report] Available from: https://www.investor.jnj.com/annual-meeting-materials/2019-annual-report (archived at https://perma.cc/PSW3-QCH5) [Last accessed 12 March 2021]

Shook, E, Knickrehm, M and Sage-Gavin, E (2019) Decoding organizational DNA: Trust, data and unlocking value in the digital workplace [Report] Accenture. Available from: https://www.accenture.com/gb-en/insights/future-workforce/workforce-data-organizational-dna (archived at https://perma.cc/UG72-6K6S) [Last accessed 7 February 2021]

Notes

1 Johnson & Johnson (J&J) is a US multinational corporation founded in 1886 that develops medical devices, pharmaceuticals and consumer packaged goods. Through its operating companies, J&J conducts business in virtually every country in the world (see https://www.investor.jnj.com/annual-meeting-materials/2020-annual-report (archived at https://perma.cc/8LEN-EYH6), last accessed 21 March 2021).

2 In 1986 J&J established a formal document outlining its beliefs and mission to help society. They called it a Credo. (Learn more about the Credo here: https://www.jnj.com/credo (archived at https://perma.cc/3V75-Z486), last accessed 12 March 2021).

3 RAG – red, amber, green – status is used in project management to indicate progress or current status of a specific element of the work. Typically, colours correspond to a standard traffic light, with users able to see at a glance what elements are 'go', 'need attention' or 'stop' (see https://pmtips.net/article/what-does-rag-status-mean (archived at https://perma.cc/85QU-DQEC), last accessed 12 March 2021).

4 The Viessmann Group is one of the leading manufacturers of heating, industrial and refrigeration systems in the world. Headquartered in Allendorf, Germany, as of 2017 the company employs 12,000 people across 86 countries (see https://www.viessmann.family/en/who-we-are (archived at https://perma.cc/EW2W-PV4W), last accessed 7 February 2021).

5   See Glossary: Fair exchange of value. In general, this refers to the exchange of two things of equal value as the basis for a reasonable and honest trade. In the context of people analytics, this describes the personal benefit employees receive from analytics in exchange for sharing their data with the organization to enable analytical work to occur.

6   See Glossary: Active (data collection). Collection of people data through 'active' mechanisms such as surveys and wearables. It is active because the employee is involved in order for the data to be collected. The opposite of active data collection is passive data collection.

7   See Glossary: Passive (data collection). Collecting data through a continual flow of data generated from a company's communication systems such as email, calendar and collaboration tools. It is passive because the employee does not have to be involved in order for the data to be collected. The opposite of passive data collection is active data collection.

8   See Glossary: Trust dividend. The impact of workforce trust on financial performance when it comes to the use of employees' data. Most notably used by Accenture in the 2019 study, Decoding organizational data: Trust, data and unlocking value in the digital workplace (Shook, Knickrehm and Sage-Gavin, 2019).

9   Syngenta A.G. is a global leader in products that protect crops and one of the world's largest seed developers, with global headquarters in Basel, Switzerland. It was formed in 2000 by the merger of Novartis Agribusiness and Zeneca Agrochemicals. It has 2019 sales of $13.6 billion at constant exchange rates, and 28,000 employees based across 90 countries globally (see https://www.syngenta.com/company/media/syngenta-news/year/2020/2019-full-year-results (archived at https://perma.cc/57HZ-BSWG), last accessed 7 February 2021).

10 Franklin D Roosevelt coined the term 'first 100 days' during a July 24, 1933, radio address. Thirteen major laws were enacted during this period. Since then, the first 100 days of a presidential term has taken on symbolic significance, and the period is considered a benchmark to measure the early success of a president. It has subsequently become a phrase used in many walks of life, including what a business leader should do when they take on a new role.

Skills 04

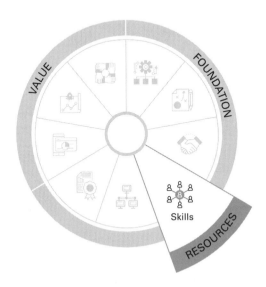

In this chapter, we discuss the skills needed for people analytics and examine the role of the people analytics leader, the specific role of an analytics translator, and the operating model required for success.

DISCOVER...

- the skills needed and responsibilities entailed in being a people analytics leader;
- an operating model for scaling people analytics to deliver value;
- why a translator enables more opportunity and clarity for success.

WITH INSIGHTS FROM...

- Standard Chartered Bank, on the people analytics leader;
- Capital One, on scaling the team;
- Royal Caribbean Cruises Ltd., on the importance of great translators.

Overview

SKILLS

Skills, as one of the Nine Dimensions, focuses on the people analytics team itself. It discusses the responsibilities and skills of the people analytics leader in particular, plus the operating model for the team and the key skill set for translating the business and human resources language into analytical language, and vice versa.

The skills necessary for people analytics have been much talked about in the past few years (Marritt, 2014; Andersen, 2016; Sharp, 2019). *The Power of People: Learn how successful organizations use workforce analytics to improve business performance* (Guenole, Ferrar and Feinzig, 2017) identifies Six Skills for Success (Figure 4.1) which we believe remains a succinct model for any human resources executive to consider as they establish and develop their people analytics team.

Figure 4.1   Six Skills for Success

Business Acumen	Consulting	Human Resources
• Financial literacy • Political astuteness • Internal awareness • External awareness	• Problem definition • Hypothesis building • Project management • Solution development • Change management • Stakeholder management	• HR sub-functions • HR interdependencies • International HR • Privacy and ethics • HR 'sixth sense'
Work Psychology	Data Science	Communications
• Industrial psychology • Organizational psychology • Research design and analysis	• Quantitative: mathematics and statistics • Computer science: databases and programming • Data awareness	• Storytelling • Visualization • Writing • Presenting • Marketing

SOURCE Guenole, Ferrar and Feinzig (2017)

While the Six Skills for Success are broadly applicable to all people analytics teams, new and additional skills are emerging in The Age of Value (described in Part One – The case for people analytics).

Some of these skills relate to deep technical expertise in data engineering, for example. While these are broadly captured in the 'Data Science' skill set, we have noticed some leading practices have recruited people with cognitive technologies and artificial intelligence expertise where needed.

A further set of skills increasingly sought after manifest in roles such as governance, including responsibility for ethics, data privacy, data management and the application of risk management frameworks. These are seen in some companies where, for example, data stewardship becomes the responsibility of the people analytics function, as we will see in the case study Managing data for business value: HSBC in Chapter 6 (Data).

Another example that has been shared is from Microsoft. General Manager, HR Business Insights, Dawn Klinghoffer explains in a 2019 article: 'We realized a while ago that having a privacy manager on the team was critical to our success. Her focus area is people analytics data privacy and security as well as partnering with other areas of Microsoft outside of HR on their use of employee data' (Green, 2019).

A final example of new skills for the people analytics team are those related to the productization of people analytics. When scaling solutions across the enterprise, having human-centred design, UX-design[1] and specialist product management skills means that people analytics teams have a stronger ability to implement solutions with more impact. Later in this chapter, we discuss these skills as part of a new operating model for people analytics.

While all the Six Skills for Success and the new skills described above are valuable, we will concentrate on what we consider to be the three most important topics for human resources leaders when talking about skills and roles. These are:

1 The people analytics leader – which of the Six Skills for Success (Figure 4.1) the people analytics leader needs the most plus the role's key responsibilities.

2 The operating model – how to organize the people analytics team to deliver value at scale most effectively.

3 The translator – a specialist role that has emerged in recent years and is an increasingly important role for people analytics.

The people analytics leader

During our research and conversations with business leaders and human resources executives over the past few years, we have concluded that having a capable leader who 'gets things done' is one of the most important aspects of people analytics teams. It is one of the key differentiators between successful people analytics teams and unsuccessful ones (Green, 2017).

This topic has been examined and discussed with many people analytics leaders themselves, including in two detailed articles with one experienced leader (Green and Chidambaram, 2018a,b), with the conclusion that there are certain key responsibilities:

1 Building and leading the people analytics team.

2 Ensuring ethics, trust and privacy remain at the heart of people analytics work.

3 Delivering value at scale.

4 Developing a culture of people analytics across the enterprise.

5 Shaping the future of the people analytics field.

We have observed that people analytics leaders originate from many different backgrounds. Traditionally, many observers and certainly several chief human resource officers we have met consider having an expert data scientist or an industrial/organizational psychologist as the key requirement. Our opinion is that a person to lead a team of 'techies and scientists' should know that language and have credibility in these skills. But they don't need to come from that background. In our experience, there is a risk they get 'into the weeds' too often and can't manage the various stakeholders.

Another option is to build the team with an expert human resources leader, who knows how to navigate the HR function to enlist support as needed from the human resources leadership team. Again, this is a solid approach and one for which a case can be made.

A further option is to bring in a consultant from outside the human resources organization (an 'internal' consultant) or even someone from a specialist consultancy firm (an 'external' consultant). This would be someone who has honed their skills in stakeholder management and project leadership. This approach can also work.

However, it is not past experience or the most recent role that are the most important factors in determining the successful people analytics leader.

Our experience and research on this topic concludes that other factors are more important: skills and reporting line.

Skills of the people analytics leader

The people analytics leader should possess a high level of expertise in certain skills more than others. Specifically, business acumen, consulting and communications (shaded darker in Figure 4.2). These are summarized below and then discussed in more detail in the following case study, The people analytics leader: Standard Chartered Bank.

Business Acumen

The people analytics leader should have a strong understanding of core services, products, customers and processes across the enterprise. They need to be able to converse with various business leaders and contribute to discussions 'in their language'.

Additionally, being aware of 'how to get things done' and having the required mix of courage, boldness, empathy and diplomacy are essential elements of being politically astute. The people analytics leader must guide their team through the right political 'landmines' to enable them to succeed.

Figure 4.2   Business acumen, consulting and communications are essential skills for a people analytics leader

Business Acumen	Consulting	Human Resources
• Financial literacy • Political astuteness • Internal awareness • External awareness	• Problem definition • Hypothesis building • Project management • Solution development • Change management • Stakeholder management	• HR sub-functions • HR interdependencies • International HR • Privacy and ethics • HR 'sixth sense'
Work Psychology	Data Science	Communications
• Industrial psychology • Organizational psychology • Research design and analysis	• Quantitative: mathematics and statistics • Computer science: databases and programming • Data awareness	• Storytelling • Visualization • Writing • Presenting • Marketing

SOURCE Adapted from Guenole, Ferrar and Feinzig (2017)

This requires having good relationships with a wide range of stakeholders, such as the chief privacy officer and financial executives.

Finally, possessing a very strong level of financial literacy will help with the people analytics leaders' understanding of and ability to deliver value – and make them a credible leader in the eyes of other executives.

Consulting

At times, the leader will be required to act as a consultant with certain stakeholders, for example, with the chief human resources officer or even the chief executive officer. It is important that in these types of situations, the people analytics leader takes the role of consultant and can use the appropriate level of problem analysis or stakeholder management skills depending on the situation, and not take on a subservient role just 'taking orders' every time.

Additionally, the people analytics leader should be familiar with project management skills. They will be expected to manage multiple projects and will require the ability to guide their team through project leadership challenges and change management programmes.

Communications

In particular, the people analytics leader should have very advanced presentation skills, including specialist skills such as data visualization and storytelling. They will need to present intricate analytical insights on complex business situations to a wide range of stakeholders, some of whom may have little time or patience.

The leader should be able to synthesize complex topics into effective stories, using a range of storytelling techniques, and to use those techniques to galvanize leaders into action.

Another communications skill is to understand and leverage the ability to communicate people analytics to employees. This is helpful in terms of communicating sensitive topics such as the approach to ethics and data privacy, for example, in a published ethics charter (see Chapter 1 – Governance) as well as marketing outcomes, and offerings to the workforce when solutions are productized.

The skills and abilities that the people analytics leader has in the three areas of business acumen, consulting and communications, will define the function's success.

Reporting line of the people analytics leader

The people analytics leader should ideally report to the chief human resources officer or another significant leader such as a chief analytics officer. At the very least, it is recommended the person should report to someone where they will get significant access to the chief human resources officer.

The reporting line for people analytics has been a topic of much discussion among leaders in the field, such as in the 2018 article by Alexis Fink and Keith McNulty which states: 'The most successful people analytics groups have consistent visibility to the CHRO or Chief People Officer. In most successful cases, the people analytics leader reported directly to the CHRO. Frustrations around impact were expressed in situations where the group was embedded in illogical parts of the organization, or where it had been 'passed around' due to a lack of buy-in as to its role and value.'

The best reporting structure for a leader is dependent largely on the size and complexity of the company. Research conducted for this book revealed that of 60 global people analytics organizations, 22 per cent of leaders report to the CHRO and 53 per cent to one level removed from the CHRO (shown in Figure 4.3). When the latter, it is best to report to someone with a strategic or transformation portfolio, such as vice president, HR strategy or digital HR.

The person to whom a people analytics leader reports and their proximity to the CHRO are the best indicators to the rest of the business as to the seriousness with which the HR function takes people analytics.

Figure 4.3   Question: To whom does the people analytics leader report? (n=60)

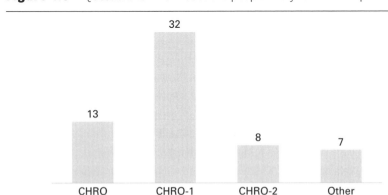

SOURCE Reproduced with kind permission from Insight222, November 2020

Searching for a suitable people analytics leader can take time. The skill set and drive needed to implement an innovative, new analytical culture and deliver results across a business is no mean feat. As we will see in the next case study with Standard Chartered Bank, the ambition with people analytics is determined by the ability of the people analytics leader. Their key message: *Getting the right person up front is key!*

 CASE STUDY

The people analytics leader: Standard Chartered Bank

Standard Chartered Bank is one of the 50 largest banks in the world by assets (Ali, 2020) and one of the oldest, having a heritage stretching back over 160 years.[2] It has over 1,000 branches located across Europe, the Americas, Asia, Africa and the Middle East, with 85,000 employees. It truly is a very diverse organization, covering over 60 markets, and its employees are at the heart of its operations, helping local consumers and businesses.

As part of the HR management team, Tom Howie is responsible for managing the group's HR operations, risk, business and HR transformation as the Chief Operating Officer in service of the design and implementation of the client-centric people strategy needed for Standard Chartered Bank. Integral to this strategy is the creation of a data-centric approach across the whole of the HR function and enabling evidence-based decision making by leaders and HR professionals across the bank.

Tom has thus been responsible for transforming the people analytics function to help realize this vision. 'Since 2017, the analytics team has been responsible for delivering scorecards and reports as needed about our people. These still continue to be very useful and we have a skilled team in India that brings this part of our operations to life.' Tom reflects, 'However, we always had another level of ambition for the analytics team, to bring enhanced insights, advanced analytics and commercial value on key business challenges.'

Tom understood that one of the most important facets of transforming people analytics would be to bring in a leader that could take people analytics to this new level: 'The team needed a different approach, and we decided this must start with the leader – an established people analytics practitioner who has "been there and done it".'

Before commencing the search, Tom spent time assessing precisely what he needed from the people analytics function and the kind of person who would thrive in the business and affect the change required.

'We spent a few months carefully noting what it took to succeed in our business as a whole,' Tom remembers. Standard Chartered Bank's operational structure is very different from most of its competitors because its operations are mostly in Asia and Africa, while its headquarters are in London. This global/regional structure and operating model brings a unique dimension when managing stakeholders across the entire business. 'So, it's critical that a leader in this space can expertly manage a large and diverse set of stakeholders and has strong cultural awareness and sensitivity,' Tom adds.

The research led Tom to identify the three key skills he would look for in a people analytics leader: strong business acumen, a consultative approach to understanding business problems, and highly developed communications skills. These were more important than having a data analysis or technology background, or a career spent purely in HR.

Standard Chartered Bank's ideal attributes for a people analytics leader (see Figure 4.4) were drawn from reading research and having discussions with numerous stakeholders from around the business.

Figure 4.4   The ideal attributes for the Standard Chartered Bank people analytics leader

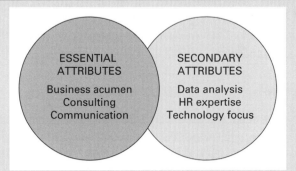

SOURCE Reproduced with kind permission of Standard Chartered Bank, October 2020

The key attributes are:

Business acumen

Standard Chartered Bank looked first for a leader who focuses on the client – ie the business – and helps them understand the value of analytics to improve their business, function and job. Practically speaking, this meant finding a leader with a financial inclination and an ability to talk business language with ease. The ideal candidate would also be able to establish and manage stakeholders inside the organization, have an extensive network in the people analytics space, and could bring leading practices from outside the organization.

'In a perfect world,' Tom reflects, 'the people analytics leader we were looking for was someone who was already a leader in the field: a prolific conference speaker, a well-networked practitioner, a member of a top-quality group of people analytics leaders. Also, someone who was passionate about learning from others and could bring leading practices and ideas into the organization. In the case of Standard Chartered Bank, we also needed someone with a broad range of business and commercial experience to draw upon – someone who had held a variety of business roles.'

Consulting

The ability to analyse business problems was at the heart of what Standard Chartered Bank wanted. 'We needed someone who would challenge the current team and take a problem-solving approach with a focus on business challenges.' Standard Chartered Bank clarified the specific skills needed to do this: high capability in problem analysis and hypothesis building; a strong ability to discuss, debate and decipher opinions from multiple stakeholders; and finally, excellent negotiation skills for prioritizing the plethora of requests.

'We felt that managing a wide set of stakeholders with a sensitive, firm and collaborative approach was going to be the most valuable element that the new people analytics leader would bring to the team.'

Communication

Due to the scale of the change needed, the new leader required well-honed communication, storytelling and change management skills. 'We knew a good communicator would make work relevant to each of the stakeholders,' says Tom. 'We've got a lot to do, and great communications skills make a huge difference – with key stakeholders and with the team. The leader would need to generate buy-in and followership from their team to deliver the required transformation.'

Standard Chartered Bank wanted to make sure that people analytics as a function would become a valuable, impact-driven partner to the business, more than it currently was. To do this, the team needed to move to a level where complex analytics solutions would be implemented and adopted broadly across the relevant markets and teams. This would be achieved through increased data democratization, increased levels of self-service and higher levels of competence and confidence in using people data by the business leaders themselves.

This integrated approach would require a full range of communications skills, some that are straightforward – like presentation skills – and others that are more complex, such as storytelling and data visualization. The ability to decipher data to get a story out across an expansive network of stakeholders was one of the most important skills required.

Equipped with this appreciation of the three key attributes required in a successful people analytics leader, Tom felt confident they would appoint the right person. Following a rigorous and extensive search, Tom and his colleagues interviewed a wide spectrum of internal and external candidates who applied for the role or were recommended through professional networks.

Tom explains that throughout the recruitment process he considered candidates' authenticity and long-term potential to thrive at Standard Chartered Bank: 'We wanted someone who would bring their energy for years to come and develop a data-driven culture across HR. This role would be integral to shaping, measuring and delivering our people strategy for years to come.'

In October 2019, Standard Chartered Bank announced that they had appointed Steve Scott. Steve had valuable experience introducing and implementing people analytics across another large financial institution. He was well networked within the people analytics community and had spoken widely on the topic at external events.

Steve had held a variety of roles across a 20-year career in financial services including finance, relationship management, operations, product management and business intelligence. With a proclivity towards business-centric strategic thinking and a natural communicator with a consulting mindset, Steve met the criteria that Standard Chartered Bank, and Tom specifically, was looking for.

'Steve is firstly a client-focused business person,' Tom reflects. 'He has already got to know a large number of stakeholders and engaged them in discussions about their business challenges and how people analytics can be used to help solve them. He has already developed a compelling multi-year vision, strategy and plan for people analytics here at Standard Chartered Bank, which is now being implemented.'

By the start of 2021, Steve had already started to transform the function through reducing the number of reporting requirements and building greater capacity for advanced analytics on key business challenges. A People Data & Analytics Council has also been established with stakeholders, enabling the team to focus on the most important topics and to build momentum across the organization.

Standard Chartered Bank is continuing with the transformation of the function and the implementation of its people strategy. But they have shown that the right leader can bring about change in an impressive way. Tom concludes, 'Steve is quickly building a data-driven approach across HR more than we have seen before. He is also working closely with business stakeholders so that Standard Chartered Bank will be a leading force in using people data to drive business outcomes.'

TOP TIP

The most essential skills for a people analytics leader are business acumen, a consultative approach and sharp communication skills.

Operating model for people analytics

One topic that prevails among chief human resource officers and their strategy and people analytics leaders is the structure needed for their people analytics operations. Key questions are: 'how should I organize my team?' and 'what is the best operating model for people analytics?'

Since most people analytics teams are growing (Figure 4.5) and are relatively young as a function (Figure 4.6), it is not surprising that these questions are being asked.

Our research for this book led us to conclude that existing systems and operating models are not appropriate for people analytics to deliver the value expected from their business leaders.

As examples, we have seen some teams 'hidden' in talent management organizations or reporting into compensation and benefits teams and other 'centres of excellence' in HR.

We have also seen people analytics teams not be a single team at all. In some companies, the activities normally associated with the people analytics team are fragmented across different departments in HR, IT and enterprise analytics. An example of this is discussed in the early part of the case study,

Figure 4.5   Question: How is the size of your people analytics team expected to change over the next 18–24 months, relative to HR? (n=60)

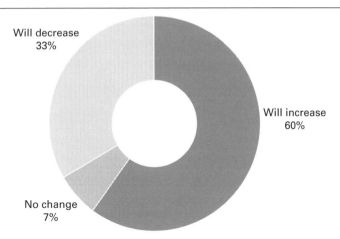

SOURCE   Reproduced with kind permission from Insight222, November 2020

Figure 4.6   Question: How 'old' is people analytics in your company? (n=60)

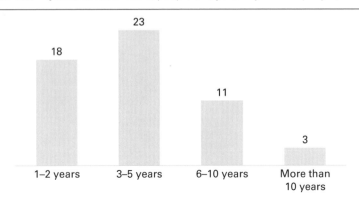

SOURCE   Reproduced with kind permission from Insight222, November 2020

Transformation in practice: Allstate (see Part Three – The next steps for people analytics), before the team leaders decided to consolidate their workforce.

The main reason why fragments of teams are located in different parts of the organization is often a result of CHROs not understanding the full potential of people analytics. In these cases, we have seen that they have decided to create efficiencies in reporting rather than focus on the value from advanced analytics. The team is split, with the reporting team typically located in a service centre of excellence, while another team of advanced analysts and data scientists is positioned in a different part of HR. We have seen this result in data scientists leaving the company in search of more exciting work and to be

Figure 4.7 Insight222 Operating Model for People Analytics

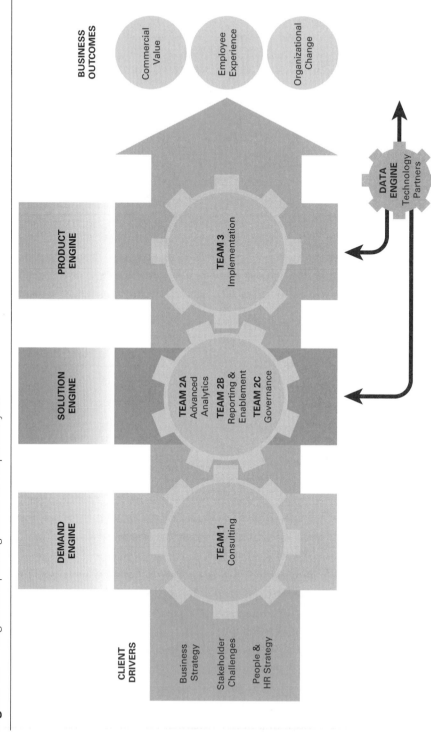

part of a bigger team, elsewhere. As such, the 'cycle of dismay' and lack of value is perpetuated.

However, in other organizations, we see that the CHRO is fully aware of the impact and potential of people analytics, and they are hungry to understand how to unleash the value.

In Chapter 8 (Business Outcomes), we outline the People Analytics Value Chain. This leads to a fresh outside-in, value-driven approach to people analytics, which requires a structure that will turn client drivers and requests into outcomes that matter. The operating model for people analytics shown in Figure 4.7 enables this through three 'engines': Demand Engine, Solution Engine, Product Engine.

Demand Engine

The Demand Engine ensures people analytics work is focused exclusively on business priorities, challenges and strategies. Consultants in the Demand Engine are responsible for understanding, prioritizing and generating the demand for people analytics work. The work includes:

- communicating with stakeholders to identify and define people-related business challenges;
- framing business questions and defining hypotheses;
- keeping stakeholders appraised of progress throughout an analytics project;
- sharing insights and recommending actions to stakeholders;
- working with the Product Engine to scale solutions.

The Demand Engine consists of a single consulting team of varying levels of consulting expertise which, depending on the organization, may be aligned by business unit and/or geography (Figure 4.8). Remembering that the business challenges should determine the skills in a people analytics function, generic skills necessary for this team include those in the 'Business Acumen', 'Communications' and 'Consulting' categories in the Six Skills for Success (Figure 4.1) specifically.

Solution Engine

The Solution Engine transforms client drivers into scalable solutions by analysing problems, delivering insights and managing the overall governance of people analytics. As shown in Figure 4.9, the Solution Engine is divided into three sub-teams.

Figure 4.8   The Demand Engine

SOURCE Adapted from Ferrar, Styr and Ktena (2020)

Figure 4.9   The Solution Engine

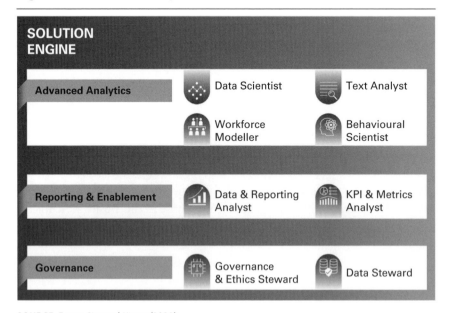

SOURCE Ferrar, Styr and Ktena (2020)

Advanced Analytics

Scientists and analysts who collaborate with the Consulting team use the most advanced techniques to test hypotheses and scenarios of the more complex people-related business challenges using any data source.

This team should possess skills in statistics, programming, research design, workforce modelling and behavioural psychology, and an understanding of cutting-edge data science techniques. One of these roles, the Text Analyst, is a specialist role emerging due to the increase in volume of new unstructured data that is, as we discuss in Chapter 6 (Data), increasingly important in people analytics.

Reporting & Enablement

A team of data analysts who are very familiar with the company's people data, how it is structured and intricate assets like data elements and the data dictionary.

The Reporting & Enablement team should have expertise in building KPIs and metrics, and experience in enabling HR business partners and implementing a business intelligence platform. They will often address ad hoc data requests (often from very senior executives), develop reports and assemble repeatable dashboards for stakeholders.

Governance

A small team of experts that formulate and maintain proper stewardship across people analytics, as mentioned in Chapter 1 (Governance). This team also significantly influences the shape and growth of the function.

It is critical that the Governance team have a firm grasp of the potential value people analytics can deliver in the company, mediating skills and up-to-date knowledge of legal and technological developments in the field, particularly regarding data use and storage.

Product Engine

The Product Engine is responsible for transforming analytical solutions into useable products and implementing them across the organization. Work typically includes:

- understanding the Solution Engine's analytics-driven recommendations and translating them into scalable products;

- building lasting consumable products using agile product management frameworks and user-centred design techniques;
- deploying effective change management programmes for implementing solutions;
- evaluating the impact and value of people analytics.

Building a Product Engine requires skills that are brand new to the majority of people analytics functions. Members of this team do not conduct analyses, but instead, they connect the raw data insights of scientists, analysts and psychologists, with the real lives of the employees, managers, executives and the workforce overall (see Chapter 7 – Workforce Experiences).

As this engine requires non-typical people analytics skills such as product design, implementation and change management, the function will likely need new resources. A list of key roles is shown in Figure 4.10. Again, always tailor the composition of this team to the demands of the business's challenge and the resulting people analytics work. Some projects may necessitate having a specialist user experience (UX) designer or a website developer, for example.

Figure 4.10   The Product Engine

SOURCE Ferrar, Styr and Ktena (2020)

A successful people analytics function comprises the skills and structure across all three engines and therefore takes an outside-in perspective, so it can scale solutions to the workforce. How a team structures itself is dependent on the organization. The 'three engine' approach of the operating model described above should be used as a guide.

An organization that has successfully scaled the team with an operating model similar to this is Capital One. As we will see in this case study, growing a team to deliver value at scale means doing many things simultaneously. It also means that the people analytics leader should be very purposeful in their approach and actions. The key messages are: *Recruit incredible talent and be useful.*

 CASE STUDY

Scaling the people analytics team: Capital One

The People Strategy & Analytics team at Capital One[3] has quadrupled in four years to almost 100 people. By early 2021, it is acknowledged as one of the most advanced functions, delivering sophisticated and business-relevant insights.

Managing Vice President, Head of People Strategy & Analytics, Guru Sethupathy PhD, has scaled and developed this team since 2017. A former academic economist and consultant, Guru remembers the mandate the chief human resources officer gave him: 'Work with senior HR executives to establish people analytics as the expectation and norm for the company's talent.'

When Guru speaks, it's with a thoughtful, erudite and business-minded approach.

The journey has thus far been defined by four missions related to business challenges (Figure 4.11).

Figure 4.11   Four missions to scale people analytics at Capital One

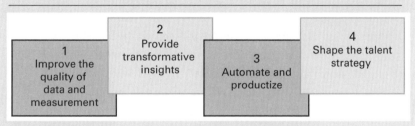

SOURCE Reproduced with kind permission of Capital One, March 2021

The magnitude of the four missions presented Guru with significant challenges: identifying the mosaic of skill sets required, building a suitable operating model and defining his own role as a leader. The key to all of the work was to recruit 'incredible talent'. There is a special lesson to be learnt from the sequence in which Guru did this.

'We focused on specialists in data quality, governance and operations, significantly improving the quality of our data in a short time. Once leaders felt they could "trust the data", we moved up the value stream. We then hired industrial-organizational psychologists to help us improve measurement, and data scientists, statisticians and advanced analytics experts to strengthen our scientific stature and insights. More recently, we have hired engineers and product specialists to build relevant products, and consultants to lead talent strategy. In this way, we have moved even further up the value chain, and now we have a focused team developing talent strategy for the enterprise.'

'In the early days, I asked our team to "just be useful!" knowing that the data would always be able to support their work.' Being useful led to high engagement with stakeholders and telling stories with data, and consequently, more demand for higher value.

Guru – who naturally works closely with Capital One's senior business and HR leaders – is passionate about influence and wants leaders on his team to be good at influencing as well. 'One of the things I look for in my senior leadership team, in particular, are people who know how to manage stakeholders and influence senior executives,' he explains. 'If we're going to deliver impact across the business effectively, we need to be able to influence a variety of stakeholders. There are a vast number of people, and it is important to see the world through their eyes.'

Today, the function consists of a full array of skill sets. Consultants, business analysts and strategists gather questions from the business, draw insights and provide recommendations and strategic council. Data stewards, software engineers and analysts manage the governance and operations of the data ecosystem. Statisticians and IO-psychologists provide expertise on measurement, surveys and research on organizational best practices. 'We have a diversity of skills across the team and I cannot say which of them, if any, are more important than the others,' Guru reflects. 'It is a full team effort from top to bottom.'

Structuring these skills into an efficient team was the next significant challenge Guru faced. His team owns the entire process from the moment data is input into systems until the insights are delivered to stakeholders, including the infrastructure, storage and movement of the data to technology partners and the cloud, productization and distribution of data and insights, and consulting and strategy. Pulling these tasks into a single team has been a great move, says Guru, as it has reduced friction, improved coordination and accelerated prioritization and action.

At Capital One, there are distinct areas of the team: consulting, data, innovation and products (Figure 4.12).

Figure 4.12   The structure of Capital One's people strategy & analytics function

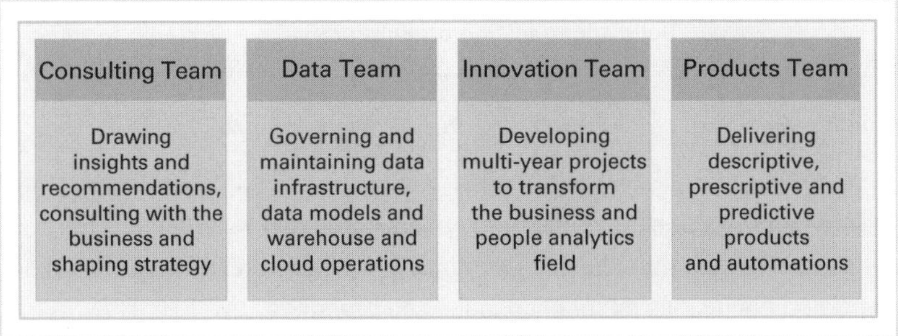

Consulting Team	Data Team	Innovation Team	Products Team
Drawing insights and recommendations, consulting with the business and shaping strategy	Governing and maintaining data infrastructure, data models and warehouse and cloud operations	Developing multi-year projects to transform the business and people analytics field	Delivering descriptive, prescriptive and predictive products and automations

SOURCE Reproduced with kind permission of Capital One, March 2021

It's also one of the aspects of his work of which Guru is most proud: 'Our team structure allows talent to move around and learn different skills and build different muscles like subject matter expertise, advanced analytics, modelling, productization, consulting and strategy. To this day, it helps us attract and retain great talent.'

Guru's most recent challenge in scaling was about himself: what is the role of the leader in a scaled analytics function?

Guru describes his role as multi-faceted (Figure 4.13). 'It's important for the leader to pick a few high-leverage projects and stay connected to the work, even in a large organization. It allows them to have tremendous influence in the broader company – and that trickles down to the rest of the team,' says Guru. 'So one part of my role is to lead and drive innovative work, and we actually own components of HR activities such as the selection processes for one of our major job families. We are not just advising on this; I am the accountable executive for implementation.'

Figure 4.13   Leadership in Capital One's rapidly scaling people analytics team

Upskill and shape the future of HR

Lead and drive innovative work

Set the vision, mission and strategy

Develop great talent and set the talent philosophy

Build a long-lasting organization

SOURCE Reproduced with kind permission of Capital One, March 2021

Another element of leading the function, Guru reflects, is to be heavily involved in hiring, retaining and developing great talent at all levels of the team, and defining its talent philosophy and practices.

Two elements of Guru's role belong in the handbook of all visionary leaders: 'Set the vision, mission and multi-year strategy,' he highlights, 'and build an organization that will outlast your leadership.'

And, the final element: 'Upskill HR!' Guru exclaims. 'Leading a scaled people analytics organization means supporting HR to harness the full power of our insights and products day to day – but also, helping to build the HR of the future.'

The People Strategy & Analytics team has delivered sophisticated people analytics work across the business, influencing talent strategy and policy, co-developed strategic and policy agendas with leaders of Capital One's businesses, and empowered better decision making at team and individual levels. 'We have business and HR buy-in because we do work that people find useful. No matter how "shiny" or exciting a project may seem, we always come back to work on the real initiatives that deliver impact.'

Reflecting on his four years of leading the team, Guru offers three tips for other people analytics leaders.

'First, start with the questions that are the most interesting and important, and work backwards to the data: build the data ecosystem around the business questions.'

'Then,' he continues, 'build out examples and proof points of value. Be useful and valuable. Once you have demonstrated impact, you will have gained the credibility that will allow you to shape the strategy of your partners and customers and to have even higher impact.'

People analytics is not some 'little HR sideshow,' as Guru confirms: 'Partner with HR but keep in mind that ultimately the business is the customer of people analytics. You don't want tension with HR, and you don't want them to feel like this is taking away from their abilities in any way or not allowing them to function in the best way possible. At the same time, don't hide behind the HR consultants. Build the credibility to be a trusted partner to sit at the table with HR consultants and the business.'

TOP TIP

Be purposeful in recruiting specialists because analytics is not some 'little HR sideshow'.

The translator

The translator is rapidly emerging as a key role in people analytics. Translators are typically storytellers with an excellent grasp of data and communication skills, and ideally a sound business acumen.

Translators are useful throughout the People Analytics Value Chain (see Chapter 8 – Business Outcomes). Chiefly, they communicate and translate business challenges into data problems, and share the insights and recommendations dictated by the data to make valuable products, then implement them across the business (see Figure 4.14).

What's the difference between a translator and a consultant?

Consultants are most adept at consulting (Figure 4.1). Translators are better able to translate data science and analytics into stories to communicate to a variety of audiences.

Figure 4.14   Translators enable work to travel throughout the People Analytics Value Chain

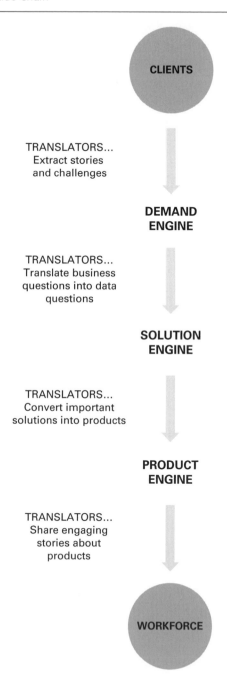

Although they share some of the same skills, the translator and consultant roles have several key differences:

- The business drives consultants' work, and thus they possess a greater knowledge of stakeholders and the context of work; translators are dedicated to bringing data to life and place a greater emphasis on developing skills such as public speaking and data visualization.

- Translators are typically better storytellers than specialist consultants.

- Consultants 'sit' in the Demand Engine, whereas translators could be any person in the people analytics team who happens to have highly honed storytelling skills. They would be brought into conversations and work, as necessary as a 'translator' from time to time.

Where does the HR business partner fit in?

Accomplished human resource business partners (HRBPs) also make great translators; they have the need to translate and bring analytics into day-to-day work. We will discuss how HRBPs can use this ability to build the culture of analytics across the business in Chapter 9 (Culture).

Let's now consider a case study that has defined the translator role to a high degree and uses it to add value. The key message of this case study from Royal Caribbean Cruises Ltd. is: *Translators convert business language to analytics, and analytics language to business.* This case study also shows that the role of translator sometimes overlaps with that of the consultant. As described above, we see these as two distinct roles; however, it is quite common that some of the skills overlap, and therefore the translator can also be a consultant. This is the case at Royal Caribbean Cruises Ltd., where the cumulative role is referred to as a People Analytics Advisor.

 CASE STUDY

The importance of great translators: Royal Caribbean Cruises

'I am not an "HR person" by background,' says Ramesh Karpagavinayagam, Head of People Analytics & Data Governance at Royal Caribbean Cruises Ltd.[4] 'I have always been part of a business and strategy team, with an interest in people and how behaviour drives business performance.'

An accomplished software engineer turned finance and people data modeller, Ramesh knows both the process and value of great analytics. With over a decade specializing in compensation and analytics with organizations including Capital One and JP Morgan, Ramesh has also developed an insight into what supports members of the workforce to give their best, and how that knowledge should translate into strategy.

'In business,' Ramesh remarks, 'decisions are often made on data-based evidence produced by armies of business analysts. Most business analysts are good at using numbers to tell a story. However, it is all too rare that they bring out the "people" elements of that story.'

Ramesh studied decision making in numerous organizations, observing how people talked to each other across landscapes big and small, and how data and information were communicated. 'I would regularly see big global product delivery teams without any supporters; no one wanted to use the products available as the solutions either weren't relevant to the business, or people simply didn't understand how a product could be useful to them.'

'The analytics service delivery model was set up to focus on technical skills. We had lots of people who could do the analysis – but few who could really tell the story. We realized that it wasn't sufficient to just have products and services readily available; we needed to explain them. "You can bring the horse to water, but you can't make it drink" – as the saying goes.'

Joining Royal Caribbean Cruises in 2019, Ramesh built the people analytics team on the premise that they would align business and people strategy to deliver exceptional employee experience through evidence-based people decisions. To do this, and drawing from his past experience, he constructed an organization with strong consultative and communication skills at the centre (see Figure 4.15). The people with these skills are known internally as 'people analytics Advisors' and make up as much as 40 per cent of the people analytics team. These people serve as 'translators', bridging the gap between data scientists and business leaders.

Translators are essential to keeping the channels of communication between the people analytics team and the wider business open. They interpret internal customer needs and help them understand the benefit of people analytics products and tools. Additionally, they translate the open data analysis back to the business line.

'Upskilling customers to use the products and processes with confidence, and in the right way to ensure accuracy and optimize simplicity

Figure 4.15   People analytics team structure at Royal Caribbean Cruises Ltd.

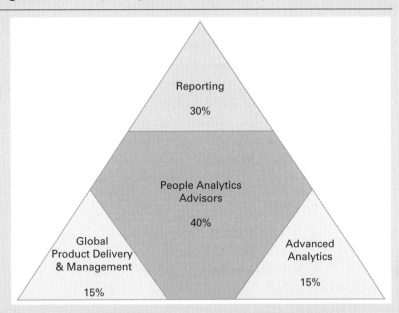

SOURCE Reproduced with kind permission of Royal Caribbean Cruises Ltd., May 2020

and efficiency, is essential to improving the people analytics team's credibility and delivering on our mission,' Ramesh explains. 'We need people on our team who are capable of doing this.'

Forming this bespoke team, the translators drive a cultural shift in Royal Caribbean Cruises that facilitates the understanding that people analytics can provide a new and better business and people solution than previously thought possible.

Skills that an ideal translator will possess are consulting skills, technical skills, and project and change management skills (see Figure 4.16).

First and foremost, translators must possess great consulting skills: 'They have to be able to feel, read and understand the customers' pulse, employing a range of listening and questioning skills. They must be good at building relationships and be able to talk about people with people.'

In addition, translators should have at least one of the other two skills:

- Technical skills: An ability – and desire – to roll up their sleeves and analyse data, understand patterns and possess enough technical expertise to understand how to develop an analytical solution.

- Project and change management skills: A keen view of building the steps needed to make analytical solutions 'sticky' and what is needed to embed them in organizations.

Figure 4.16 Skills required by Royal Caribbean Cruises Ltd. People Analytics Advisors

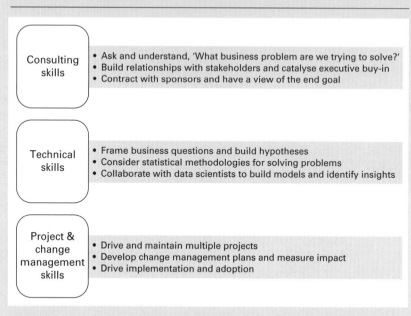

- **Consulting skills**
  - Ask and understand, 'What business problem are we trying to solve?'
  - Build relationships with stakeholders and catalyse executive buy-in
  - Contract with sponsors and have a view of the end goal

- **Technical skills**
  - Frame business questions and build hypotheses
  - Consider statistical methodologies for solving problems
  - Collaborate with data scientists to build models and identify insights

- **Project & change management skills**
  - Drive and maintain multiple projects
  - Develop change management plans and measure impact
  - Drive implementation and adoption

SOURCE Reproduced with kind permission of Royal Caribbean Cruises Ltd., May 2020

Ramesh personally has found that few people have all three skills. 'As long as a candidate has good consulting skills and one of the other two, they will become a good translator.'

Working across no more than three high-priority projects at any one time, the translators communicate between the people analytics team, human resources business partners (HRBPs), business leaders and more than 80,000 employees.

Ramesh has created an operating model to guide the role of the translators (see Figure 4.17). 'The operating model is simple and practical,' Ramesh outlines. 'High-performing People Analytics Advisors listen to the customer and their challenges, and are able to convert their people problems into analytical problems.'

The People Analytics Advisor begins with a 1:1 consultation with a customer. This conversation is based on a set of predefined questions. The Advisor explains that they are going to understand the business challenges first, the people challenges second, and then consider a data-driven approach.

Advisors are careful to avoid using complicated jargon and instead keep to language that works for the customer. 'The ability to adapt their

Figure 4.17 Principles for People Analytics Advisors at Royal Caribbean Cruises Ltd.

Develop deep client relationships with high-touch servicing

- Be trusted partners for HRBPs in strategic business discussions
- Take a proactive approach to spot opportunities to solve business problems

Serve as a point of entry for people analytics

- Prioritize the most impactful work
- Use Agile techniques to develop and test solutions

Create seamless connections between line of business and centres of excellence

- Connect HR
- Look for opportunities to scale across the enterprise

SOURCE Reproduced with kind permission of Royal Caribbean Cruises Ltd., May 2020

conversation, coupled with an understanding of business, are indicators of a good translator,' Ramesh adds. 'We look for all-rounders who can understand and talk the language of the business during recruitment.'

Once they have a picture of the problem, People Analytics Advisors regroup with the rest of the team, where they discuss the 'answers' from the consultation. Together, the team assesses the impact of the solution, categorizing it as 'low, medium or high' impact and forming a streamlined process in an Agile[5] framework.

The development team produces minimum viable products over a series of customized week-long sprints. The People Analytics Advisor then discusses and explores these solutions with the customer in an iterative fashion.

'Establishing a strong and personal relationship with the customer means that People Analytics Advisors have the opportunity to introduce and sell the analytical solution to them,' Ramesh describes. 'They can explain the benefits to the customer, always making it relevant and focused on the problem at hand.'

'Crucially, the People Analytics Advisor has the customer's ear and can explain how the solution is going to make their decision making or processes even more efficient and simpler to use going forward. It secures customer buy-in for the long run and can develop a deeper rapport that helps the team to develop bespoke, customized products. The people analytics team can also use information from the Advisors' discussions to anticipate issues and offer proactive solutions to customers' challenges before they even emerge.'

As Ramesh refines his team and impact, he is keen that the focus of People Analytics Advisors remains on high-impact work and the most important business challenges. His strategy to achieve this involves perhaps the greatest 'translation' of all: the people analytics team is transforming Royal Caribbean Cruises' HR culture to become data-driven.

TOP TIP

Build the translator skill set in your people analytics team.

Summary

The skills required by a successful people analytics function encompass a team of 14 different roles. As the conductor, the people analytics leader plays a crucial role in organizing the team, setting it up for success and engaging the business. Things to pay particular attention to include:

- Hire and develop a capable leader who 'gets things done': this is one of the most important differentiators between successful and unsuccessful people analytics teams.

- Develop the leader to be a master consultant, communicator and business influencer.

- Encourage the chief human resources officer to have the people analytics leader as one of their direct team and a part of the human resources leadership team (HRLT). Don't hide people analytics deep in the organization.

- Take an outside-in, value-driven approach to people analytics that takes client drivers and transforms them into scalable solutions and usable products that drive business outcomes.

- Build a translator skill set into the people analytics team – people who can translate business challenges into analytical work and convert insights into actionable recommendations.

References

Ali, Z (2020) The world's 100 largest banks, 2020 [Blog] Standard & Poor, 7 April. Available from: https://www.spglobal.com/marketintelligence/en/news-insights/latest-news-headlines/the-world-s-100-largest-banks-2020-57854079 (archived at https://perma.cc/K8EM-TYD3) [Last accessed 7 February 2021]

Andersen, M K (2016) Six must-have competencies in a world-class analytics team [Blog] LinkedIn, 16 June. Available from: https://www.linkedin.com/pulse/six-must-have-competencies-world-class-analytics-team-andersen/ (archived at https://perma.cc/Z2RT-HBMN) [Last accessed 7 February 2020]

Ferrar, J, Styr, C and Ktena, A (2020) Delivering Value at Scale: A new operating model for people analytics [Report] Insight222, 24 November 2020. Available from: https://www.insight222.com/people-analytics-operating-model-research (archived at https://perma.cc/7UEH-2QYJ) [Last accessed 13 March 2021]

Fink, A and McNulty, K (2018) If you haven't invested in analytics, start now. Here's how, TLNT, 19 September. Available from: https://www.tlnt.com/if-you-havent-invested-in-analytics-start-now-heres-how/ (archived at https://perma.cc/TX3Z-7AE2) [Last accessed 13 March 2021]

Green, D (2017) What constitutes best practice in people analytics? [Blog] LinkedIn, 16 January. Available from: https://www.linkedin.com/pulse/what-constitutes-best-practice-people-analytics-david-green/ (archived at https://perma.cc/82QR-VF4K) [Last accessed 13 March 2021]

Green, D (2019) People analytics for good [Blog] myHRfuture, 25 March. Available from: https://www.myhrfuture.com/blog/2019/3/22/how-to-create-a-people-analytics-function-for-good (archived at https://perma.cc/UU7N-BXMX) [Last accessed 13 March 2021]

Green, D and Chidambaram, A (2018a) The role of the people analytics leader – Part 1: building capability [Blog] myHRfuture, 22 January. Available from: https://www.myhrfuture.com/blog/2018/1/22/the-role-of-the-people-analytics-leader-part-1-building-capability (archived at https://perma.cc/7EGE-BC7Q) [Last accessed 22 March 2021]

Green, D and Chidambaram, A (2018b) The role of the people analytics leader – Part 2: Creating organisational culture & shaping the future [Blog] myHRfuture, 25 February. Available from: https://www.myhrfuture.com/blog/2018/2/25/the-role-of-the-people-analytics-leader-part-2-creating-organisational-culture-shaping-the-future (archived at https://perma.cc/DMN2-86BP) [Last accessed 13 March 2021]

Guenole, N, Ferrar, J and Feinzig, S (2017) *The Power of People: Learn how successful organizations use workforce analytics to improve business performance*, Pearson, London

Marritt, A (2014) The skills needed to build a HR Analytics team [Blog] LinkedIn, 20 November. Available from: https://www.linkedin.com/pulse/20141120213648-78008-the-skills-needed-to-build-a-hr-analytics-team/ (archived at https://perma.cc/28WG-9TT7) [Last accessed 7 February 2020]

Sharp, R (2019) How to build a people analytics team, *HR Magazine*, 24 December. Available from: https://www.hrmagazine.co.uk/article-details/how-to-build-a-people-analytics-team (archived at https://perma.cc/8R2F-K6EK) [Last accessed 13 March 2021]

Notes

1 UX refers to user experience; a specific set of skills that has developed in the digital and mobile age whereby designers understand the experience that people have of their interactions with digital processes and mobile and desktop devices.

2 Standard Chartered Plc is a British multinational banking and financial services company headquartered in London, England, operating in 60 markets and employing 85,000 people globally (see https://www.sc.com/en/about/ (archived at https://perma.cc/PG69-NN7D), last accessed 13 March 2021).

3 Capital One Financial Corporation (Capital One) is one of the largest credit card issuers in the US. It was founded in 1994 and is headquartered in McLean, Virginia, with almost 52,000 employees worldwide (see https://www.capitalone.com/about/corporate-information/corporate-offices/ (archived at https://perma.cc/L7RZ-RCRU), last accessed 11 March 2021).

4 Royal Caribbean Cruises Ltd., doing business as Royal Caribbean Group (NYSE: RCL), is a cruise vacation company that owns four global brands: Royal Caribbean International, Celebrity Cruises, Azamara and Silversea (see https://www.rclinvestor.com/ (archived at https://perma.cc/AEM2-QLTB), last accessed 13 March 2021).

5 See Glossary: Agile. A collection of software and project development techniques and approaches under which solutions evolve through the collaborative effort of cross-functional teams and their end users.

Technology

05

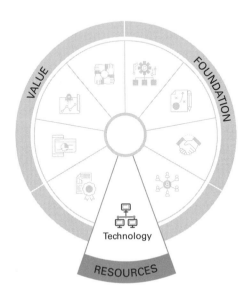

In this chapter, we discuss technology options for people analytics, why it can enhance business value, employee benefits and HR's credibility, plus topics related to procuring and building technology, and the productization of analytics.

DISCOVER...

- Three Waves of Technology for people analytics;
- topics to consider for buying and building technology;
- what to consider when scaling and productizing analytics.

WITH INSIGHTS FROM...

- Vertex Pharmaceuticals, on buying technology;
- Bosch GmbH, on building a technical architecture for workforce planning;
- Microsoft Corporation, on scaling analytics across the enterprise.

Overview

TECHNOLOGY

Technology, as one of the Nine Dimensions, consists of all types of analytics technology needed for successful people analytics. In particular, it outlines the topic of 'build versus buy', using technology to scale analytics solutions and emerging technologies to accelerate data gathering, analysis, insights and the democratization of data.

Technology – and technology companies – dominate the world. Technology giants such as Apple, Microsoft, Amazon, Google and Facebook are now five of the world's top 10 largest companies by market capitalization.[1] The dominance of technology in the last 10–15 years is staggering, as smartphones, tablets and social media have captured human attention. The firms – four of which the *New York Times* refers to as 'The Four Horsemen of the Techopolypse' in a 2020 article (Swisher, 2020) – and the CEOs that lead them influence the public and politicians worldwide. And they have achieved all of this at unimaginable speed: only two of the companies we mention above existed before 1990.

As technology dominates the consumer world (and the world in general!), it also dominates the world of HR. HR technology is one of the most talked-about topics in the whole of HR, and this dimension is the source of many questions and discussion. Top influencers lists like *HR Weekly*'s 100 Most Influential People in HR (2021) are filled with influencers in HR technology and related topics. So it is not surprising that chief human resources officers (CHROs) are influenced by technology giants, too.

Large HR specialist technology companies such as Oracle,[2] SAP SuccessFactors[3] and Workday[4] have or are developing products to support the delivery of people analytics work. Other technology companies such as Microsoft have also focused on people analytics solutions as they have grown their footprint in the overall HR technology market.

As the people analytics field has grown, a new category of HR technology has emerged: the people analytics technology market. Increasingly, technology companies emerge and self-categorize as 'people analytics', which is not only an indication of the overall growth of the field, but that technology is an important dimension in people analytics.

A 2020 study of the people analytics technology market by RedThread Research (Garr and Mehrotra, 2020) found that, despite the adverse economic situation caused by the pandemic, the market grew by 35 per cent between 2019 and 2020. The study identified over 120 people analytics technology companies and estimated the value of the market at $2 billion.

The proliferation of new people analytics technologies has fed fierce competition in the market, which has witnessed a number of significant acquisitions in recent years: Microsoft reportedly acquired LinkedIn for $26.2 billion in 2016 (Microsoft, 2016); SAP SuccessFactors spent an estimated $8 billion in 2018 to acquire Qualtrics (SAP, 2018); LinkedIn paid a reported $400 million to buy Glint in 2018 (LinkedIn, 2018), and Workday announced its intention to acquire Peakon for an estimated $700 million in early 2021 (Somers, 2021).

Research conducted by Insight222 in 2020 asked 60 global organizations, 'Are you currently using the following technology?' (Ferrar, Styr and Ktena, 2020). The results gave us an indication of how companies are able to address stakeholders' most complex and business-focused topics. An analysis of the results and a review of people analytics technology and how the market has developed three phases or 'waves', is shown in Figure 5.1.

The remainder of this chapter discusses the business topics each technology can address, how to procure technology, tips for the internal building process and a guide to scaling people analytics, all rooted in these three waves.

Although they are a significant part of people analytics work, this book does not include a description of the underlying technology required for data models or statistical analysis, as it has been extensively covered by experts

Figure 5.1 Three Waves of People Analytics Technology Adoption

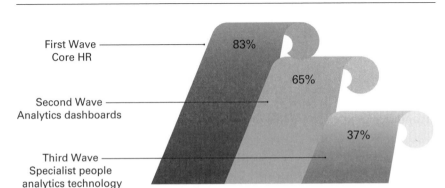

First Wave
Core HR — 83%

Second Wave
Analytics dashboards — 65%

Third Wave
Specialist people
analytics technology — 37%

SOURCE Ferrar, Styr and Ktena (2020)

such as Keith McNulty in his 2020 *Handbook of Regression Modeling in People Analytics: With examples in R and Python*, nor does it address data visualization, which can be studied with resources such as Cole Nussbaumer Knaflic's book *Storytelling with Data* (2018)and its follow up, *Storytelling with Data: Let's practice!* (2019).

The Three Waves of People Analytics Technology

First Wave: core HR

Technology adoption in the latter stages of The Age of Discovery and in The Age of Realization (see Part One – The case for people analytics) was largely characterized by the emergence of cloud-based core HR systems. Companies scrambled to move from 'on-premise'[5] to SaaS-based[6] core HR technologies that enabled them to take advantage of regular software updates. Our above-mentioned survey observed that 83 per cent of 60 global organizations had made this shift to the cloud by 2020. We were surprised it wasn't 100 per cent!

In the First Wave, core HR providers (principally Oracle, SAP SuccessFactors and Workday) captured the attention of CHROs, column inches and exhibition floor space at industry events. The hype around these technologies created a notion that these systems could do anything – some actually thought they could do everything – and that investing in other technologies, particularly for analytics, was unnecessary.

In reality, however, while a cloud-based core HR system undoubtedly provides a foundation for people data and analytics, it is not enough on its own. People analytics professionals with these core HR platforms typically encounter the following hurdles:

Data models   Similar to a beautiful house built on poor foundations, there is a lack of quality data models underlying the SaaS-based core HR system.

Incomplete story   A combination of difficulty accessing data quickly and being unable to incorporate data from outside HR systems into reports and dashboards means that managers, HR leaders and executives have only a partial view of their people.

Predictive analytics   The lack of predictive analytics capability means that there are limited insights and virtually no ability to prescribe recommendations for action. These core HR technologies were not initially typically designed with predictive analytics outcomes as their core solution.

Data inclusion   Core HR technologies are typically unable to add specialist data from emerging technology platforms meaning that complex business-focused topics are less likely to be undertaken using core HR platforms alone.

Human resources functions that have cloud-based core HR systems are able to deliver consistent HR processes and consumer-like experiences to employees for those processes. However, from an analytics perspective, those core HR systems can be seriously lacking, despite claims to the contrary, in our experience. They often do not have the necessary capability to deliver analytics beyond reporting, dashboards and some scorecards – and even these are usually limited to data within their own system. This is a common complaint we hear from human resources executives and people analytics leaders.

Another common pain-point for people analytics leaders is when their CHRO has been 'sold' a core HR system under the impression it will solve all their problems. The only solution is to raise the topic of the Second and Third Waves.

In short, core HR technologies alone just aren't good enough to achieve excellence in people analytics.

Second Wave: analytics dashboards

In the late 2000s, towards the end of The Age of Discovery we described in Part One (The case for people analytics), scorecards, reports and dashboards for HR were typically amalgamated by technologists on request, and using 'on-premise' technology. The processes of consolidating data and producing reports were largely a mystery to CHROs and other C-suite executives. So long as the reports were available, the time, expense and technology needed to produce them were of little interest.

Unfortunately, some leaders are still ignorant of the complexities involved today and their companies continue to utilize people analytics on an 'as needed' basis. We still hear of people analytics leaders complaining about the hours and 'all-nighters'[7] spent consolidating these reports just to show the CEO the latest attrition rate – or worse, to provide an accurate figure for the headcount of the company.

The Second Wave has gone some way to address this problem. Developing at an increasing speed throughout The Ages of Realization and Innovation, the largest HR technology companies, including Oracle, SAP SuccessFactors and Workday, created dashboard capabilities for people data processed in their systems. However, this proved to be inadequate as organizations needed HR dashboards that aggregated all people data – irrespective of the system that the data was created in. This led to new providers entering the marketplace, including Crunchr,[8] One Model,[9] Panalyt,[10] PeopleInsight,[11] SOLVE,[12] SplashBI[13] and Visier.[14]

Although the ability to aggregate all people data into dashboards supported by powerful visualizations is desirable, providers – and the people analytics leaders looking to procure their solutions – face a number of challenges:

Cost   The additional costs involved in procuring these platforms are often seen as 'additive', and 'expensive', even if they are substantially less expensive than core HR. Convincing senior HR and IT executives that these technologies are needed can be a complex and lengthy process.

Value   Second Wave technologies deliver significant value, but companies often view that value only through the lens of HR, instead of focusing on business benefits, such as how putting the information needed to manage people in real time in one platform at managers' fingertips, with additional insights and recommendations for action, leads to substantial, quantifiable benefits to the business. Sadly, many business leaders view these as 'soft benefits' (such as saving managers' time) rather than quantifying the 'hard benefits' such as increased sales performance, improved productivity or profit enhancements through increased retention and reduction in hiring.

HR capability   HR professionals often do not possess the technical expertise required to utilize these tools. This greatly hinders their efforts – in particular those of HR business partners (HRBPs) – to drive conversations with business stakeholders and limits the potential benefits of people analytics initiatives.

When buying and implementing Second Wave technologies, it is advisable to develop an analytical culture in HR at the same time. This is discussed in Chapter 9 (Culture) and in detail in the case study, Scaling people analytics adoption: Merck KGaA, in the same chapter.

When implemented successfully, analytics dashboards can provide huge benefits to any business. Examples include:

Executive insights C-suite executives receive consistent, accurate information about their workforce in real time.

Democratization of data The opportunity to democratize data to all managers in the business improves decision making around people and teams.

Speed of decision making The speed of decision making greatly increases as HR professionals are able to lead evidence-based conversations with people data in real time rather than relying on a few analytics 'geeks' to crunch the data by request.

Improved credibility The impact and credibility of HR as a function with its internal clients increases as the consistency of data improves. This is due to the ability for the aggregation of all data across people from all systems: core HR, non-core HR and other business applications, which enables the provision of insights at the 'click of a button' to senior executives without huge investment in time, money and resources on data engineering.

Cost savings The 'wasted time' undertaken by technologists and analysts in piecing together reports can deliver significant cost savings.

Organizations that have adopted Second Wave technologies (65 per cent as shown in Figure 5.1) have accelerated their ability to deliver scorecards, dashboards and reports at scale for data related to their workforce.

Some companies we have encountered achieved many of the benefits mentioned above through building their own Second Wave technology as opposed to buying solutions from vendors. The people analytics teams in the majority of these organizations are over 10 years old – before many Second Wave technology vendors existed. Typically, we advise functions to strongly consider buying Second Wave technologies to deliver excellence in people analytics.

Third Wave: specialist people analytics technology

As described in Part One (The case for people analytics), a key characteristic of The Age of Innovation for people analytics is the emergence of specialist technologies such as workforce planning, talent market intelligence, behavioural skills, relationships, productivity and organizational network analysis (ONA). As shown in Figure 5.1, these technologies are rapidly gaining traction: they were in use in 37 per cent of companies in the study by 2020, and an additional 44 per cent planned to invest in them by 2022.

In addition to those categories of technologies listed above, advancements in technology related to other categories such as assessment, employee engagement and talent management have been reinvigorated by a new breed of cloud-based companies. Some of these categories have been managed by people analytics teams for years, but it is the onset of these new companies that is injecting contemporary approaches to solve 'old' problems as well as new business demands.

The list below[15] considers some of the most prominent providers to emerge in The Age of Innovation:

1 **Assessment analytics**: Arctic Shores,[16] Hirevue[17] and pymetrics.[18]

2 **Employee engagement and listening**: Culture Amp,[19] Glint,[20] Humu,[21] Medallia,[22] Peakon,[23] Perceptyx,[24] Qlearsite,[25] Qualtrics[26] and Reflektive.[27]

3 **Employee text analytics**: Workometry by OrganizationView.[28]

4 **Labour and talent market intelligence**: Burning Glass,[29] Claro,[30] Emsi,[31] Faethm,[32] Gartner TalentNeuron,[33] Horsefly[34] and LinkedIn Talent Insights.[35]

5 **Relationship analytics and ONA**: Cognitive Talent Solutions,[36] Microsoft Workplace Analytics,[37] Polinode,[38] TrustSphere,[39] Worklytics[40] and Yva.ai.[41]

6 **Talent management and skills inference**: Clustree (Cornerstone),[42] Cobrainer,[43] Degreed,[44] Gloat[45] and TechWolf.[46]

7 **Workforce planning and organizational design**: Anaplan,[47] Dynaplan,[48] eQ8[49] and orgvue.[50]

The possibilities of Third Wave technologies are incredibly exciting! With these, people analytics professionals are able to provide insights to meet some of the most valuable and interesting business opportunities and challenges. Used well, the technologies enhance the work of the people analyst and data scientist, and excite business leaders to take action. Used poorly, they can be an expensive mistake.

As such, we recommend the following considerations before investing:

Start with the business question   The first rule of people analytics still applies. Don't jump to buying technology without understanding 'what the problem is'; there might be a redundant technology 'looking for a problem to solve' and, worst-case scenario, it damages the credibility of the people analytics and HR functions. Third Wave tools can help provide new insights around topics like productivity, sales effectiveness through the lens of networks, inclusion and company culture through listening tools, but leaders must prioritize the choices made and focus on the tools for supporting the business's primary challenges.

Use the right combination of technologies   Consider this metaphor: you cannot use a Swiss Army knife to build a wardrobe out of planks of wood – you need a screwdriver and specialist tools such as a chisel, hammer and saw. While some Third Wave providers are broadening their product portfolios, many of these are highly specialist in nature. Like building the wardrobe, solving complex analytical questions often requires more tools than a single multi-element core HR system. It may even be necessary to use a combination of technologies to solve a complex business problem. It might sound like a lot of work, but gathering specialist tools to solve an important challenge can deliver extraordinary value.

Be mindful of privacy and ethics   Some Third Wave technologies gather and analyse data that can be considered invasive. Considering whether or not to use the solution is therefore not just a technological question, but one for employee relations, privacy, ethics and legal, too. Challenging tightly-held beliefs and assumptions about the collection and use of people data in an organization is a powerful way to test, validate and reconfirm the company's governance and approach towards privacy and ethics. Third Wave technology demands a sound and solid approach to governance and stewardship of data. Read Chapter 1 (Governance) and Chapter 6 (Data) for guidance.

Buying people analytics technology

An entire book could be devoted to the topic of buying and implementing First, Second and Third Wave technology – and it still wouldn't be enough to share everything!

From our experience, buying technology for people analytics work presents several challenges. Among them are five key considerations:

1 Indicators that buying technology is needed.

2 How to navigate the vendor market.

3 Working with procurement specialists.

4 Ten key questions to consider when buying technology.

5 What to look for in a vendor partnership.

Indicators that buying technology is likely

Typical indicators for buying technology include:

Lack of existing solutions   The technology currently available will not help analyse a clearly defined and highly prioritized business problem, as described in Chapter 2 (Methodology).

Technology experts are not available   It is not possible to access the right skills in the people analytics team or technologists elsewhere in the company.

Time is limited   There is not enough time to build the right solution internally due to the importance or urgency of the problem based on the sponsor's needs.

How to navigate the vendor market

The people analytics and wider HR technology markets are highly complex and growing more so by the day. There are hundreds of vendors and this complexity will only increase as the number and categories increase. A proactive approach is essential for people analytics leaders who need to navigate the vendor market. This may include:

Keep abreast of the market   At a minimum, people analytics leaders should study resources such as the People Analytics Technology Market study by RedThread Research (Garr and Mehrotra, 2020) and the annual HR Technology Market report from Josh Bersin (2021). Further, leaders should nominate a member of their team to be responsible for undertaking routine and periodic vendor marketplace overviews and regularly updating the team.

Build a good network of peers in other organizations   One of the most frequent requests that we receive from people analytics leaders is to connect them with peers who already work with a specific HR technology company. A peer network makes it possible to develop a thorough practical understanding of the 'unfiltered' pros and cons of each vendor and areas of focus for potential discussions with them.

Have a shortlist of companies by category in mind   Leaders can save significant time if they have an understanding of the pros and cons of vendors by the time the business demands a solution. A ready-to-go shortlist, existing relationships and understanding of the marketplace also enhance the credibility of the people analytics team and HR.

Working with procurement

It is very important to nurture the relationship with the procurement team. Procurement experts can be invaluable in building an investment case, identifying and selecting the most suitable technology vendor and navigating what can be complex negotiations. Procurement executives also often have strong partnerships with finance.

The case study, Procuring technology: Vertex Pharmaceuticals, later in this chapter, provides a helpful template for working with the procurement team. Three highlights are:

Treat procurement colleagues well   Move away from a relationship based on 'immediate need'. The relationship with procurement will succeed based on trust and partnership. Not only is this good for harmonious internal relationships; it increases the likelihood that the solution that is procured is the best for the company overall. Start building the relationship before 'needing them'.

Involve procurement in the vendor selection   Let procurement specialists do their job. Don't be patronizing and tell colleagues what to buy. They have built expertise for a reason and should be respected, like all people, for the skills they bring to the business.

Involve procurement in the business problem   Support its understanding of the detail of the people analytics work, the specific problem to be solved and why a vendor is needed.

Ten key questions to consider when buying technology

Naturally, there are a number of general questions relating to the cost, license and commercial aspects that it would be expected to encounter when agreeing contractual terms with any technology vendor, and many more that would constitute a request for proposal (RFP).[51]

The 10 most important additional questions to ask are:

1 Does the product address the needs of all countries in scope?
2 What are the hidden costs?

3 What is the approach to privacy?

4 What is required of the people analytics team, both time and resource?

5 What is the policy for access to raw data that is gathered by the vendor?

6 What are the implementation stages for conducting a pilot and for implementing across the enterprise?

7 How quickly is the technology integrated into core systems?

8 What failures have occurred with the product/solution and what was learnt?

9 What customer and technical support is provided?

10 What is the vendor's financial stability (if a small firm)?

What to look for in a vendor partnership

From our experience and research, there are three areas to focus on when developing a partnership with a new people analytics technology vendor. These are:

1 'Real' partnership. This includes the influence on their product road map, what levels of support will be provided during implementation and after 'go-live', and whether the vendor will make raw data available (if they are a data gatherer) at no extra cost. Remember that any data collected is the personal data of the employees and collective data of the company. Provided appropriate access, security and disclaimers are in place, it should be available for analysis and integration.

2 Conducting pilots. Is the vendor open to an initial pilot period? Conducting a pilot where technology is implemented in only a portion of the company to analyse a fraction of the data needed can be helpful in evaluating the suitability of potential partners and their solutions. Conducting a pilot implementation project can also help in making a bigger investment case if benefits are realized from that pilot.

3 Privacy. It is important to understand the vendor's approach to data security, privacy, storage and ownership. Where necessary, be ready to involve the company's data privacy team and ethics council described in Chapter 1 (Governance). In some cases, openness from the vendor to work together to design policies and processes relating to ethics and the use of their technology will be extremely helpful.

As mentioned above, Vertex Pharmaceuticals provides a helpful example of how to 'buy' technology in the case study below. The approach and structure taken fit the profile we see of many people analytics teams looking to procure some of the more specialized analytics technologies. Its key message is: *Don't buy technology in a vacuum*.

CASE STUDY

Procuring technology: Vertex Pharmaceuticals

When you buy any technology, you should consider several factors: the purpose, price, safety and post-sale customer service. In the People Strategy and Analytics team at Vertex Pharmaceuticals (Vertex),[52] it is no different. The team has made both an art and science out of buying people analytics technology. It knows how to skilfully buy technology, put it to use and deliver a return on investment (ROI).

Vertex is an innovation-driven company that has had much success in the pharmaceuticals sector. With just 3,000 employees, Vertex reported revenues of $4.16 billion in 2019.[53] The People Strategy and Analytics team has embraced the same organizational values of creativity and research to become an innovative function delivering substantial value.

When Senior Director of People Strategy and Analytics, Jimmy Zhang, joined Vertex in 2018, the organization faced two challenges: a lack of data, and limited resources for people analytics.

The lack of data was due to the company's slim workforce; there was simply not enough data – let alone clean data – for deep people analytics work. The People Strategy and Analytics team quickly established solid foundations, and a new partnership with a third-party vendor to create a structure and database for gathering more and different types of data from the workforce.

This partnership would inspire the solution to the second problem: building a scalable people analytics function with limited resources required a new, collaborative structure. Vertex had a history of acquisition and collaboration with highly specialized solutions providers – and Jimmy knew that having partners who are invested in mutual success was the best way for the function to build capability. Today the team utilizes a combination of buying in solutions and building its own, blending the two to create scalable solutions that solve business challenges.

Figure 5.2   Three key elements of technology analysis at Vertex

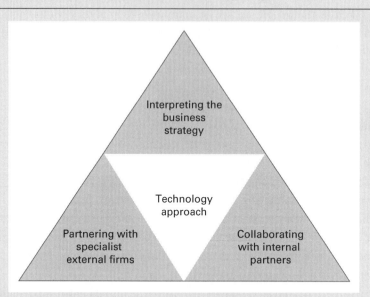

SOURCE Reproduced with kind permission of Vertex Pharmaceuticals, December 2020

Linking the acquisition of technology to the business strategy is the first of three defining characteristics of the team's approach to new purchases (see Figure 5.2).

A good example of procuring technology was in response to a need for external sensing to help understand the external talent environment. As Jimmy explains: 'The business strategy required a robust 10-year plan. For this, we wanted to build an internal capability for gathering external labour market data by "scraping". Very quickly, however, we realized it was cheaper to buy the technology from a specialized external firm that would give us the market data we needed.'

On the opposite end, Vertex decided to build the AI-enabled talent marketplace internally using their own bespoke skills-matching algorithm. As Jimmy explains: 'We followed our strategy of scanning the marketplace for an external vendor that we can partner with, but quickly realized that our internal skills algorithm performed a lot better than existing vendor solutions. Our team decided to go down the path of building a "Career Hub" to help people stay and grow their careers at Vertex.' Vertex decided to build this Career Hub using their own algorithm, their own technology platform and then partnering with a specialist vendor to develop a custom user interface.

A second characteristic of the approach had emerged: where there is a strategic need for technology, look for partnerships internally to help operationalize initiatives. Jimmy suggests building relationships with IT, privacy, strategic sourcing, data science and communications to enable success.

Together with internal partners, the team examined and leveraged external data to decide in what cases it should build versus buy. 'Buy' won this time.

Instead of contacting vendors himself, Jimmy involved procurement specialists. 'People strategy and analytics professionals are experts in people analytics. We know what requirements we have,' Jimmy observes. 'But the internal partners are experts in understanding the supplier marketplace and the mechanics of buying technology. Furthermore, everything goes through rigorous security and privacy reviews.'

'Going to our internal partners with a list of vendors we had in mind would have defeated the entire purpose of working with them. We really want their expertise in helping select the vendors, and this starts with working with them at the beginning of the process.'

The relationship with internal partners took time to get started. Jimmy devised a five-point plan to guide the conversation (Figure 5.3). 'We had to explain the relevance of the external sensing solution in terms they would understand – ROI, impact on the business strategy, the kind of business challenges we were solving and,' Jimmy stresses, 'why we wanted their help.'

Figure 5.3 Jimmy Zhang's 'quick tips' for partnering with procurement specialists

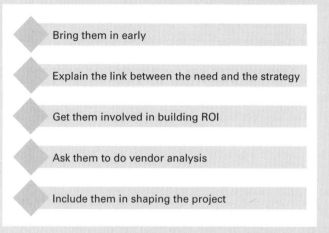

Bring them in early

Explain the link between the need and the strategy

Get them involved in building ROI

Ask them to do vendor analysis

Include them in shaping the project

SOURCE Reproduced with kind permission of Vertex Pharmaceuticals, December 2020

'I see our internal partners as key collaborators who have a strong voice in everything we do. Bringing them into the conversation at the beginning of the process, and spending time explaining the value of work in a business context – especially when it is leading-edge and something they have never heard of – is the best way to work with them.' Strong cross-functional collaboration helps with vendor proposals and selection criteria in an agile way.

And that brings us to the third element of the approach (Figure 5.2): partnering with a highly specialized external partner.

The process of choosing the technology partner for the provision of external talent market data was as follows: a series of discussions with the companies established if they could provide exactly the solution Jimmy and the team needed. Then, the companies were asked to analyse sample data – in this case, all historical postings over a three-year period. On delivery, the data scientists validated the results, comparing them to Vertex's own data, to assess accuracy.

One vendor was more suitable for Vertex's needs. The entire process and purchase cost less than internal development. In addition, the vendor was able to provide the team with raw data from outside Vertex, which contributed to the team's data-gathering efforts. The initial work was quickly assessed for impact and, as it exactly fulfilled the business's need and strategic goals, was scaled.

'We work quickly and undertake pilots wherever possible,' Jimmy reflects. 'When a solution isn't quite what we need, the relationship is terminated, and the team moves on. When we do find the right solution, however, we validate the work and build a deep partnership.'

Curiously, the deciding factor is not usually the technology itself, Jimmy says, but the vendor's approach to collaboration that tips the balance: 'We only invest in vendors who want to really partner with us – not just supply a tool. We are a team of innovators and subject matter experts and we want to work hand-in-glove with our partners. If a vendor invites our internal development team to meet and is excited to collaborate with us to develop their product, then we know it will be a successful relationship.'

Since the initial project, the People Strategy and Analytics team has invested heavily in a blend of buying and building technology to cement its position as a value-adding function. Some examples of this include buying technology for research, employee listening, data aggregation and visualization, and building technology to create an internal hub to help employees stay and grow their careers at Vertex.

Figure 5.4 Jimmy Zhang's five tips for buying technology

1

Technology purchase or building should always be aligned under one strategy – don't buy tech because you feel like it. Buy it because it aligns to the strategy and work you are doing.

2

Partner with experts – buy them in for the job you want them to do. Don't try to compromise with a technology vendor who doesn't have deep expertise in what the work is.

3

When you buy something, try it out first – piloting. If it works, move ahead. If it isn't solving what you want, cut it off quickly.

4

Don't be tied to a Build or a Buy strategy – be flexible in your approach.

5

Don't look at a technology vendor as a supplier – look at them as a partner. When you do the analysis, talk to their tech team, their product management team, their data scientists. Get to know them.

SOURCE Reproduced with kind permission of Vertex Pharmaceuticals, December 2020

One project in particular that epitomizes the team's three-pronged approach to technology acquisition is its work on organizational network analysis (ONA). 'The business wanted a deep understanding of how employees impact productivity with the hypothesis that networks between people were important,' says Jimmy.

'We collaborated with our internal partners in the first week of this project. We started the conversation with – as always – "We want to do good things for the business, and we need your help".' The team explained how each function could support the work, making sure the right tool was selected and that the right processes were put in place.

Strategic sourcing and IT submitted a list of the three leading companies aligned with the strategy and goals. 'They even gave us names that we weren't familiar with!' Jimmy recalls.

Jimmy has learnt valuable lessons working with Vertex to build and buy multiple technologies. When it comes to procuring new technology, he offers five tips (Figure 5.4).

'Interpreting the business strategy and collaborating with internal teams gives us the framework for selecting the right technologies. It is this three-pronged approach that allows us to take our work to the next level.'

TOP TIP

Buy technology only when it makes sense.

Building people analytics technology

Developing or 'building' technology to productize people analytics solutions can be complex to undertake. But since occasionally it is the only route to take, sometimes it's necessary.

This section of the chapter focuses on four factors to consider when building, rather than buying, technology to support people analytics work:

1 Indicators that building technology is needed.

2 How to work with the enterprise and HR technology teams.

3 Ten key questions to consider when building technology.

4 What to look for in an internal technology partnership.

Indicators that building technology is needed

Typical indicators that will likely lead to choosing to 'build' rather than 'buy' technology include:

Use cases are complex   Once a vendor marketplace assessment has been completed, it is key to understand if they meet the necessary 'use cases'. If not, then building technology 'in-house' is likely. Such an example is provided in the case study, Architecture for the skill world: Bosch, described later in this chapter. In this case study, they concluded that of 40 'use cases' identified, no vendor could address more than two with their 'pre-built' solutions.

Long-term corporate strategy   If the business needs are complex and important to the long-term corporate strategy, it may be more sensible to build the long-term technical infrastructure 'in-house'. That is especially true if there is serious sponsorship of the analytics and resulting recommendations since, in these scenarios, the resource will likely be made available alongside a strong investment case. Such an example is provided in the case study, The analytical CHRO: The Viessmann Group in Chapter 3, Stakeholder Management. In this case study, Viessmann built its own ViGrow product following a drive for skills development and retention that was sponsored by the CEO in line with the group's strategy.

Investment case   A well-constructed investment case shows there is a need for deep technical skills for the duration of the project analysis and productization. The case indicates that there will be a greater return on investment if the technology is built in-house and that it will deliver a better, faster, more cost-effective solution with greater employee benefits.

How to work with the enterprise and HR technology teams

Building technology in-house for analytics – either the analysis or the productization – is not simple and may require significant time and commitment from the people analytics team throughout.

These are steps to consider when working with enterprise and HR technology teams:

Learn their language   Take time to understand the language of technology. If key points being discussed are not understood due to 'tech jargon', the solution risks being designed without meeting project requirements.

Involve them in the business rationale   Include colleagues from enterprise and HR technology teams as part of the overall team for the analytics project. Involving people in the discussion from the earliest stage of the analytics methodology (see Chapter 2, Methodology) is wise. Allow the technology team to hear directly from the project sponsor and other key stakeholders.

Build expertise within the people analytics and HR team   While technology is built or delivered outside of the people analytics team, data stewardship and the data model should be owned from within the people analytics team. The same is true of analytics productization. The accountability for product management of an analytics solution rests with the people analytics leader, not with the technology team. These roles and responsibilities are discussed as part of the section on the Product Engine, within Chapter 4 (Skills).

Ten key questions to consider when building technology

There are many questions to ask an internal technology team, but since both the people analytics and enterprise technology teams already work in the company, it is expected that strategic and behavioural alignment is strong. However, there are still many topics to discuss in detail.

Some of the questions to consider, once it is decided to build a people analytics technology solution in-house, are:

1 Who is the key business sponsor for the project? (See Chapter 2, Methodology, for more details on sponsorship.)

2 Is the investment case validated and has it been 'signed off' by relevant colleagues in finance and technology?

3 Is the right level of representation from HR, technology, privacy and finance involved for executive support and decision making?

4 Will a governance board be needed (see Chapter 1, Governance) to manage the project?

5 Who is assigned from technology, HR and legal to build the product?

6 Is there access to human-centred design skills to support the implementation of the analytics solution?

7 If the product being built involves data gathering and storage, has consideration been given to data privacy?

8 How will employee communications be managed?

9 How will the relevancy of the technology offering be maintained over time?

10 How will the technology meet the potential changing demands of the business?

What to look for in an internal technology partnership

Interestingly, the same three areas we highlighted earlier in the chapter (What to look for in a vendor partnership) also apply, albeit framed slightly differently, when developing a technology partnership internally. These are:

1 **'Real' partnering.** Is the in-house technology team invested for the duration of the analytics project/product? Are they passionate about the problem that is being solved and prepared to work together on the analysis, implementation, product road map and long-term development and maintenance of the product?

2 **Conducting pilots.** Is flexibility offered? The technology team must be willing to pilot and implement across the enterprise or significant business unit(s). Any pilots conducted for either the analysis or implementation phases will allow iteration and co-creation of solutions. The internal technology colleagues will need to have the tenacity and the courage to scale solutions.

3 **Privacy.** Will the internal technology partner be supportive of the work and prepared to work together to address any data privacy challenges? Or will it cite that the project has not been 'signed-off' and simply 'stop work'? It is important to work with technology and legal colleagues to overcome any hurdles related to data privacy.

Bosch provides a practical example of building technology. Specifically, its people analytics team permitted us to discuss a project related to skills and strategic workforce planning. During our discussions, the team's leaders emphasized one key message for others: *Technology enables the strategy. Technology does not become the strategy.*

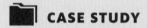 **CASE STUDY**

Architecture for the skill world: Bosch

This is the story of how Bosch put strategy ahead of technological capability, reached new technological heights and added real business value in the field of people analytics skill management.

Bosch's Skill platform is a bit like the film, *Avatar*. It is said that film director James Cameron first dreamt up the blue-hued alien world of *Avatar* in the 1960s – but it took until 2009 for the film to be made because the technology needed to bring the idea to life did not yet exist (Johnson, 2009). In fact, the only way the movie made it to screens at all is because Cameron and his team built the necessary technology themselves.

And this is what Steffen Riesenbeck, Head of People Analytics at Bosch,[54] explained to us: 'Delivering against the new Bosch strategy, I remember having 40 use cases but each vendor could only manage a maximum of two. So we had to build the technology ourselves.'

Speaking with Steffen's former boss, Rosa Lee, then Senior Vice President of Global Human Resources Management at Bosch, in 2019, we got a strong sense that people analytics was a new and expanding capability for the organization.

'We should be absolutely aligned to the business strategy,' Rosa said. 'And we need to bring a data-driven approach to all our work, irrespective of how complicated the business challenge may be.'

Steffen's breakthrough came about in response to Bosch's transformation into an Artificial Intelligence of Things (AIoT) company. This journey required Bosch to scale and automate its operations to an advanced level. Every aspect of the business was impacted. As the leader of people analytics, Steffen knew that he needed to transform his own team and the organization into an AIoT company.

Steffen met with dozens of stakeholders around the business in 2019 to discuss the skills needed in the wake of the transformation. His research revealed that many employees were concerned about the rapid changes in the business and how they would fit into the new strategy and Bosch's future. People analytics combined with digital solutions, Steffen realized, could add value, both to employees and the business, planning, facilitating and contributing to Bosch's transformation. Steffen drew up a vision for people analytics: the team would implement a business-wide, analytics-driven, instantly accessible and actionable strategic skill solution. Every member of Bosch's workforce would be able to access their own and aggregate data on what skills currently exist and how they should be developed to be aligned with the new business.

Figure 5.5   Strengths, weaknesses, opportunities and threats to a skills management platform as defined by Bosch's people analytics team

STRENGTHS	WEAKNESSES
Bosch is an advanced engineering company Bosch has a culture of technology	Small people analytics team Products must be available in multiple languages Hundreds of vendors on the market to search through
OPPORTUNITIES	THREATS
Senior executives and key stakeholders want the project	If the product is not built quickly, talent will leave

SOURCE   Reproduced with kind permission of Bosch, February 2021

Steffen and his team undertook a thorough assessment of the strengths, weaknesses, opportunities and threats (SWOT) it would face as it produced the highly complex project (Figure 5.5). The SWOT analysis revealed a major challenge the team faced: with just five people, most of whom were without significant experience of projects at this scale, the team needed help. Wanting to execute the project at speed and in line with the timelines laid out in the business strategy, buying in the expertise and technical capability necessary to complete the work seemed the smoothest way forward.

Before reaching out to vendors, the team needed to clarify the vision for the project and understand the ways it could impact and add value to the business. Working with the aforementioned stakeholders in different functions, Steffen was able to produce a clear outline for the platform with detailed descriptions of 40 use cases that the business and employees required in a future skills platform. Once the use cases were defined, Steffen reached out to the vendor market.

One after the other, the meetings with vendors proceeded in the same fashion: Steffen would share the project outline and its 40 use cases, and the vendor would say, 'Yes, we can help you… with maybe one or two of those!'

It became clear that buying technology solutions to power the platform would mean one of two things: either a compromise on delivering value to the business, or the team would need to stitch different technologies together, which would take time and money, and potentially wouldn't solve the challenge. 'Neither of these options felt right, so we stuck to basics. We would not compromise the strategy to fit the technology.'

'We wanted to be true to the vision,' Steffen reflects. 'We didn't want a partial solution that would patch a hole during Bosch's transformation; we wanted this platform to be whole and robust, able to support Bosch today and for years in the future as an AIoT company.' An analytically-derived skills platform was believed to be so important for Bosch that Steffen decided the team needed to build the technology to meet all 40 use cases.

Steffen smiles as he remembers the reaction of internal stakeholders: 'Bosch's consumer products and external-facing functions were already run on technology developed internally. There was lots of precedent for what we wanted to do.' This was a pivotal moment for HR and the people analytics team in Bosch, as it aligned the organization with the business transformation and became more digital.

In mid-2020, with help from internal partners from Bosch's technology-centric consumer products and marketing functions, the team started to build its skills management platform. The architecture is sound and truly reflects Bosch's strategic objectives.

As shown in Figure 5.6, the platform is built on natural language processing and machine learning algorithms and developed iteratively based on feedback from a variety of users and key stakeholders. In practice, the platform looks something like a search engine. Type in a question or a term like 'B2C sales', and the platform will give you all the insights around that skill or skill set for you, the individual, and – if you have access – a team or organization. The platform is intuitive, does not require training to use and, due to its similarity to the user experience of most popular internet search engines, the platform's use has spread throughout the company.

Figure 5.6 The technical structure of Bosch's 2020 Skills Platform

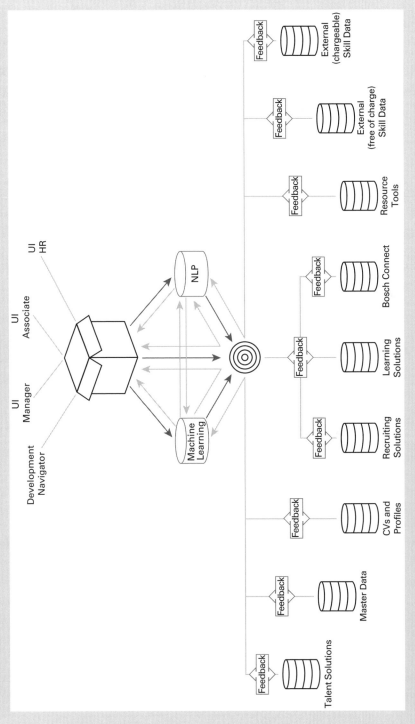

NOTE UI = User Interface; NLP = Natural Language Processing

SOURCE Reproduced with kind permission of Bosch, February 2021

The new technology project is fully aligned with the business strategy. But the work is not over. 'Building technology in a large business with an AIoT focus is an ongoing project,' Steffen reflects. 'I now realize that we may never reach the end of the solution. But continuously iterating in response to stakeholder feedback means that the solution will always add value, especially as it is designed with the strategy in mind.'

TOP TIP

Don't be afraid to build technology when it is needed.

Using technology to scale and productize analytics

Analytics does not stop when the analysis is complete, the prediction is calculated or the recommendations shared with stakeholders. If the analysis provides valuable insights with strong recommendations, and there is a desire to implement, then the hard work of productization begins. As former British Prime Minister Winston Churchill said, 'Now this is not the end. It is not even the beginning of the end. But it is, perhaps, the end of the beginning.'

These words are true for analytics projects when hypotheses are validated, solutions are created, predictions calculated and recommendations delivered. Then the really hard work starts. Technology is fundamental to scaling, productizing and personalizing people analytics. It enables the shift from a solution that benefits maybe 1,000 employees to one that benefits a whole organization of tens or hundreds of thousands of people.

Chapter 4 (Skills) discusses our recommendation for an operating model for people analytics that is premised on an outside-in, value-driven approach that turns client drivers and requests into business outcomes that matter. As shown in Figure 4.7, this is enabled through three engines: a Demand Engine, a Solution Engine and a Product Engine.

The Product Engine is responsible for transforming analytical solutions into useable products that are then implemented and scaled across the organization. This requires the move from the traditional focus of people analytics as a series of 'experiments' and 'projects' to one that instead focuses on 'products' and 'offerings'.

This requires a mindset shift – don't think only of experiments, think of experiments as a lead-in to products. This shift is enabled by people as well as technology and leads to the requirement for a range of non-typical people analytics skills such as product management and specialist user experience designers.

Product management

Product managers are commonplace in organizations when it comes to designing, developing and scaling products for customers but have hitherto been absent from people analytics. We have observed only a very few people analytics teams that have developed a 'product' and enlisted the sort of 'product managers' that are commonplace in technology software organizations.

Since most products to people analytics solutions result in technology applications – mobile or desktop – it is important to think of the Product Engine as a software factory, where the 'product' is transformed into a 'piece of software' that the users – that is, employees – will be delighted to use and interact with.

However, this is complex, especially since the 'product' might be a range of products in response to many recommendations for the 'solution'. One example we encountered was explored in The right sponsor: Swarovski, in Chapter 2 (Methodology), where six recommendations emerged as the 'solution' to the conversion rate of customers: employee retention, staffing and scheduling, the store manager's leadership characteristics, sales consultants' behaviour, attributes and skills, employees being trained to the correct level at the right time, and team composition in mid to larger size stores.

While some of the products for these recommendations may be relatively simple – training guides for HR professionals on how to assess for the new leadership characteristics of store managers – others are more complex. For example, there may be an application designed for store managers that shows them when their scheduling of staff meets the required characteristics of 'good scheduling'. Or an application for store managers to help them know which staff require training to enable staff retention. These notification and 'nudge' apps would take some considerable software engineering to perfect.

In other words, be thoughtful about how to deliver analytics solutions and consider what skills and processes are needed to bring 'projects' into the workplace as 'products' or 'offerings'. Other case studies that might help are those by Santander Brasil in Chapter 7 (Workforce Experiences) and IBM in Chapter 8 (Business Outcomes).

To learn more about product management, just searching the term 'product management skills' online returns more than 900 million results. Digestible articles providing a good starting point include Julia Austin's 'What it takes to become a great product manager' published in *Harvard Business Review* (2017), and Olivia Tanuwidjaja's 'Introducing analytics product manager' (2020).

Human-centred design

Consumer experiences are based around productization models, reinforced with intuitive user interfaces and highly personalized experiences. People analytics is now on the same journey.

In the same way that product managers are needed to develop solutions, so are the complex and much needed skills of human-centred user design as it specifically applies to software.

Design is key to ensuring employees actually use offerings – if a product is not user-friendly, it simply won't be used. The key to great design is not to think of the product in the traditional sense of an HR process – but to think of it as an interface to improve the experience of the employee, manager or executive, depending on its application.

User-design skills are also mentioned in Chapter 4 (Skills) in the topic about the Product Engine as part of the operating model for people analytics.

Finally, in this chapter, we highlight a case study from Microsoft Corporation that shares in practice why scaling analytics is important. The key message from this case study is: *Value is created when analytics is scaled to the enterprise, and to scale it you need technology.*

 CASE STUDY

Scaling people analytics: Microsoft

From the late 1990s until the present day, Dawn Klinghoffer has steered people analytics into the spotlight at Microsoft. 'I was – and always am – looking for creative and data-driven ways to influence people decisions with confidence,' Dawn says.

Now, General Manager for HR Business Insights – the People Analytics leader – at Microsoft,[55] Dawn originally started her career as an actuary. Early on in her tenure at Microsoft, she was tasked with creating a P&L for people accountability. It was a lightbulb moment for her. Dawn realized that people represent more than just a cost to the business. Effective management of people leads to innovation, business impact and top-line growth opportunity. Since that moment, her passion and vision have led Dawn to devote her professional life to what is now known in the business world as 'people analytics'.

'In its simplest form, people analytics requires good data, solid analyses and effective processes. But to really make a difference to employees and the business, people analytics must be scaled. Like most things, the value of analytics is limited unless people – employees, managers and executives – actually use it.'

Figure 5.7   How Microsoft's HR Business Insights team scales people analytics

SOURCE Reproduced with kind permission of Microsoft, September 2020

With this in mind, Dawn explains the mindset of her organization (see Figure 5.7) is wrapped around the vision that 'people represent more than a cost to the business, they represent business impact'. This vision is realized by four elements: a strong commitment to ethical and legal aspects of data; an experienced team of professionals in science, data, behaviour and HR; an armoury of simple and sophisticated technologies; and powerful internal and external communications that ensure transparency and engagement with the outcomes of her work.

All of these together contribute to scale, says Dawn. But of these four elements, 'technology' has been by far the most pivotal: 'We are a business of more than 150,000 employees. Almost all of them – including 20,000 managers – interact with our insights and are affected by the actions resulting from them.'

The twin crises of 2020 – the COVID-19 pandemic and the global anti-racism Black Lives Matter movement – highlighted the need for scaling people analytics more than ever before, as companies needed to understand how their workforce was reacting, feeling and working, at speed.

In the years leading up to 2020, Dawn realized that in order to be able to listen to the complete voice of the employee, she would need more than a one-size-fits-all employee engagement survey. Dawn and her team worked with an external partner to develop a new employee listening tool. They built a daily pulse survey that could pose open questions to a random sample of employees every day, aggregate their insights and monitor the culture of the organization.

When COVID-19 hit in early 2020, employees were forced to transition into home-working environments. Dawn was thankful for the employee listening technology they had previously implemented. It proved to her that scaling the technology would now work to their benefit and the benefit of the organization and every employee within it.

At this time, the employee voice and impact had never been so important, nor so difficult to hear. The events during the first three months of the global pandemic unfolded at a speed never before seen. And on top of that, the Black Lives Matter anti-racism movement made listening to employees all the more critical.

The Daily Pulse allowed the HR Business Insights team to survey a representative sample of employees across the globe in a non-invasive and truly valuable way. Every day through March 2020, 1,500 randomly sampled employees were invited to respond to the survey. During COVID-19 the Daily Pulse became increasingly important as a way to understand the sentiment of the organization, and Dawn's team 'upped the ante' by sending 2,500 survey invitations out every day from April 2020.

Both quantitative and qualitative questions were included in the survey. Using open questions such as 'Please provide any comments or questions you have for Microsoft Senior Leadership regarding COVID-19' and 'Share what is on your mind about what is going on inside and outside Microsoft,' allowed employees to provide real insights about what was going on at Microsoft and across the globe.

Furthermore, Dawn and her team could add in, remove and edit questions within 24 hours. This agility, coupled to the bite-size nature of the Daily Pulse, also allowed the business to keep pace with the spread of the pandemic and the Black Lives Matter movement. Questions and answers were always relevant and immediate. In a crisis, feedback is more important than ever. The insights from the Daily Pulse were aggregated and communicated weekly to the HR leadership team.

Responses were analysed with both human and machine intervention. Dawn's team began by coding comments manually, developing a comprehensive coding system to categorize the comments. That coding system was then leveraged to develop several supervised natural language processing models, which enabled scalable categorization of the comments with minimal human intervention.

Insights and recommendations are shared with Microsoft's 20,000 managers in regular emails sent from Chief People Officer Kathleen Hogan, and an alias it created to share content and insights regularly to managers. For employees, the team works closely with Learning & Development to develop entire content streams around insights and outcomes. Dawn has hopes that this will soon also be complemented by a dedicated platform for employees to access all of their personal data and insights.

The information the team gathers from the Daily Pulse helps the business provide the right support to employees across the company, continuously informs programmes and facilitates collaboration and teamwork. Comments gathered through the Daily Pulse lead to an additional worksite survey – location by location – to plan the transition from remote working back to the workplace. 'Being able to listen to and respond to our workforce at this scale and in this detail has proved invaluable to informing how we should be supporting employees in their new flexible working conditions in every country we operate in.'

'If I have learnt anything from the twin crises of 2020, it's that people analytics is at the centre of everything,' Dawn reflects. 'I am so glad my team invests so heavily in employee listening and in particular, pulsing, because it's giving us a technology that allows us to listen and communicate with our workforce at scale.'

Some might say that it is no surprise that Microsoft – a large, global technology firm – could do this. But what Dawn discovered was that no matter how technologically proficient your company is, it's always the same: if you don't have a model that can be adapted to scale you cannot derive insights at scale. So, it wasn't that Microsoft happened to be a technology company, it was the fact that Dawn had the foresight to think about scaling analytics so that when a crisis occurred, she had the infrastructure in place.

With all the right technology and processes in place, Dawn was ready when the world changed to help the business respond with up-to-date insights. This should be the goal of every people analytics leader.

TOP TIP

Be bold in using technology to scale.

Summary

Technology is a key enabler of people analytics, helping data gathering and analysis, supporting the democratization of data and providing the basis to scale analytics solutions across the enterprise. Key messages regarding technology include:

- Keep abreast of the people analytics technology market through research and peers, but only consider buying technology if it helps solve a defined business problem.

- Demand a sound and solid approach to privacy and ethics, especially with regards to some of the emerging technologies.

- Nurture the relationship with the procurement team, help them understand the business problem and involve them with vendor selection.

- Focus on vendors that seek to partner, provide flexibility around road maps and pilots, and have a clear approach to data privacy.

- Secure sponsorship to build a technology solution, work with finance on the investment case and partner in a transparent way with enterprise and HR technology teams.

- Scale and productize analytics through implementing technology across the enterprise, when possible. Build product management and human-centred design skills into the people analytics team.

References

Austin, J (2017) What it takes to become a great product manager, Harvard Business Review, 13 December. Available from: https://hbr.org/2017/12/what-it-takes-to-become-a-great-product-manager (archived at https://perma.cc/E2SK-XKDB) [Last accessed 29 January 2021]

Bersin, J (2021) HR Technology 2021: the definitive guide [Blog] Josh Bersin. Available from: https://joshbersin.com/2021/03/hr-technology-2021-now-published-shattering-changes-in-the-market/ (archived at https://perma.cc/PJ69-C3GK) [Last accessed 21 March 2021]

Ferrar, J, Styr, C and Ktena, A (2020) Delivering Value at Scale: A new operating model for people analytics [Report] Insight222, 24 November. Available from: https://www.insight222.com/people-analytics-operating-model-research (archived at https://perma.cc/7UEH-2QYJ) [Last accessed 7 February 2021]

Garr, S and Mehrotra, P (2020) People Analytics Tech 2020 Overview [Report] RedThread Research, 3 December. Available from: https://redthreadresearch.com/pat-2020-overview (archived at https://perma.cc/EY8H-Z4FM) [Accessed 1 January 2021]

HR Weekly (2021) The 100 most influential people in HR – 2021 edition, *HR Weekly*, 25 January. Available from: https://hrweekly.co/experts (archived at https://perma.cc/LD8P-NUTA) [Last accessed 26 January 2021]

Johnson, B (2009) The technological secrets of James Cameron's new film Avatar, *Guardian*, 20 August. Available from: https://www.theguardian.com/film/2009/aug/20/3d-film-avatar-james-cameron-technology (archived at https://perma.cc/QEE7-YQ7A) [Last accessed 7 February 2021]

LinkedIn (2018) LinkedIn closes on acquisition of Glint: helping leaders build winning teams [Blog] LinkedIn Corporate Communications, 16 November. Available from: https://news.linkedin.com/2018/11/linkedin-closes-on-glint-acquisition (archived at https://perma.cc/LL7G-WHUW) [Last accessed 14 March 2021]

McNulty, K (2020) *Handbook of Regression Modeling in People Analytics: With examples in R and Python,* Open source and available from: http://peopleanalytics-regression-book.org/ (archived at https://perma.cc/L3GX-9U96) [Last accessed 27 January 2021]

Microsoft (2016) Microsoft to acquire LinkedIn [Blog] Microsoft, 13 June. Available from: https://news.microsoft.com/2016/06/13/microsoft-to-acquire-linkedin/ (archived at https://perma.cc/P8K5-B8DB) [Last accessed 14 March 2021]

Nussbaumer Knaflic, C (2018) *Storytelling with Data: A data visualization guide for business professionals,* Wiley, New York, NY

Nussbaumer Knaflic, C (2019) *Storytelling with Data: Let's practice!* Wiley, New York, NY

SAP (2018) SAP SE to acquire Qualtrics International Inc, sees experience management as the future of business [Blog] SAP, 11 November. Available from: https://news.sap.com/2018/11/sap-to-acquire-qualtrics-experience-management/ (archived at https://perma.cc/7K5L-D8CB) [Last accessed 14 March 2021]

Somers, D (2021) Workday to acquire Peakon: why employee engagement matters [Blog] Workday, 28 January. Available from: https://blog.workday.com/en-us/2021/workday-acquire-peakon-employee-engagement.html (archived at https://perma.cc/GPS5-XTK3) [Last accessed 1 February 2021]

Swisher, K (2020) Here come the 4 horsemen of the techopolypse, *New York Times*, 1 July. Available from: https://www.nytimes.com/2020/07/01/opinion/anti-trust-tech-hearing-facebook.html (archived at https://perma.cc/4FDY-BX2T)

Tanuwidjaja, O (2020) Introducing analytics product manager [Blog] Medium, 16 August. Available from: https://medium.com/swlh/introducing-analytics-product-manager-d0073ed9cf47 (archived at https://perma.cc/5GHF-WRQM) [Last accessed 29 January 2021]

Notes

1 According to https://companiesmarketcap.com (archived at https://perma.cc/V6H8-G24A) as of 7 February 2021.

2 Oracle Corporation is an American multinational computer technology corporation headquartered in Austin, Texas, originally founded in 1976 (see www.oracle.com (archived at https://perma.cc/3NUJ-3FMR), last accessed 7 February 2021).

3 SAP America, Inc is a US-based company providing cloud-based software for human capital management, originally founded in 2001 and acquired by SAP in 2011 (see https://www.sap.com/products/human-resources-hcm.html (archived at https://perma.cc/E5ZS-PQ3Z), last accessed 7 February 2021).

4 Workday, Inc, is a US on-demand financial management and human capital management software vendor founded in 2005 (see www.workday.com (archived at https://perma.cc/CS95-XZR2), last accessed 7 February 2021).

5 See Glossary: On-premise technology. Software that is installed and run on computers that are located on-site (on the premises) at an organization.

6 See Glossary: SaaS (or Software as a Service). An approach to software licensing and delivery in which software is hosted remotely in the cloud and accessed via an internet browser.

7 The phrase 'all-nighters' relates to workers who have to work through the night to complete tasks and activities due to the pressure of deadlines and complexity involved in solving problems that the requestors typically don't understand or care about, or because of other intense deadlines.

8 The online Crunchr platform was created in 2015. Crunchr is part of Focus Orange, an HR advisory firm based in Amsterdam, Netherlands (see https://www.crunchrapps.com (archived at https://perma.cc/Y8SZ-VUCS), last accessed 7 February 2021).

9 One Model, Inc is based in Texas, USA and was founded in 2014 (see https://www.onemodel.co (archived at https://perma.cc/BXD3-F7C2), last accessed 7 February 2021).

10 Panalyt, Pte Ltd is headquartered in Singapore and was founded in 2017 (see https://www.panalyt.com (archived at https://perma.cc/QP83-MXEB), last accessed 7 February 2021).

11 QuIRC, Inc (doing business as 'PeopleInsight') is headquartered in Ottawa, Canada and was founded in 2002 (see https://www.peopleinsight.com (archived at https://perma.cc/9CT9-5FSF), last accessed 7 February 2021).

12 SOLVE is part of HCMI, based in Los Angeles, CA, USA and founded in 2008 (see https://www.hcmi.co/solve (archived at https://perma.cc/6SWB-LENW), last accessed 7 February 2021).

13 Splash Business Intelligence, Inc is headquartered in Georgia, USA and was founded in 2014 (see https://splashbi.com (archived at https://perma.cc/3MGF-7CGJ), last accessed 7 February 2021).

14 Visier, Inc. is headquartered in Vancouver, Canada and was founded in 2010 (see https://www.visier.com (archived at https://perma.cc/WGB9-S254), last accessed 7 February 2021).

15 Data as of 7 February 2021.

16 Arctic Shores Limited is headquartered in Manchester, UK and was founded in 2013 (see https://www.arcticshores.com (archived at https://perma.cc/C4QM-G5BA), last accessed 7 February 2021).

17 Hirevue, Inc is based in South Jordan, UT, USA and was founded in 2004 (see https://www.hirevue.com/ (archived at https://perma.cc/TL3Y-USBZ), last accessed 7 February 2021).

18 Pymetrics, Inc is headquartered in New York, NY, USA and was founded in 2013 (see https://www.pymetrics.ai/ (archived at https://perma.cc/NQ94-SA33), last accessed 7 February 2021).

19 Culture Amp Pty Ltd is headquartered in Richmond, Australia and was founded in 2009 (see https://www.cultureamp.com (archived at https://perma.cc/X9NM-P3W2), last accessed 7 February 2021).

20 Glint, Inc, based in Sunnyvale, CA, USA was originally founded in 2013 and was acquired by LinkedIn Corporation in 2018 (see https://www.glintinc.com/ (archived at https://perma.cc/2UCZ-NX26), last accessed 7 February 2021).

21 Humu, Inc is headquartered in Mountain View, CA, USA and was founded in 2017 (see https://humu.com/ (archived at https://perma.cc/VS78-56MV), last accessed 7 February 2021).

22 Medallia, Inc is headquartered in San Francisco, CA, USA and was founded in 2001 (see https://www.medallia.com/ (archived at https://perma.cc/YS9G-RTZH), last accessed 7 February 2021).

23 Peakon ApS is headquartered in Copenhagen, Denmark and was founded in 2015 (see https://peakon.com/ (archived at https://perma.cc/3SWP-6DZW), last accessed 7 February 2021).

24 Perceptyx, Inc is headquartered in Temecula, CA, USA and was founded in 2008 (see https://www.perceptyx.com/ (archived at https://perma.cc/Y6MW-7JY7), last accessed 7 February 2021).

25 Qlearsite Ltd is headquartered in London, UK and was founded in 2015 (see https://www.qlearsite.com (archived at https://perma.cc/E3RH-3AY8), last accessed 7 February 2021).

26 Qualtrics International Inc has co-headquarters in Seattle, WA and Provo, UT, USA, was founded in 2002 and was acquired by SAP SE in 2020 (see https://www.qualtrics.com (archived at https://perma.cc/2HGK-MEH5), last accessed 7 February 2021).

27 Reflektive, Inc is headquartered in San Francisco, CA, USA and was founded in 2013 (see https://www.reflektive.com/ (archived at https://perma.cc/NU7P-3ZUU), last accessed 7 February 2021).

28 Workometry is a product of OrganizationView GmbH, which is based in St Moritz, Switzerland. OrganizationView GmbH was founded in 2010 (see https://www.workometry.com/ (archived at https://perma.cc/PP96-5G2W), last accessed 7 February 2021).

29 Burning Glass Technologies, Inc is headquartered in Boston, MA, USA and was founded in 1999 (see https://www.burning-glass.com (archived at https://perma.cc/CJ27-ZB4J), last accessed 7 February 2021).

30 Joberat, Inc (doing business as Claro Workforce Analytics) is headquartered in Nashua, NH, USA and was founded in 2014 (see https://claroanalytics.com/ (archived at https://perma.cc/BDR3-BMSG), last accessed 7 February 2021).

31 Economic Modeling LLC or 'Emsi' is headquartered in Moscow, ID, USA and was founded in 1987 (see https://www.economicmodeling.com (archived at https://perma.cc/TB74-DV92), last accessed 7 February 2021).

32 Faethm Holdings Pty Ltd is headquartered in Sydney, Australia and was founded in 2016 (see https://www.faethm.ai (archived at https://perma.cc/6WWM-UUZH), last accessed 7 February 2021).

33 Gartner TalentNeuron is a division of Gartner, Inc and is based in Stamford, CT, USA. TalentNeuron was incubated in 2012 by Zinnov, a Bangalore-based management consulting firm. It was acquired by CEB in 2014, which in turn was acquired by Gartner, Inc in 2017 (see https://www.gartner.com/en/human-resources/research/talentneuron (archived at https://perma.cc/XN2J-B6JQ), last accessed 7 February 2021).

34 Horsefly is part of AI Recruitment Technologies Ltd, founded in 2011 and headquartered in Liverpool, UK (see https://horseflyanalytics.com (archived at https://perma.cc/5438-CGGA), last accessed 7 February 2021).

35 LinkedIn Talent Insights is a product of LinkedIn Corporation, based in Sunnyvale, CA, USA, originally founded in 2002 (see https://business.linkedin.com/ (archived at https://perma.cc/E9MZ-V2WQ), last accessed 7 February 2021).

36 Cognitive Talent Solutions, Inc is headquartered in Palo Alto, CA, USA and was founded in 2018 (see https://www.cognitivetalentsolutions.com (archived at https://perma.cc/Z2K7-RTHT), last accessed 7 February 2021).

37 Microsoft Workplace Analytics is a product of Microsoft Corporation, which is headquartered in Redmond, WA, USA and was founded in 1975 (see https://www.microsoft.com/en-gb/microsoft-365/business/workplace-analytics (archived at https://perma.cc/S8GW-HRUG), last accessed 7 February 2021).

38 Polinode Pty Ltd is headquartered in Sydney, Australia and was founded in 2014 (see https://www.polinode.com (archived at https://perma.cc/7ASS-GEZG), last accessed 7 February 2021).

39 TrustSphere PTE Ltd is headquartered in Singapore and was founded in 2011 (see https://www.trustsphere.com (archived at https://perma.cc/HP4D-KRHY), last accessed 7 February 2021).

40 Worklytics, Co is headquartered in New York, NY, USA and was founded in 2015 (see https://www.worklytics.co (archived at https://perma.cc/64MU-QF87), last accessed 29 January 2021).

41 Yva.ai, Inc is headquartered in Santa Clara, CA, USA and was founded in 2016 (see https://www.yva.ai/ (archived at https://perma.cc/C9N6-BRSB), last accessed 7 February 2021).

42 Clustree is headquartered in Paris, France and was founded in 2014 (see https://www.clustree.com (archived at https://perma.cc/TR3W-U8GY), last accessed 7 February 2021).

43 Cobrainer GmbH is headquartered in Munich, Germany and was founded in 2013 (see https://www.cobrainer.com (archived at https://perma.cc/FJA2-SWUY), last accessed 7 February 2021).

44 Degreed, Inc is headquartered in Pleasanton, CA, USA and was founded in 2012 (see https://degreed.com (archived at https://perma.cc/G83R-BJ7L), last accessed 7 February 2021).

45 Gloat Ltd is headquartered in New York, NY, USA and was founded in 2016 (see https://www.gloat.com (archived at https://perma.cc/2RFY-JHUM), last accessed 7 February 2021).

46 TechWolf BV is headquartered in Gent, Belgium and was founded in 2018 (see https://techwolf.ai/ (archived at https://perma.cc/DT55-NLXT), last accessed 7 February 2021).

47 Anaplan, Inc is headquartered in San Francisco, CA, USA and was founded in 2006 (see https://www.anaplan.com/ (archived at https://perma.cc/978Y-G3MC), last accessed 7 February 2021).

48 Dynaplan AS is headquartered in Manger, Norway and was founded in 2004 (see https://www.dynaplan.com (archived at https://perma.cc/3CQC-4T42), last accessed 7 February 2021).

49 eQ8 is headquartered in Sydney, Australia and was founded in 2020 (see https://www.eq8.ai/ (archived at https://perma.cc/8LEY-78PK), last accessed 7 February 2021).

50 orgvue is a division of Concetra Analytics, founded in 2011 and headquartered in London, UK (see https://www.orgvue.com (archived at https://perma.cc/2EPC-YKVN), last accessed 7 February 2021).

51 See Glossary: Request for proposal (RFP). A document outlining requirements requested from potential vendors who wish to deliver those requirements to the requestor (ie the customer). The vendors deliver their document as a proposal. It normally consists of, or is accompanied by, a number of questions that the customer wishes each vendor to answer as part of their proposal. Issuing an RFP document is typically a signal to invite vendors to 'bid' for the business of delivering the requirements.

52 Founded in 1989 and headquartered in Boston, Massachusetts, USA, Vertex Pharmaceuticals Inc comprises a staff of approximately 3,000, located in South Boston and London and across research and development sites and commercial offices in North America, Europe, Australia and Latin America (see https://investors.vrtx.com/news-releases/news-release-details/vertex-reports-full-year-and-fourth-quarter-2019-financial (archived at https://perma.cc/XWH7-2EN5) and https://www.forbes.com/companies/vertex-pharmaceuticals/#6d84f9ca58e9 (archived at https://perma.cc/R3ME-7X93), last accessed 7 February 2021).

53 Vertex Pharmaceuticals according to the S&P 500, reported by *Forbes* Magazine (see https://www.forbes.com/companies/vertex-pharmaceuticals/#6d84f9ca58e9 (archived at https://perma.cc/R3ME-7X93), last accessed 7 February 2021).

54 Bosch is an engineering and technology company headquartered in Gerlingen, Germany. Made up of approximately 400,000 employees in 60 countries, the privately-owned company was founded in 1886, with the majority stake held by a charitable foundation, Robert Bosch Stiftung (see https://www.bosch.com/company/ (archived at https://perma.cc/58BH-K3B4), last accessed 7 February 2021).

55 The Microsoft Corporation is a US multinational corporation headquartered in Redmond, Washington that develops, manufactures, licenses, supports and sells computer software, consumer electronics and personal computers and services (see https://www.microsoft.com/en-gb/about/ (archived at https://perma.cc/22UV-T3E6), last accessed 7 February 2021).

Data   06

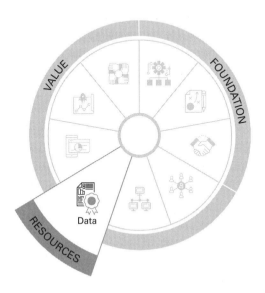

In this chapter, we discuss why the people analytics leader should also be the chief data officer for HR, the most important aspects of data management and why leveraging other data sources internally, externally and from the use of emerging technologies will enhance the business outcomes delivered.

DISCOVER...

- why data stewardship is important;
- how to make data management an enabler and not a distraction;
- why leveraging data from emerging technologies can turbo-boost people analytics.

WITH INSIGHTS FROM...

- HSBC, on the role of chief data officer for HR;
- Nokia Corporation, on leveraging a burning platform for data management;
- Tetra Pak, on partnering with finance to standardize data for a key business objective.

Overview

DATA

Data as one of the Nine Dimensions, consists of data stewardship, data management and how to use data to deliver more value to the business. Of particular importance is the use of data sources, especially emerging data, that will add incremental value and expand people analytics far beyond the focus on human resources policies and process, to those that address the most complex business issues.

Data is everywhere. Based on the five-year compound annual growth rate (CAGR), the amount of data created, captured, copied and consumed between 2020 and 2024 could amount to more data than that created over the past 30 years (International Data Corporation, 2020; Press, 2020).

That's a lot of data! And the exponential growth in data is both challenging companies and providing the opportunity for competitive advantage.

Data is the raw material of all analytics and therefore key to its success. It has been characterized as such, even before the term analytics came into the general lexicon, such as how it was outlined as the Data-Information-Knowledge pyramid (see Figure 6.1) described in the *Public Administration Review* in the 1970s (Henry, 1974).

Figure 6.1   The Data-Information-Knowledge Pyramid

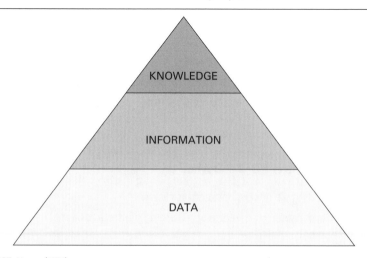

SOURCE Henry (1974)

However, data can be the Achilles' heel[1] of the people analytics team because, in our experience, many of these functions seem to believe that all people data should be 'fixed' before analytics can begin. Of course, organized data is important – very important – but to suggest that to create perfect data first before beginning people analytics projects is crazy.

What is not crazy is to focus on key topics that will enhance data availability, quality and accessibility. It is key:

- to have an understanding of what data is available;
- to have the comprehension, computational and software skills that allow data to be captured, cleaned, processed, analysed and presented;
- to know how to structure, manage, govern and secure people data;
- to know what new data sources to seek in order to meet ever-increasing requests, challenges and opportunities.

The first two of these are not discussed in this book. In *The Power of People: Learn how successful organizations use workforce analytics to improve business performance* (Guenole, Ferrar and Feinzig, 2017) there is an entire chapter focused on the pragmatic use of people data including knowing what is good enough [data], missing data, outdated data, what to do when no data is available, non-normal data distributions, data outliers, and inconsistent data definitions, as well as concise sections on data from inside and outside the HR function and non-traditional data sources. We do not intend to repeat what has already been written on these topics.

Nevertheless, we now continue to address the third and fourth points in the list above throughout the rest of this chapter.

The people analytics leader as the chief data officer of HR

The first known chief data officer (CDO) role was created by Capital One in 2002 (Forbes Insights, 2019), and most large organizations now have someone in place with this title at the enterprise level.

The role of chief data officer for HR emerged very recently and in our research for this book we found that only 28 per cent of people analytics leaders had some level of chief data officer, governance or stewardship responsibilities as part of their people analytics responsibilities.

We believe that the people analytics leader should also be the CDO for HR. In their 2020 article titled 'Are you asking too much of your chief data officer?' Tom Davenport and Randy Bean identify seven types of CDO. In the context of people analytics, three of these should be combined into the key CDO responsibilities for the people analytics leader: the chief data and analytics officer, data governor and data ethicist. Let's discuss each of these in turn.

The chief data and analytics officer

Data is one of the critical ingredients required to be successful with people analytics, so combining responsibility for data management, data science and analytics enables the people analytics leader to be in control of their destiny. The sensitivity around people data means it is important that the people analytics leader should also take overall responsibility for the governance of people data and the wise and ethical use of this data in the organization.

The methods, benefits and governance structures overall for people analytics are outlined in Chapter 1 (Governance). In that chapter, we show that data stewardship is one of six types of governance that are needed for excellence in people analytics. Our suggestion to tie data governance together with analytics governance dovetails well with the role of the people analytics leader described in Chapter 4 (Skills).

Data governor

For more insight on the CDO role and how it evolves over time, we recommend reading an article from Boston Consulting Group, 'A show-don't-tell approach to data governance' (Aractingi *et al*, 2020). This explains how the CDO shifts from a 'doer' in the initial phases as they set their vision and build the foundations, to a 'facilitator' ensuring best practices around data governance once capabilities have been established.

Setting a clear strategy for people data

One of the main benefits for the people analytics leader with the role of data governor is that they can set a clear vision about the strategy for using people data in their organization.

Figure 6.2 A suggested people data strategy

> A people data strategy leverages *all data* in a manner that drives *business value*, *protects* the business and employees and encourages and enables *innovation*.

Figure 6.2 highlights the components of a suggested people data strategy and why they are important. Let's examine the key elements of such a strategy:

All data This includes all people data across the enterprise as well as non-people data where appropriate (eg financial, customer, operational, sales, real estate).

Business value People analytics should be all about delivering value to the business. It should never be about the department or team. This requires strong partnerships and an ethos of 'shared data is power'.

Protects The wise and ethical use of people data is paramount with robust processes for all aspects related to data privacy. It is not just about following the law and regulations, but about doing 'what is right'.

Innovation By working together and sharing data across the organization, there will be more opportunity for creativity, new solutions and improved outcomes for the business and its workforce.

A rigorous strategy and approach to people data delivers three key outcomes (Figure 6.3). First, it puts the onus on driving business value and improving performance. Next, in terms of providing strong governance around ethics, it protects the business and the workforce and creates the climate for employees gaining personal benefit in exchange for sharing their data.

Figure 6.3 Outcomes from a people data strategy

VALUE	ETHICS	CULTURE
Drives business value and improves performance	*Protects the business and employees*	*Drives innovation and builds momentum*

Finally, it helps create a healthy culture around the use of people data, how it can drive innovation across the business and create the momentum for people analytics to grow and flourish.

Establishing a strong governance framework

As data governor, the people analytics leader has an important role in setting the framework for all people data governance. We suggest a model for this that has a number of sub-components arranged around three key categories, shown in Figure 6.4.

This figure resembles a house, where some elements are built into the foundations while others are visible. This is similar in that some elements of people governance are foundational and often not seen – and often not appreciated – by other people, whereas the elements 'above ground' are items that are more frequently shared with other stakeholders.

Strategy and culture   This category relates to aligning people data governance to the values of the organization plus the regulatory, compliance and risk management frameworks that help govern the company as a whole. Like the roof protects the house from the elements, these are governing aspects to give protection to the entire data policies, frameworks and model.

Figure 6.4   The 'house' of people data governance

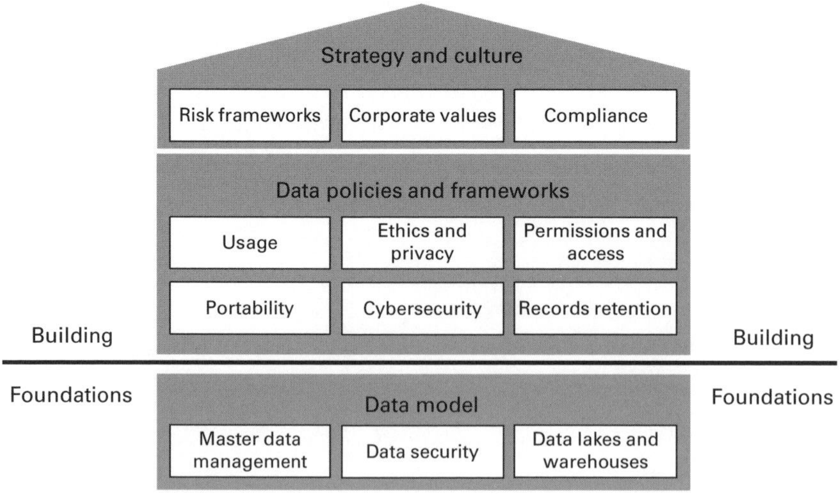

Data policies and frameworks This category ensures that specific elements of people data governance meet jurisdictional and company ethical, legal and regulatory obligations relating to data privacy. It also includes policies and frameworks on the usage and portability of data, the permission, access and records retention frameworks needed, as well as the important topic of cybersecurity. Like a house has rooms of differing shapes and sizes, these topics come with varying levels of complexity.

Data model This category provides the basic foundation and principles for all people data within the organization. It ensures data is identified, stored, provisioned, processed and governed properly, as well as creating and maintaining good quality data, which is findable, accessible, interoperable and reusable. It also focuses on the storage and security for people data including both data warehousing[2] and data lakes,[3] which are both needed according to Amazon Web Services, 'a typical organization will require both a data warehouse and a data lake as they serve different needs and use cases'.[4] Like a house has solid foundations, the data model serves as the underpinning for people data – and indeed all people analytics.

With regard to data governance for people analytics, we believe that all of these elements if implemented well will significantly enhance the credibility of the people analytics team, as well as HR in general. We specifically believe that the role of people analytics in being a data ethicist is key and we discuss this more now.

Data ethicist

Ethics and data privacy are two of the most important topics in people analytics. We discuss the set-up and development of an ethics and privacy council in Chapter 1 (Governance) as a means to manage the components of ethics and data privacy. Our recommendation is that the people analytics leader, as a data ethicist, leads an ethics and privacy council with key representation from the chief privacy officer, significant works councils and employee relations experts.

By being transparent about the approach to ethics, an organization is likely to gain more trust from employees and workers across the company. This is important if the 'fair exchange for value' is to be delivered. By creating trust, and through that trust receiving more people data from employees, then more value can be delivered.

According to the seminal Accenture study on trust and workforce value, where an organization 'adopts responsible strategies, the trust dividend could be worth more than a 6 per cent increase in future revenue growth' (Shook, Knickrehm and Sage-Gavin, 2019). The responsible strategies are:

Give control. Gain trust.   Empower people with greater control of their own data.

Share responsibility. Share benefits.   Involve people in designing systems and identify accountable executives.

Elevate people. Use technology responsibly.   Use technology in responsible new ways to elevate people and to fix its own unintended consequences.

Our own advice to create an ethics charter is one of the systems that can be put in place to create the 'fair exchange for value' – to share responsibility and share benefits. The case study, Ethics, ethics, ethics: Lloyds Banking Group, in Chapter 1 (Governance), outlines the key aspects of building an ethics charter.

Being a chief data officer for HR

Coupling the chief data officer for HR responsibilities with leading the people analytics team doesn't just enable the people analytics leader to be in control of their destiny. Ultimately it increases the likelihood of delivering sustainable value on a consistent basis to the business in the long term, with high trust garnered from employees.

For an example of how this works in reality, the following case study from HSBC is very relevant. Their key message: *A keen focus on data governance opens doors to value.*

 CASE STUDY

Managing data for business value: HSBC

Few companies with mature people analytics organizations have established strong data governance models designed by the analytics team. Even fewer use their data stewardship to guide their analytics. And only a handful have asked their people analytics leader to also be the company's Chief Data Officer for HR.

HSBC[5] is one of the rare organizations that have taken people data stewardship to this level, and it can carefully analyse and securely store data from more than 250,000 workers. HR data-driven insights are supplied and actioned at the highest levels, every employee has self-service access to varying levels of bank data, managers can view their team's people data right alongside information from across the business, and HR and the CFO/COO communities can access daily information – on demand.

To emphasize the level to which the data architecture has allowed it to develop the analytical value to the business, the bank is launching a people analytics chatbot to enable users of the self-service platform to ask a question in a conversational style and have the insight immediately shown to them in the bot itself. This could not be done without the focus HSBC has applied to governance, managing data and defining its metadata models. Consider just one element: data is drawn from many different systems and covers more than 60 countries. The data modelling, privacy, security and data quality requirements of this kind of work alone is staggering.

The person behind this strategy and approach is Eden Britt. He is the Global Head of People Analytics & HR Chief Data Officer (CDO) at HSBC and has been leading this strategy since 2016.

'Really strong data governance makes it possible for people analytics to add value to our employees and the business,' Eden explains. 'Ultimately, solid data structures allow us to work with confidence and speed. Establishing and continuously improving our data management is one of the most valuable things the bank has done.'

With more than 20 years in HR, a degree in information technology ('pre-internet!') and an interest in design and coding, Eden has both an accomplished HR background and a strong data and systems background. This gives him the rare ability to understand the HR function and how it operates, the employee life cycle, data handling and data structures, and the business context for analytics. As part of the bank's Group Data leadership team, Eden's role as CDO for HR is to help develop and carry out both the HR data strategy and the bank's data strategy, which sees HSBC establish much better controls around data management, data quality, integrity, governance and data architecture. His 'double hat' role of CDO and Head of People Analytics also means Eden is responsible for defining, developing and implementing the people data, analytics and data science strategy, helping build capability to deliver a strong foundation in people data.

'The dual nature of the role is crucial,' says Eden, 'as it allows me to consider where the organization is going and how HR fits into its strategy, and then, how to structure a strategy around good data management "what data we need" and analytics "what data should we leverage?" to ultimately improve the organization and help HSBC address business challenges.'

Eden and his team started with establishing governance. 'HR data is used across the bank, in HR processes and services, and from managers performing a people management role to driving security profiles, group directory information and business systems access,' Eden explains. 'For this, we needed data structures to be clear and precise to ensure all people data is safe, clean, robust and accurate.'

Eden started with basic questions, similar to those discussed in Chapter 1 (Governance): Who is the data steward? Who are the data owners? How does that link to the process? How do we document a data dictionary? A data glossary? How do we manage controls? How do we run continuous monitoring on those controls to ensure that they are effective? And how do we run good data management?

'When I think about data governance and data management, there are a lot of different elements to contemplate,' Eden reflects. 'I don't only think about the ethics, data privacy and controls, documentation and rigour. I also think about how we capture data into an environment that allows us to be able to use it for analytics purposes. That helps us define the prioritization of which critical data elements we should focus on for quality assurance purposes, and which ones we take from core platforms and put into our data warehouse, and how we structure the data within the warehouse. I also think about how we might evolve the operational side of the HR function to take advantage of automation, straight through processing and robotic process automation.'

This perspective only typically exists in organizations that combine the CDO role with the people analytics leader role. Leaders who only have a CDO role do not have the accountability to deliver analytics with business value. They can, therefore, sometimes classify data management as simply 'the overall handling of the data and issues with data quality, management, integrity management'. Having the analytics perspective and accountability drives a mindset for using data to deliver business value.

The team's multi-faceted approach to people data governance and documentation has certainly helped Eden. More so, he has been given the authority to challenge 'cottage industries' capturing data outside of HR and provide vigorous checks on data warehouse integrity. This has delivered HR's 'Golden Source' of data – the single source of truth for all people data across the bank. And with the CDO hat, Eden can manage the Golden Source. 'Stakeholders know that they can be confident that when they use our data, it is correct – where we do see challenges, it is often based on systems not yet being updated.'

An excellent example of what Eden describes is attrition, where a manager has not yet entered the exit into the HRMS platform, but the business has already considered the employee a leaver. His advice is always to refer back to the process and ensure that the data is updated in the core platform, which drives accuracy, versus 'adjusting' data off system. 'Update in the system today, it will be present in your report tomorrow!' Eden explains.

And that credibility means people and business decisions can be made based on high-quality quantitative and qualitative data. People data is now submitted to and accepted by the group executive committee regularly. 'Establishing confidence in HR data at the top of the house and in other functions like finance is a big part of proving credibility and success,' Eden notes.

Strong data governance also helps the team solve problems. In the case of any new data from outside the function, or challenges on people data, Eden conducts root cause analysis: 'And then we'll fix both the data issue and the root cause. It means we will continue to improve this iterative cycle so that the data that we provide supports the business requirements.'

Eden credits an engineering mindset with being able to instil and manage data governance with such success. 'Pragmatism and a good logical understanding of processes and data structures, business context and a view to manage risk management all help us decide how we use data, which data is important and reference structures. I think that people who are problem solvers and big-picture thinkers make for the best data governors.'

Reflecting on his dual role, Eden believes he can get more value from analytics because of his CDO role. And in his CDO role, he takes a pragmatic risk management approach rather than a purely technical perspective: 'People looking through a technical lens can often get lost in documentation of architecture and flow of data and linkage to process,' he says. 'That's fine. But documentation alone will not always allow you to see the big picture.'

'I find that having a practical, action-oriented mindset is better. When you have the business goal in mind as your ultimate outcome, you approach work more like a strategist or business owner than a technician— you're ready to work, to stand up and make a difference, but you fully understand the risks involved with taking action. When you are able to navigate the spectrum of risk, analytics and data science are easier to deliver.'

> **TOP TIP**
>
> Make the people analytics leader chief data officer for HR.

Data management

There are many books and articles about data management, indeed whole degree courses are dedicated to the intricacies of data management and related topics. This book is going to address some key insights that we have learnt during the course of our research that adds some guidance to this area.

As we've already outlined, it's important not to allow the need to improve the quality and management of data to prevent an organization from doing people analytics. However, to create long-term sustainability and consistency in people analytics, it is important to spend time on it in order to develop a dynamic and repeatable solution for data management.

Be prepared, though – effective data management takes considerable effort and time. The case study, Great data infrastructure unlocks value: Nokia Corporation, included later in this chapter, describes how data management took several years. But the effort was worth it, as evidenced by the speed with which the people analytics team was able to respond to the requirements of the business for information about their people during the initial stages of the COVID-19 pandemic.

One very strong reference that is helpful is McKinsey & Co's article, which includes the Stairway to Impact model (Ledet *et al*, 2020). In this article, 'How to be great at people analytics', which was informed by qualitative interviews with 12 people analytics teams in global organizations, the authors highlight the following points for leading people analytics teams:

Align data management with the vision for people analytics Before spending time extracting, shaping, cleaning and recoding data, make sure this is aligned to the overall vision. Don't spend time continually repeating this process for data that is not needed, or that is related to low-impact projects.

Establish a common language, definitions and standards for data   Work across the business, especially with finance, to agree data hierarchies and dictionaries for all data elements that are essential for the serious analytics leader. These will allow consistent language across the business and bring credibility to the function (also see the case study, The financial side of productivity: Tetra Pak, later in this chapter).

Take a cross-functional approach to technology   The people analytics team should collaborate in an agile manner with their peers across the organization with regard to technology and infrastructure that supports good data management at an enterprise level.

Get data scientists involved   Using programming languages such as R and Python, data scientists are able to take data to a higher level by joining disparate sources, building models and providing actionable recommendations to executives.

Invest in dedicated data-engineering resources   The greatest team differentiator that McKinsey & Co found was the level of dedicated data-engineering resources. When there was significant investment in this, leading teams showed 'full ownership of their own data repositories, allowing them to rapidly test new ideas, iterate, and reduce dependencies on enterprise-level technology resources'.

Breadth and depth of data sources   Leading people analytics functions have invested heavily in building strong HR-data foundations. They also go far outside the boundaries of core HR (see Chapter 5 – Technology) to add additional internal sources of data, so they can deliver more advanced insights and solutions.

Data management overall should not be viewed as an activity in isolation. Indeed, when undertaken well, it provides the route to impactful people analytics work. So, our recommendation is that the people analytics leader should always look to own and steer the people data strategy and then guide the management of data and the processes involved therein as described above.

Sometimes a 'burning platform'[6] is needed to make this happen, as described in the case study that follows from Nokia Corporation. Their key message to fellow analysts and HR executives is: *Build a dynamic and repeatable system for data management, quickly.*

 **CASE STUDY**

Great data infrastructure unlocks value: Nokia

When the COVID-19 pandemic struck in early 2020, Nokia[7] was able to quickly assemble external and internal people and other business data to provide information that supported business continuity and employee safety. This was only possible because of the company's purposeful approach to data management of people and human resources data.

The clear and defined approach to managing high-quality data came about because a burning platform appeared in January of 2016: the acquisition of the French–US telecom company, Alcatel-Lucent by Nokia. At the time of the merger, both organizations were of similar size with tens of thousands of employees and with presence in dozens of countries, which presented the opportunity to take the best of both worlds when looking at process transformation. In relation to workforce analytics, both companies had a patchwork of embryonic reporting and analytics teams spread across the globe with no obvious technology or system in place for managing data.

'The merger was a giant red flashing arrow that said, "Start Here!"' Nokia's Head of Workforce Analytics & Organization Management, David Shontz, recalls. 'The only way the newly merged business was going to be effective in delivering value from analytics was if it had solid data governance through simplified systems. To do that, we knew we needed to act quickly to bring systems and data together.'

The project team for the system and data integration was led by Hendrik Pieters, Head of HRIS Business Transformation. The first step in the process was to establish a clear strategy. Hendrik and his team agreed on four strategic drivers (see Figure 6.5):

- Enhance end-user experience – a strategic driver to positively influence employee experience.

- Simplify HR processes and associated technology – a strategic driver that improves the daily life of all line managers and employees, leading to measurable benefits for the business.

- Implement dynamic change management – a strategic driver to ensure that the Nokia and Alcatel-Lucent teams would allow choices of systems and HR processes to be made more quickly and therefore speed up cultural integration.

- Refine downstream systems and interfaces – a strategic driver aimed at reducing overhead and cost.

Figure 6.5 Strategic drivers of the Alcatel-Lucent integration with Nokia

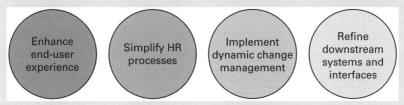

SOURCE Reproduced with kind permission of Nokia, December 2020

With its clearly defined strategy, the team was able to begin selecting technology. This was the most challenging and complex part of the integration. After compiling a list of data and technology in both companies, the team established a process by which it could quickly decide which of the systems would be the appropriate one for the merged company.

In some cases – such as the choice of core HR system – the choice was relatively simple: as Nokia's processes were considered the baseline for the newly merged Nokia company, and speed was of importance, it was a natural choice to select its core HR system to use going forward. Performance and Compensation, which needed to be up and running very quickly due to annual compensation processes, were a priority and also relatively simple: again, as Nokia processes were the baseline, the choice was easy. Similarly, when it came to Learning and Development, Alcatel-Lucent had placed significant emphasis on its system, and thus it was decisively chosen over Nokia's.

However, for other systems like Recruitment, there were no 'perfect fits'. In these cases, the team worked on a case-by-case basis, selecting legacy systems occasionally enriched with other candidates as part of a request for quotation-based selection process.[8]

The core HR system was implemented in a wave-like, case-by-case pattern. The first wave focused on those countries with workforces who would experience less disruption from the team's work, ie those countries with either the smallest combined workforces or those that hosted more Nokia employees than Alcatel-Lucent employees. The last waves saw the team work with more complex markets such as those with similarly sized employee populations or even Alcatel-Lucent dominant workforces such as the United States (where there were 4,000 Nokia employees and 6,000 Alcatel-Lucent employees) and China (9,000 Nokia employees and 11,000 Alcatel-Lucent employees).

In countries with local systems and technologies, country systems were changed to globally chosen systems. Over time Hendrik and the team were able to streamline everything into one series of technologies.

Integration was tough in an unstable environment and even with quick decision making, there was no shortage of challenges: the yearly compensation campaign started three months after the acquisition, requiring a new calculation engine, budgets to be spread over twice as many legal entities and five times the number of business units, reviews with Working Councils of both legacy organizations, and many more challenges. Still, thanks to their clear and methodical approach, the first annual salary review took place just four months from Day Zero!

During the integration process, the team evolved a common data model, which brought together all data items and their relationships, security and access protocols from the various systems. Today this data model is the basis for all of Nokia's corporate people analytics. It is kept up to date through integrations with the different HR systems.

The team has reformatted data management underneath to fit the new approach with the chosen technologies. 'One approach we took was to start considering the types of insights we might need in the future,' David explains. 'This approach meant that we always implemented systems and data management in the best way so that we would be able to deliver the most valuable insights to the business and employees.' The aim was to get as few and efficient tools as possible so that data and people from both businesses could be easily consolidated.

Data and system integration were undertaken at incredible pace. Quick decision making led to speedy implementation. The whole data management and technology selection process took just over 18 months, with implementation continuing throughout this period and for a further 12 months (see Figure 6.6).

Key successes included:

- The Annual Salary Review process was supported by one process and one system within four months of the integration date.

- Sales Incentive, Employee Recognition, Employee Incentive and Employee Equity Purchase were all available as one system unified around one process within 12 months of the integration date.

- The core HR system – including the integration of Payroll – was harmonized into one single technology and data management platform within just two and a half years.

Figure 6.6 A timeline of Nokia's data management transformation

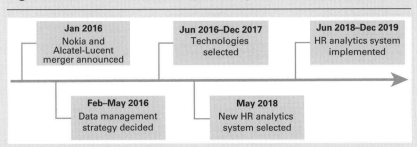

Jan 2016	Jun 2016–Dec 2017	Jun 2018–Dec 2019
Nokia and Alcatel-Lucent merger announced	Technologies selected	HR analytics system implemented

Feb–May 2016	May 2018
Data management strategy decided	New HR analytics system selected

SOURCE Reproduced with kind permission of Nokia, December 2020

Finally, David's Workforce Analytics team could consider how to change people analytics across the newly merged Nokia organization. With the consolidated armoury of technology and a single cohesive data management system, the team only had to choose a data democratization and visualization platform that could support people analytics globally.

'If it had been down to just HR, we would have persevered with our existing system,' says David. 'But in talking with business stakeholders and other functions, we realized their technology was far superior to ours. Our strategy from the outset of the work was to bring people data and business data together, so we went with the technology platform being used enterprise-wide.' It was the right decision; within a couple of years, all Nokia HR and business leaders had access to people-data-driven insights on a daily basis to support decision making using a platform familiar to them.

David reflects on the entire strategy of unifying systems and data: 'We were clear from the outset: the streamlining must enable real, repeatable success. That meant that the "outputs" had to be insights – actionable insights.' The team has since worked with Nokia managers and users to understand what insights they need to do their job and, using a design thinking approach, has provided useful and engaging products for the global HR and leadership organization.

The refined, embedded processes enable the Workforce Analytics team to respond quickly and add value when it really matters, such as when the COVID-19 pandemic hit in early 2020. Having the recently transformed HR analytics platform meant the team could respond with confidence and accuracy at a speed it would never have been able to do before.

'We had two things we did not have before 2016: a strong foundation for all of our workforce analytics, and the capability to integrate new data sources quickly and easily. We just needed the questions from the business or the vision to supply it with what it might need. We did not anticipate a global pandemic would test the system, but we had to be ready to respond to anything. And we were.'

'Our message to others out there is this: Don't underestimate the difficulty of bringing all HR data together – and don't underestimate how useful the end product will be.'

On reflection, it is clear that David, Hendrik and the whole team involved at Nokia were successful due to their approach, which had three core principles (Figure 6.7).

Figure 6.7   Nokia's guiding principles for data management system integration

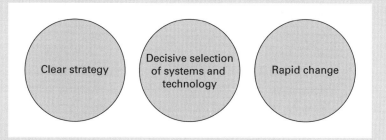

SOURCE   Reproduced with kind permission of Nokia, December 2020

First, the clarity in strategy and the four drivers used enabled strong direction. Second, the team made decisions on systems and technology based on the best process, best technology, or system with the deepest penetration among employees, which made for simple decision making. Finally, decisions and actions were taken at speed – much faster than we have seen in most organizations. There was no lengthy dithering, and when procurement processes were used, they were undertaken rapidly.

The entire focus was on what the team had, using it well and acting fast. Because of that, it had data and system management in place across a merged organization quickly, allowing people analytics to deliver value immediately.

> **TOP TIP**
>
> Think about data management proactively, with the business goal in mind.

Leverage data across the enterprise to generate business outcomes

Bringing people data and business data together is a strong example of the 'two plus two equals five'[9] concept, where the sum is greater than adding together the individual parts.

Throughout this book, we advocate an outside-in approach to people analytics based on taking client demands from across the enterprise and converting them into tangible business outcomes. This requires the people analytics team to partner with other functions in the business, combine their data and expertise, and together solve the business challenge in front of them.

In the case study, People analytics in practice: National Australia Bank, included in Part One (The case for people analytics) of this book, we explain how the bank has an 'Enterprise Analytics Data Council', which fosters collaboration, provides access to centrally located technical expertise and drives learning and career opportunities for all analytics professionals across the bank. Companies like National Australia Bank and others that have formed similar councils or communities of practice at an enterprise level have created the ideal climate for multiple analytics teams to collaborate on important business challenges.

For those people analytics leaders who don't have these types of structures in place, we recommend working together with peers across the enterprise, probably leveraging a chief analytics officer elsewhere in the company, if one exists.

In practical terms, working together involves sharing data, resources and technology – and accepting differences. We notice that teams that do this follow the principle of 'shared data is power' and, as such, they tend to be more successful at solving complex business-relevant topics.

Business outcomes that can be delivered by merging people and other business data together are almost infinite. Some common shared data opportunities are shown below with examples of relevant 'use cases'.

Customer data plus people data   This includes merging customer data such as cNPS[10] scores, conversion rate of customers and customer service data. For example, ISS identified the impact of eNPS[11] on cNPS and contract profitability (Kamp Andersenet et al, 2015). Similarly, the case study, People analytics in practice: National Australia Bank, in Part One (The case for people analytics) found that employee engagement in the bank branches had a direct impact on cNPS.

Finance data plus people data   This includes revenue, profit, cost, expense, departmental cost data, overhead and other 'fully loaded'[12] costs, and earnings per share. The case study below, The financial side of productivity: Tetra Pak, examines how the people analytics team and finance came together to work on a business challenge relating to employee productivity.

Sales and revenue data plus people data   This includes new customer sales, existing customer growth rates, renewal and retention rates of customers, and market share data. For example, Virgin Media found that customers who were cancelling their subscriptions following a poor experience when they applied for a job at the company was costing $5 million per annum (Steiner, 2017).

Safety and accident data plus people data   This includes safety incidents and accident reports and absenteeism data related to accidents. For example, Maersk Drilling established a value chain linking leadership quality on its rigs to lower crew turnover and better safety performance.

These are just four examples, but other business data we've seen being combined with people data to realize business outcomes include real estate (for example, footfall, CCTV, office dynamics, building location to help inform workplace design and collaboration) and IT data (for example, use of computers and applications to measure remote working effectiveness, productivity, collaboration, well-being and inclusion).

The following case study, as mentioned above, reflects the benefit of sharing data to solve organizational topics that can only be solved when departments – and their data – are shared. The key message from the case study from Tetra Pak is: *Work with finance to increase the credibility of people data so it can be used to guide financial decision making.*

 CASE STUDY

The financial side of productivity: Tetra Pak

Tetra Pak[13] is a name that many people know of, but perhaps don't realize the extent to which they use its products. The company is best known for its manufacture of food packaging such as milk cartons. It has seen phenomenal organic growth since its foundation in 1951, and in 2019 alone it achieved €11.5 billion in net sales, with its approximately 25,000-strong workforce delivering products and services in more than 160 countries.[14]

In the last 20 years, Tetra Pak's HR team has focused on workforce planning as it related to expansion and the activities associated with a growing business. As the company has matured – and certainly in the latter part of the 2010s – the emphasis has shifted to measuring and managing productivity and anticipating potential future issues. Many maturing organizations reach a point when productivity becomes a challenge, when resource costs are growing at a greater rate than sales (see Figure 6.8). When the need for managing Tetra Pak's productivity has arisen, the global HR function at the company has also had to change its focus. This means working with a broader range of stakeholders.

Figure 6.8   Typical costs and productivity indices of a generic maturing business. Values are representative, only.

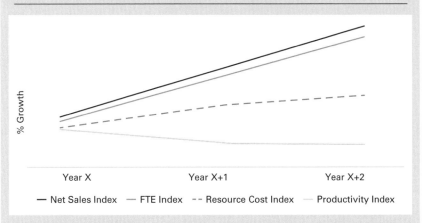

NOTE   FTE: full-time equivalent

Director of HR Technology, Process & Projects, Eva Åkesson, concluded that the team needed relationships with three stakeholders in particular: a sponsor within the HR leadership team who would champion the work; finance colleagues; and business executive support.

John Argabright, Vice President of Human Resources at Tetra Pak Processing Systems AB, was excited by the potential value this work could deliver and grabbed the initiative with both hands, becoming the main sponsor from the HR leadership team. Together with Adrian Benvenuto, Tetra Pak's People Analytics Lead, they formed an effective collaborative team on this project.

Upon inspecting much of the past data and business planning processes, they realized the planning scenarios and models would be much more powerful and more widely accepted by stakeholders with active collaboration in partnership with finance. Additionally, John and Adrian understood from research that only 8 per cent of HR functions that lead strategic workforce planning trust talent data and insights derived from HR data, fewer than one in five believe HR analytics focus on the right business questions, and only 15 per cent have ever changed a decision in the past year as a result of HR data. They knew that if they didn't work with multiple stakeholders, the likelihood of work being embedded in Tetra Pak's decision making would be significantly lower.

'We were faced with a storm in a teacup,' says John. HR was beginning to make a lot of noise about productivity, but the team knew that to garner trust, its finance colleagues should be involved throughout. Finally, John and Adrian knew that board level business decisions are fundamentally more credible if finance actively supports them.

HR and finance joined forces to collaborate and focus on the business opportunity. They prioritized the co-development of a new Productivity Report with key indices to shine a spotlight on the topic and provide the insights needed for business action. Everyone was pleased when it became clear that the two groups were aligned. As Eva recalls, 'As soon as people peeled back the labels of "I'm in HR", and "I'm in finance", it was easy. We were one team, one force, trying to solve a business challenge.' John agrees: 'We all wanted to work together to create something of value to the business. Once our goals were aligned, it was just semantics.'

HR and finance worked together on all aspects of the analytics methodology.[15] In practical terms, this involved clarifying the business question and hypotheses, defining data elements, validating the quality of data, developing the models produced, conducting the analyses, agreeing on visualization, testing products, defining metrics, reviewing insights and implementing recommendations. It also included selecting the right technology and visualization systems that would have the highest impact with executives. 'Creating a common understanding of what the data represents, how it is defined, and how analytics can support the Tetra Pak leadership team was a significant breakthrough,' says Adrian.

The most important test of the business planning and analytics work was to ensure that executive stakeholders adopted the recommendations. This meant presenting to – and gaining approval from – the Global Leadership

Team (GLT). HR couldn't simply show some slides and move on; it had to inform and motivate top business leaders to take action. HR and finance instilled a level of excitement among members of the GLT to take action on productivity. The joint approach resulted in one of the team's most memorable moments: gaining acceptance at an executive meeting in April 2019, side-by-side with finance, with whom it was in total agreement. Presenting the material to the GLT alongside financial allies created a forum for collaborative discussion.

'The analytics work that went into producing our visualizations motivated the GLT to take action,' John recalls. 'Credible data that backs up simple visualizations around a business problem that people care about creates energy across the business: it's exciting to see how invested executives become.'

The initiative continues to be a success. Furthermore, the partnership between HR and finance continues to strengthen and has laid the foundation for working on business-critical challenges.

The teams have an understanding and can accelerate other work. Adrian puts it best, simply: 'We spotted somewhere to make a difference to the business. Together with finance, we made it happen.'

TOP TIP

Put functional silos to one side to focus on the problem in hand.

Emerging data sources

People analytics functions have an increasing plethora of data sources available to support their work. These sources, and the technologies that enable them, help people analytics teams to address more complex business problems that are requested by stakeholders. Some of the technologies that enable these data to be sourced are outlined in the Third Wave, as described in Chapter 5 (Technology).

During our research and experience, we encountered human resources teams that are reluctant to invest in these data sources – and the technologies that allow them to be sourced – since they appear complex and expensive, and challenge organizational acceptance of data privacy. Those organizations are often then unable to address these complex and advanced analytical topics and try to find proxy data sources. Invariably teams are left wanting.

Leading people analytics practices are often those that always seek new ways to solve the business questions their stakeholders want answered, irrespective of the complexity. Those teams have solved issues through using these new data sources. These emerging data sources provide a tremendous opportunity to deliver value, as reflected in Accenture's study, Decoding organizational DNA: Trust, data and unlocking value in the digital workplace (Shook, Knickrehm and Sage-Gavin, 2019).

Four data sources that we recommend people analytics teams pay particular attention to are:

- voice of the employee data;
- unstructured data;
- labour and talent market data;
- collaboration and productivity data.

Voice of the employee data

What is it?   This is detailed employee data that helps organizations learn about the 'voice' and detail behind a traditional employee engagement survey. The data is usually qualitative but might also be quantitative. It is usual to procure or develop in-house an employee listening platform to capture this data.

What is it used for?   Just as marketing functions follow a similar approach to understand the voice of the customer, so people analytics teams and the HR functions they serve use employee listening platforms to understand the voice of the employee. This data can be used to analyse a series of use cases including employee well-being, how employees feel about the company, the impact of remote working, employee sentiment on ways to improve customer and other business outcomes, etc.

One example of gathering employee voice data is described in the case study Scaling people analytics: Microsoft Corporation (Chapter 5 – Technology), where the team used multiple channels to collect both active and passive data sources as a daily pulse. The data is integrated to create an enterprise picture of the employee voice to provide insights to topics on a daily basis. It is important to consider:

a Purpose: Develop a clear understanding and strategy around employee listening since the commitment needs to be long term, given the investment required.

b Sponsorship: Enlist the most senior business executive possible as a sponsor. This will ensure alignment with strategy and also provide employees with a sense of importance, which will help create more powerful data collection, as well as make the employee experience better.

c Data: Investing in data integration is key to any employee listening platform, especially between qualitative data from the platform and the underlying core HR and business data.

d Ethics: Embed ethical practices in the listening strategy, work with the ethics and privacy council (or set one up) we describe in Chapter 1 (Governance). As part of this, conduct transparent and continuous communications with employee representative groups like works councils as well as employees themselves. Work with the chief privacy officer and works councils from an early stage to ensure commitment and demonstrate benefits.

e Vision: Implementing an employee listening platform is complex and requires a long-term vision and agile approach to building it in stages.

Unstructured data – text analytics

What is it? Analysing unstructured data in the people analytics field typically requires analysing large volumes of text from workers, recruitment candidates or alumni using specialist software and resources skilled in areas such as natural language processing (NLP). Typical sources of data could be both internal to the organization, such as comments on open questions from employee surveys, or external to the organization, such as comments on Glassdoor[16] reviews.

What is it used for? Particularly with regard to employees' comments in surveys, open-text questions provide richer and deeper data for analysis and to drive action from executives. The case study, Measure employee experience: ABN AMRO in Chapter 7 (Workforce Experience), provides a prime example of the richness of data that open text provides.

Other common uses of text data for people analytics include employee skills inference to support workforce planning, analysing requests to HR help desks in order to develop chatbots, analysing performance management review data to answer questions around bias, using external data to understand internal and external trends in employee engagement, etc. It is important to consider:

a   Skills: Recruit, develop or procure the specialist skills needed to analyse text. In the operating model described in Chapter 4 (Skills), we dedicate an entire role to this in the Solution Engine. Some would say that this is 'just' another analysis that any data scientist can conduct, but we have seen that leading people analytics teams develop or hire dedicated people to focus on the growing role of text analysis. If hiring into the team is not possible, leverage skills from elsewhere in the business, such as from the consumer analytics team.

b   Prioritization: According to text analytics specialist Andrew Marritt, 'great models (for text analysis) will work well for one question but rarely are generalizable' (Green, 2018). In other words, think carefully about the business problems and the outcomes and prioritize the most important.

c   Privacy: Most unstructured data, when analysed, is more interesting if merged with other business and people data, such as core HR. This will usually mean that attributable data and confidentiality are more important than anonymity. Ensure that encryption, data security and privacy controls are well understood and managed.

d   Communication: Employees are more likely to provide unstructured comments if they understand why it is requested, and that everything is fully secure. Spend a lot of time on employee communications.

Labour and talent market data

What is it?   This is the collection and analysis of external data as it relates to geographies, people, skills, jobs, salaries, functions and competitors, which, when combined with internal data, enables easier decision making.

What is it used for?   This type of data is typically used to analyse and provide insights on external market factors affecting recruitment of skills, workforce planning, talent availability and workforce forecasting. It can also be used in enterprise-wide topics such as location strategy, real-estate planning and risk management. Additionally, it can provide useful information about competitor organizations and their talent.

It is important to consider:

a Purpose: Be clear as to the reason for using talent market data. Think carefully about why this data is needed because if unclear, it is possible that the data received from the external vendor may not be useful.

b Data integration: Depending on the scope of the work to be undertaken, it may be necessary to integrate data from more than one vendor depending on the geographies and talent categories in scope.

c Measurement: Think about how to measure success up front, since this data can be overwhelming and the effort taken to analyse it may well outweigh the benefits.

Collaboration and productivity data

What is it? This data is commonly referred to by its scientific name, Organizational Network Analysis (ONA). It is the study of how information flows across the company and how people collaborate within and between teams beyond the formal reporting structures. ONA is not new, but it is now becoming more prevalent due to the ability to analyse large volumes of data and merge it with internal business data to drive significant insights. ONA can be active (collected through 'active' mechanisms such as surveys) or passive (collecting data through a continual flow of data generated from a company's communication systems such as email, calendar and collaboration tools).

What is it used for? Much has been written about what ONA data can be used to analyse (Leonardi and Contractor, 2018). Typical 'use cases' include the study of networking behaviour of successful sales teams and leaders (Green, 2019), the impact of remote working on collaboration (Green and Goel, 2019), employee well-being and burnout (Irwin, 2019), using employee networks to drive innovation (Arena *et al*, 2017) and providing new insights on diversity and inclusion (Newman, 2019). In short, there are a lot of possibilities for collecting and analysing ONA data.

It is important to consider:

a Purpose: Start with the business problem. Don't just use ONA because it sounds 'cool'. Use it when appropriate to help solve a real business problem.

b Vendors: Each vendor's capabilities are slightly different, so the choice of vendor will depend on the business challenge. There is no 'typical' vendor profile. Some are better for investigating productivity while others specialize in topics such as collaboration and inclusion.

c Ethics: We have seen a number of initiatives to use passive ONA data fail because the company was not prepared for the very robust processes needed in security, privacy and ethics. Have a clear business reason for including this data as part of the analysis, work with the ethics and privacy council described in Chapter 1 (Governance), and be transparent about areas such as the data to be analysed and the potential benefits for the organization and the workforce.

d Test and learn: We recommend conducting a pilot project with ONA first. Start small, test the appetite, then scale. There are many insights and benefits, but using this data is not for the faint-hearted people analytics leader or chief human resources officer. However, the opportunity for business impact and value is very large indeed.

Summary

Data is the raw material for all analytics. Structuring, managing, governing and securing data is key to the success of people analytics, as is understanding what new data sources can potentially provide new insights for business outcomes.

- Have a chief data officer for HR.
- Combine responsibility for data management, data science and analytics into one role.
- Deliver strong governance for people data, which provides clear guidelines on the privacy and management of data.
- Pay attention to data management, align it with strategy, create clear definitions and standards, and invest in data-engineering resources.
- Take a cross-functional approach and leverage data and skills from across the enterprise to collaborate on work that generates enhanced business outcomes.
- Leverage emerging data sources – both internal and external to the organization – and seek new ways to solve business challenges.

References

Aractingi, A, Baltassis, E, Khendek, Y and Quarta, L (2020) A show-don't-tell approach to data governance, Boston Consulting Group, 4 February. Available from: https://www.bcg.com/en-gb/publications/2020/show-tell-approach-data-governance (archived at https://perma.cc/8KCQ-6MSH) [Last accessed 15 March 2021]

Arena, M, Cross, R, Sims, J and Uhl-Bien, M (2017) How to catalyze innovation in your organization, *MIT Sloan Management Review*, 13 June. Available from: https://sloanreview.mit.edu/article/how-to-catalyze-innovation-in-your-organization/ (archived at https://perma.cc/P9Z6-88UQ) [Last accessed 7 February 2021]

Davenport, T and Bean, R (2020) Are you asking too much of your chief data officer? *Harvard Business Review*, 7 February. Available from: https://hbr.org/2020/02/are-you-asking-too-much-of-your-chief-data-officer (archived at https://perma.cc/VN46-W9DL) [Last accessed 7 February 2021]

Forbes Insights (2019) Rethinking the role of chief data officer, *Forbes*, 22 May. Available from: https://www.forbes.com/sites/insights-intelai/2019/05/22/rethinking-the-role-of-chief-data-officer/?sh=4f1147021bf9 (archived at https://perma.cc/T5GE-662H) [Last accessed 7 February 2021]

Green, D (2018) Using employee text analytics to drive business outcomes [Blog] myHRfuture, 21 November. Available from: https://www.myhrfuture.com/blog/2018/11/21/using-text-analytics-with-people-data (archived at https://perma.cc/9A29-SJXE) [Last accessed 7 February 2021]

Green, D (2019) How McKesson Used ONA to Drive Sales Performance with RJ Milner [Podcast] Digital HR Leaders, 3 December. Available from: https://www.myhrfuture.com/digital-hr-leaders-podcast/2019/12/3/how-mckesson-used-ona-to-drive-sales-performance (archived at https://perma.cc/R4YQ-RMCH) [Last accessed 7 February 2021]

Green, D and Goel, M (2019) The role of network analytics (ONA) in ensuring team collaboration and well being [Blog] myHRfuture, 27 April. Available from: https://www.myhrfuture.com/blog/2020/4/27/the-role-of-network-analytics-ona-in-ensuring-team-collaboration-and-well-being (archived at https://perma.cc/LT72-QQEW) [Last accessed 7 February 2021]

Guenole, N, Ferrar, J and Feinzig, S (2017) *The Power of People: Learn how successful organizations use workforce analytics to improve business performance*, Pearson, London

Henry, N L (1974) Knowledge management: a new concern for public administration, *Public Administration Review*, **34** (3), May–Jun, pp 189–96

International Data Corporation (2020) IDC's Global DataSphere Forecast shows continued steady growth in the creation and consumption of data [Press realease] 8 May. Available from: https://www.idc.com/getdoc.jsp? containerId=prUS46286020 (archived at https://perma.cc/747L-YED2) [Last accessed 7 February 2021]

Irwin, N (2019) The mystery of the miserable employees: how to win in the winner-take-all economy: the business unit was doing well, but the employees were sad. Could data offer a clue? *New York Times*, 15 June. Available from: https://www.nytimes.com/2019/06/15/upshot/how-to-win-neil-irwin.html (archived at https://perma.cc/U88L-TXCF) [Last accessed 7 February 2021]

Kamp Andersen, M, Svegaard, S and Ankerstjerne, P (2015) Linking Customer Experience with Service Employee Engagement [Report] ISS World, Service Management 3.0 Series, November. Available from: http://www.publications. issworld.com/ISS/External/issworld/White_papers/LinkingEmployeeand CustomerEngagement/ (archived at https://perma.cc/K4X5-TVQY) [Last accessed 7 February 2021]

Ledet, E, McNulty, K, Morales, D and Shandell, M (2020) How to be great at people analytics, McKinsey & Co, 2 October. Available from: https://www. mckinsey.com/business-functions/organization/our-insights/how-to-be-great-at-people-analytics (archived at https://perma.cc/9RL7-4VKU) [Last accessed 7 February 2021]

Leonardi, P and Contractor, N (2018) Better people analytics, *Harvard Business Review*, November – December. Available from: https://hbr.org/2018/11/ better-people-analytics (archived at https://perma.cc/3TGR-9NFZ) [Last accessed 7 February 2021]

Newman, G (2019) How organizational network analytics is transforming diversity and inclusion through data, HR Zone, 10 July. Available from: https:// www.hrzone.com/engage/employees/how-organizational-network-analytics-is-transforming-diversity-and-inclusion (archived at https://perma.cc/ATJ7-233K) [Last accessed 7 February 2021]

Press, G (2020) 54 Predictions about the state of data in 2021 [Blog] *Forbes*, 30 December. Available from:https://www.forbes.com/sites/gilpress/2021/12/30/54-predictions-about-the-state-of-data-in-2021/?sh=5e88f6d6397d (archived at https://perma.cc/L6XJ-JYHV) [Last accessed 7 February 2021]

Shook, E, Knickrehm, M and Sage-Gavin, E (2019) Decoding organizational DNA: Trust, data and unlocking value in the digital workplace [Report] Accenture. Available from: https://www.accenture.com/gb-en/insights/future-workforce/ workforce-data-organizational-dna (archived at https://perma.cc/KPV9-4BXV) [Last accessed 7 March 2021]

Steiner, K (2017) Bad candidate experience cost Virgin Media $5m annually – here is how they turned that around [Blog] LinkedIn Talent Blog, 15 March. Available from: https://business.linkedin.com/talent-solutions/blog/candidate-experience/2017/bad-candidate-experience-cost-virgin-media-5m-annually-and-how-they-turned-that-around (archived at https://perma.cc/Q6NA-FTKK) [Last accessed 7 February 2021]

Notes

1 Someone's Achilles heel is the weakest point in their character or nature, where it is easiest for other people to attack or criticize them. It is applied in business to point to a weak point in a system, process or team that leads to vulnerability and potential disruption of activity. Collins Dictionary (see https://www. collinsdictionary.com/dictionary/english/achilles-heel (archived at https://perma. cc/4S78-SVA7), last accessed 7 February 2021).

2 See Glossary: Data warehouse. A central repository of integrated data from one or more sources, storing current and historical data in one single place. Often formatted such that data is stored using predefined structures and protocols.

3 See Glossary: Data lake. A centralized repository that allows the storage of structured and unstructured data at scale, without having to first structure the data into any order or pre-described format.

4 See https://aws.amazon.com/big-data/datalakes-and-analytics/what-is-a-data-lake/ (archived at https://perma.cc/43NL-C8EX), last accessed 7 February 2021.

5 HSBC Bank plc was founded in 1836 in Birmingham, UK and has its global headquarters in London, UK. Serving more than 40 million customers around the world, it employs upwards of 85,000 people (see https://www.about.hsbc. co.uk/ (archived at https://perma.cc/S87E-BTCV), last accessed 7 February 2021).

6 See Glossary: Burning platform. Term used to describe the process of helping people see the consequences of not changing. By sparking just enough concern about what happens if the status quo remains the same, people begin to embrace change.

7 Nokia Corporation is a Finnish multinational telecommunication, information technology and consumer electronics company founded in 1865. As of 2020, Nokia employs approximately 103,000 people across over 100 countries and conducts business in more than 130 countries (see https://www.nokia.com/ about-us/ (archived at https://perma.cc/NC33-VFV5), last accessed 7 February 2021).

8 See Glossary: Request for quotation. A document similar to an RFP but usually shorter and used as a precursor to the RFP, to request a quotation for services or products from potential vendors.

9 2+2=5 is the theory that when two companies or organizations join together, they achieve more and are more successful than if they work separately. *Cambridge Business English Dictionary* (see https://dictionary.cambridge.org/dictionary/english/2-2-5 (archived at https://perma.cc/8VM9-X63B) (Last accessed 7 February 2021).

10 See Glossary: Net Promoter Score (NPS) is a customer loyalty metric developed by (and a registered trademark of) Fred Reichheld, Bain & Company, and Satmetrix Systems, Inc. Reichheld introduced NPS in his 2003 *Harvard Business Review* article, 'One number you need to grow'. cNPS is another way to describe NPS and means customer Net Promoter Score, and is usually used to differentiate it from eNPS.

11 See Glossary: eNPS means employee Net Promoter Score and is a version of NPS. eNPS usually refers to organizations asking their staff one question: Would you recommend [name of company] as a great place to work? The methodology for working out the score of eNPS is the same methodology as for NPS.

12 See Glossary: 'Fully loaded' refers to the costs of an employee that include the direct costs of a person (that is their salary, other compensation and benefits) plus standard incremental costs. The finance function usually has a calculation for these incremental costs that includes such items as real estate occupancy, IT costs and cost for headquarters staff.

13 Tetra Pak is a multinational food packaging and processing company, headquartered in Lund, Sweden and Pully, Switzerland and founded in 1951 (see https://www.tetrapak.com/about/our-identity-and-values (archived at https://perma.cc/Z3G3-GPUE), last accessed 7 February 2021).

14 See https://www.tetrapak.com/about/facts-figures (archived at https://perma.cc/G553-BTXZ), last accessed 7 February 2021).

15 The team effectively followed the Eight Step Methodology described in Chapter 2 (Methodology).

16 Glassdoor is a website where current and former employees anonymously review companies.

Workforce Experiences

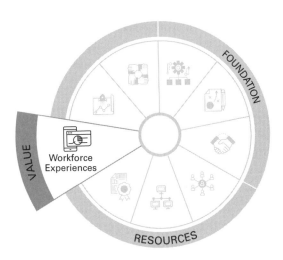

07

In this chapter, we consider the concept of the consumerization of HR and how this leads people analytics to have a responsibility to four key audiences – the employee, the manager, the executive and the workforce.

DISCOVER...

- the opportunity that 'consumerization' offers human resources;
- how the employee experience impacts people analytics;
- the responsibilities the people analytics function has for employees, the workforce, managers and executives.

WITH INSIGHTS FROM...

- ABN AMRO Bank N.V., on measuring employee experiences;
- FIS, on using data to change the performance management system across the company;
- Banco Santander S.A., on bringing analytics to life in front of executives.

Overview

> ## WORKFORCE EXPERIENCES
>
> Workforce Experiences, as one of the Nine Dimensions, describes how audiences across any organization benefit from people analytics. It outlines key topics such as consumerization and personalization of employee experiences, the democratization of data to all managers, how to excite executives with interactive analytics and how to change organizational processes for improving the entire workforce experience.

People analytics consists of two words: 'people' and 'analytics'. It is the word 'people' that is key to this chapter. Delivering the benefits of analytics to the people who provide the data – namely employees – positively impacts business performance.

The Accenture study, Decoding Organizational Data: Trust, data and unlocking value in the digital workplace (Shook, Knickrehm and Sage-Gavin, 2019) found that 92 per cent of employees are open to their data being collected and analysed by their company provided there is a 'fair exchange of value'[1] whereby employees get personal benefit in return. The same study found that the difference that this 'trust dividend'[2] makes to growth rates is 12.5 per cent, equating to $3.1 billion globally. Delivering workforce experiences with people analytics is therefore not just the right thing to do, it also provides enormous benefit to the company.

We note in Part One (The case for people analytics) that 'workforce experiences' is one of the core outcomes of people analytics (see Figure 7.1).

We will now explore the topic of workforce experiences in more detail across the following elements:

- Consumerization of HR: We will explore consumerization as it relates to the human resources function and its responsibilities.
- Four Responsibilities of people analytics: We will discuss how consumerization applies to four audiences and why the people analytics function has a responsibility to each: the employee, the workforce, the manager and the executive.

Figure 7.1 People analytics consists of multiple activities and outcomes

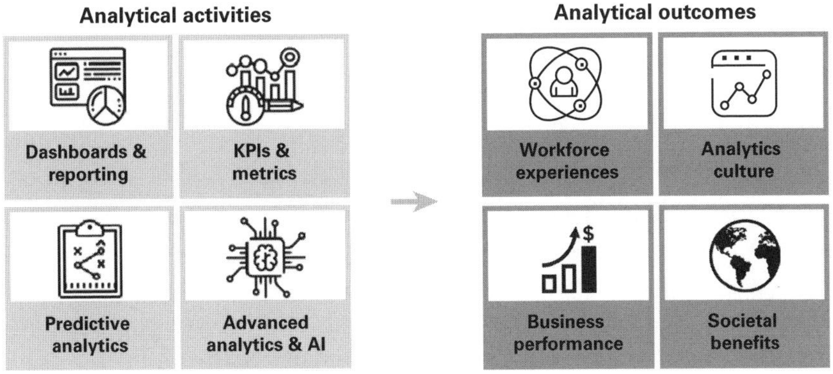

The consumerization of HR

As Peter Hinssen explains in his 2018 *Forbes* article on what HR can learn from marketing about employee experience: 'Marketing used to be all about broadcasting: we had a product or service and pushed that to the customer. We had no idea what they wanted, only the belief that our solution was so positively awesome that – if we could just reach enough people – a big percentage of them would buy what we had.'

Sound familiar? It should because this is typically how the majority of organizations have treated their workforce for decades. Companies develop an HR programme such as a training course or performance management system with little input from employees relative to its size. They then scale the programme, sometimes – but not always – following a pilot implementation in part of the business, then deliver the programme across the enterprise often irrespective of geography, business line, audience demographics or culture. Feedback that is collected is often about the implementation of the programme. In our experience, business outcomes are rarely measured.

Okay – we may be being a little harsh! Some companies have started doing things differently, using data to inform decision making. And some human resource executives have an outstanding perspective on delivering employee experiences in a more differentiated and segmented fashion. But based on our research, relatively few companies and their HR executives are using employee data and analytics pervasively to inform decision making for the majority of their HR programmes.

In this respect, the human resources function can definitely learn from the experiences of the marketing function and how customers have become consumers. For HR, this means looking at employees as consumers. We call this the 'consumerization of HR'.

Over the last 15 years, marketing has been transformed by data, analytics and technology. Companies now harness customer data and by using analytics are able to treat each customer as a single individual or 'customer of one' (Howell, 2020), personalizing offerings accordingly. Companies like Amazon and Netflix have built incredibly successful businesses based on sophisticated personalization engines that provide recommendations based on customer preferences. Indeed, Amazon's recommendation engine reportedly generates 35 per cent of its revenues (Morgan, 2018).

Leading HR functions are now treading a similar path, and employee experience (EX) promises to provide a similarly positive impact to the function and the workforce as customer experience (CX) did for marketing and the consumer. A 2015 paper by Accenture, Managing your people as a workforce of one, helped point the way with its clarion call of: 'When it comes to managing talent, one size no longer fits all' (Smith and Cantrell, 2015).

As companies increasingly focus on EX, a new leadership role emerges in HR: the employee experience leader. One of the first organizations to embrace this change was Airbnb, who appointed Mark Levy into this role as early as 2013. As Mark revealed in an interview with Jacob Morgan in *Forbes* in 2016, 'If Airbnb had a Customer Experience Group, why not create an Employee Experience Group?' (Morgan, 2016).

So what is EX? Mark Levy defines it as such: 'Employee experience is about doing things with and for your employees, not to them' (Levy, 2020), which we believe captures the essence perfectly. EX is often confused with employee engagement, but although they are related, they are very different: EX can be described as what the employee observes and how they feel about every interaction they have with the company throughout their tenure. Engagement, instead, is a measure of experience, whether perceived or real.

Pioneers like Airbnb and others such as IBM (Burrell and Gherson, 2018), Microsoft (Hougaard, Carter and Hogan, 2019) and ABN AMRO (see the case study later in this chapter) helped pave the way. By 2019, a study of 200 companies by KennedyFitch (2019) found that every company with over 50,000 employees had begun their EX journey. In its State of Employee Experience 2019 study, TI People identified that the 'Head of Employee Experience' reported directly to the CHRO in 23 per cent of companies.

In many respects, the growth of EX mirrors that of people analytics in The Age of Realization (see Part One – The case for people analytics).

Indeed, EX and people analytics are two of the fastest-growing areas of HR, whose importance is consistently cited by business leaders and HR professionals in research studies. Two examples include the World Economic Forum's HR 4.0: Shaping People Strategies in the Fourth Industrial Revolution report (2019), which highlighted EX and people analytics as two of six key imperatives that business and HR leaders need to implement. The second example is LinkedIn's Global Talent Trends 2020 report, in which HR professionals ranked EX and people analytics as the two most important trends changing the way talent is attracted and retained. This is not a coincidence – EX and people analytics are intrinsically linked, and the growth of each is partly dependent on the other.

Let's now turn to the implications of the consumerization of HR and how this affects the role of people analytics. We will do this by looking at The Four Responsibilities of people analytics.

The Four Responsibilities of people analytics

People analytics plays a significant role in the consumerization of HR. This can be looked at through the eyes of four audiences – or segments of the workforce – and their expectations as consumers. We define these as The Four Responsibilities of people analytics (see Figure 7.2):

- The Responsibility of people analytics to the 'Employee as an "Employee of One"';
- The Responsibility of people analytics to the 'Workforce as a Consumer of People Processes';
- The Responsibility of people analytics to the 'Manager as a Consumer of People Data';
- The Responsibility of people analytics to the 'Executive as a Consumer of People Insights'.

The Responsibility of people analytics to the 'Employee as an "Employee of One"'

People analytics is an indispensable component of designing, measuring, communicating and improving an effective end-to-end journey for employees.

Figure 7.2 The Four Responsibilities of People Analytics in the Consumerization of HR

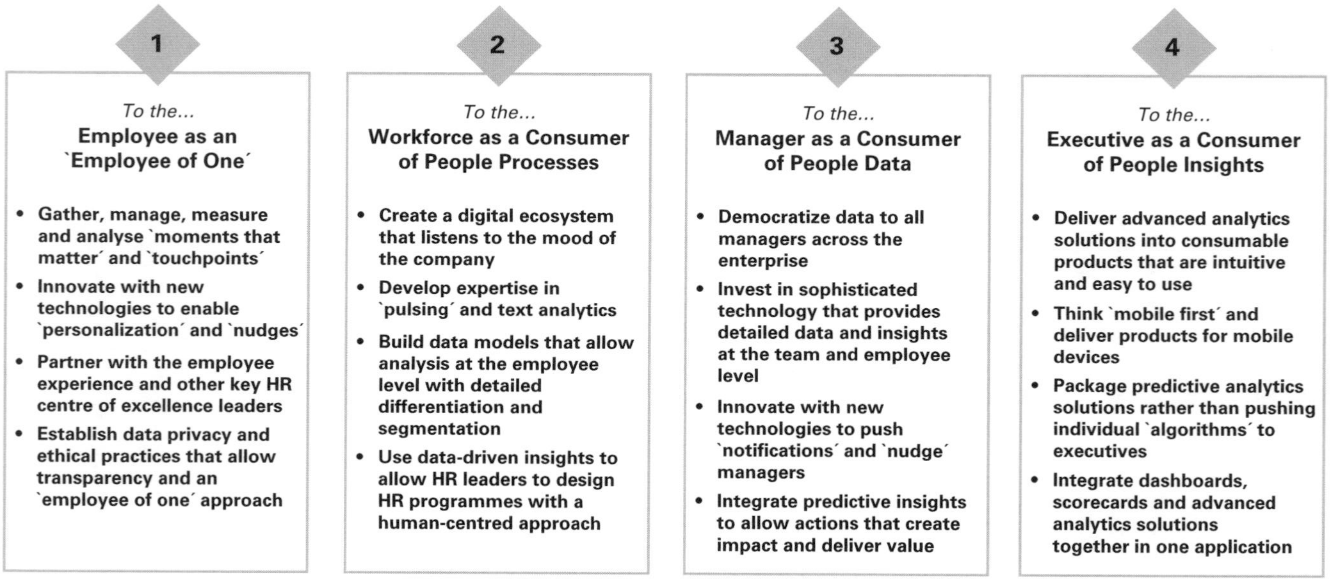

1

To the…
Employee as an 'Employee of One'

- Gather, manage, measure and analyse 'moments that matter' and 'touchpoints'
- Innovate with new technologies to enable 'personalization' and 'nudges'
- Partner with the employee experience and other key HR centre of excellence leaders
- Establish data privacy and ethical practices that allow transparency and an 'employee of one' approach

2

To the…
Workforce as a Consumer of People Processes

- Create a digital ecosystem that listens to the mood of the company
- Develop expertise in 'pulsing' and text analytics
- Build data models that allow analysis at the employee level with detailed differentiation and segmentation
- Use data-driven insights to allow HR leaders to design HR programmes with a human-centred approach

3

To the…
Manager as a Consumer of People Data

- Democratize data to all managers across the enterprise
- Invest in sophisticated technology that provides detailed data and insights at the team and employee level
- Innovate with new technologies to push 'notifications' and 'nudge' managers
- Integrate predictive insights to allow actions that create impact and deliver value

4

To the…
Executive as a Consumer of People Insights

- Deliver advanced analytics solutions into consumable products that are intuitive and easy to use
- Think 'mobile first' and deliver products for mobile devices
- Package predictive analytics solutions rather than pushing individual 'algorithms' to executives
- Integrate dashboards, scorecards and advanced analytics solutions together in one application

Figure 7.3   The top areas where people analytics adds value

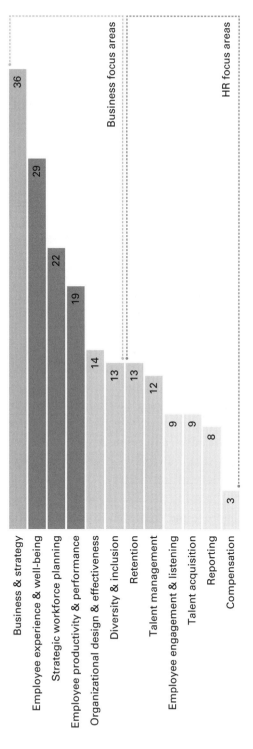

SOURCE Ferrar, Styr and Ktena (2020)

Companies with a good grasp of EX use people analytics to segment employees into personas. They also identify the key employee 'touchpoints' or 'moments that matter', create journey maps and provide insights that shape human resources programmes and company processes.

Chapter 6 (Data) highlights some emerging sources of data that people analytics teams can use to analyse EX. This includes survey data (from annual surveys and monthly or even daily pulse surveys), collaboration data (such as ONA) and data from core HR systems.

One important aspect to remember, especially in the context of people analytics is that managing EX requires HR to engage and involve line managers and work in concert with IT, real estate and other functional areas. This is because nearly all of the touchpoints that matter most to employees are actually owned by the business. Indeed, research by TI People in 2019 found that of the 36 most important employee touchpoints, only one is owned by HR.

Additionally, to engage in EX at the detailed analytical level, there will need to be more detailed approaches to data privacy. The entire ethics policies of using people data might need to be reconsidered, given the level of detail required to capture useful data at the individual employee level. This may give rise to uncertainty from employees, unions, works councils and other employee representative bodies, that this collection of employee data is too invasive and raises concern about a 'Big Brother'[3] culture within the organization. Nothing could be further from the truth; that is why the data privacy, data security, employee relations and people analytics teams are advised to create a modern ethics charter (see Chapter 1 – Governance) with full transparency to the employees to enable the trust dividend to be realized.

The key is this: it is not possible to measure, personalize, productize and consequently improve the employee experience without analysing people data. Therefore, people analytics as a function is essential. And consequently, the chief human resources officer will need to invest in people analytics even more if they want to 'move the needle'[4] on EX.

That means investing in gathering data on individual employee experiences becomes key. It also means investing in a data model that allows all qualitative and quantitative data to be integrated at the employee level to create a 'Big Data platform' of people data that delivers the necessary micro-segmentation. This might need more governance and new levels of stewardship (see Chapter 6 – Data).

Additionally, investment in new technologies will allow insights to be personalized. 'Nudging' can also be developed to help employees take action when most needed. With the use of these technologies, companies will get nearer to the goal of reaching people at the individual level – as an 'employee of one'.

Finally, there will need to be an investment in data analysis, especially expert skills such as text analysis, plus investment in communications and management of privacy and ethics in a much more deliberate way.

With all this investment, the CHRO is key as an enabler of EX. But the quality of the people analytics leader is paramount, too.

Any people analytics leader who does not want to work with their EX colleagues and gather, manage, measure and analyse EX data puts the whole concept of EX in jeopardy, therefore affecting the potential of every employee's experience in the entire company.

Now that is a big responsibility. And it is one that the people analytics leader and their team should embrace.

The case study that follows, Measure employee experience: ABN AMRO, provides a compelling example of how people analytics can be used to listen to employees, analyse what they are saying, communicate insights and drive action in an agile way. The key message is: *If you are serious about employee experience: start listening, love the problem and take action.*

 CASE STUDY

Measure employee experience: ABN AMRO

'Using people analytics to identify employee insights is imperative. But the real value lies in bringing these insights into action. This is when human resources truly can affect the employee experience,' says Patrick Coolen, Global Head of people analytics, Strategic Workforce Planning and HR Survey Management at ABN AMRO.[5]

This philosophy has served Patrick for almost a decade, since he started building the people analytics function at the bank. Patrick has always had a 'business first' approach and a mindset that focuses on segmenting employees and not just data.

'Our ethos is to create actionable insights that enable better decision-making on workforce topics that are linked to key business performance indicators such as customer satisfaction, revenue and cost optimization.'

Over the years, as the team's reputation has grown within the bank, their responsibilities have broadened to incorporate strategic workforce planning and the measurement of employee experience as well as advanced analytics. Since early 2019, the team has been heavily involved in transforming how the bank defines and measures the employee experience.

One of the three core pillars of ABN AMRO's corporate strategy[6] is to build a 'future-proof bank'. To operationalize this, the bank recognizes that: 'Our employees are the foundation of a future-proof bank'. This strategy places employee experience at the heart of corporate and HR strategy for the bank.

The dual emphasis on transforming the employee experience and the customer experience and linking them together under the belief of 'Happy People, Happy Clients' has proved to be an important milestone for the bank and a guiding principle for Patrick and his team (Sexton-Brown, 2018).

'We want to provide our employees with the best career they can possibly have, from start to finish,' Patrick explains. 'This means we need to "listen" to what our employees are telling us, learn from what they say and act to help them do their jobs more easily, smartly and swiftly.' By using the word 'listen', Patrick explains he is talking about the analytical nature of capturing what employees are writing about and asking for collectively. This is very different from the traditional approach of 'listening' to employees one by one and repeating their phrases in an anecdotal manner.

This approach to 'listening' is an evolving territory for the discipline of people analytics, and Patrick has mastered it well by learning from colleagues in Customer Experience. Recognizing that employee experience extends beyond HR and the people analytics team – explicitly, that it is a joint effort with Facilities Management, IT and Internal Communications – a Continuous Listening Framework was developed collaboratively.

Having worked in people analytics since 2013, Patrick identified that this project created an important moment in his own evolution as a people analytics leader. The first, that he needed to gather different data and master all the elements of that data. The second, that he needed to collaborate much more extensively with other functions than he'd ever had to before.

This raised Patrick and his team's own level of analytics proficiency to new levels. In doing so, they created a framework for continuous listening, shown in Figure 7.4.

Figure 7.4 ABN AMRO Continuous Listening Framework

1. START LISTENING	2. LOVE THE PROBLEM	3. TAKE ACTION
• Conduct EX surveys • Conduct business pulse surveys • Collect transactional data	• Understand the data • Analyse with passion • Make recommendations	• Communicate • Iterate solutions • Collaborate with functional partners

SOURCE Reproduced with kind permission of ABN AMRO, May 2020

The people analytics team has developed an active and multi-pronged approach to listening to the bank's approximately 18,000 employees. Previously existing tools like the annual engagement survey are now augmented with a short targeted 'pulse' survey (see Figure 7.5) sent every month to a 10 per cent sample of the workforce.

'This is how we capture data to bring our "listening" approach to life. These questions help us really understand the needs of our employees.'

Figure 7.5 A sample pulse survey for ABN AMRO employees

Example question 1: *How likely are you to recommend ABN AMRO as a good employer to a friend or relative?*
Input: Numeric score
Output: NPS-style rating

Example question 2: *What is ABN AMRO doing well as an employer?*
Input: Open text
Output: 'Top' score, indicating what ABN AMRO is doing well

Example question 3: *What could ABN AMRO do better as an employer?*
Input: Open text
Output: 'Tip' score, indicating what ABN AMRO could do better

SOURCE Reproduced with kind permission of ABN AMRO, May 2020

Sampling is very important and is one of the elements that differentiates Patrick's approach from other organizations that we have studied. The people analytics team uses techniques such as stratified sampling[7] to ensure that the 10 per cent of employees who receive the monthly pulse survey are representative of the total workforce. This helps the team to mitigate the risk of survey fatigue while ensuring effective 'listening'.

The people analytics team is focused on various topics for employee experience. This uses advanced text mining. To help kick-start the process, Patrick called text analytics expert Andrew Marritt, Founder and CEO of workforce data company OrganizationView.[8] Andrew trained the ABN AMRO people analytics team in text analytics, so the team could improve its proficiency and enable the bank in the long term.

His principle is rooted in text analysis being specific about what you are looking for. Then, use strong methods and a rigorous approach to allow detailed information to be gathered. It is Andrew's perspective that many organizations seem to endlessly fish in an ocean of text data, hoping to find something useful, without first asking themselves 'what are the key topics?'

'We learnt to fall in love with the problem we are trying to solve for our employees,' Patrick explains. 'Your employees deserve to be taken seriously, and that requires a good understanding of the problem. The text mining or topic detection provides us with a much deeper insight into what employees are really talking about.'

Overall, the ABN AMRO people analytics team have concluded six learning points from this approach to listening to employees: detection, trend analysis, modelling, focus, action and monitoring (see Figure 7.6).

'By listening to employees, working with our colleagues to take action and then measuring the impact of our interventions, we are making a real difference to employee experience in the bank.' Patrick concludes: 'ABN AMRO's senior management is fully engaged with improving the employee experience and is using the insights provided by the people analytics team to help make the organization better and "future proof" the bank.'

Employee listening is only as good as the communication back to employees and management. Patrick and his team cover this in their 2020 LinkedIn article (Coolen et al, 2020) by emphasizing three points.

The first is the importance of sharing the insights directly with all employees. This not only is respectful because, ultimately, it is employees for whom we are trying to improve the experience, but it also improves the response rate of surveys.

Figure 7.6 Six elements for text analysis at ABN AMRO

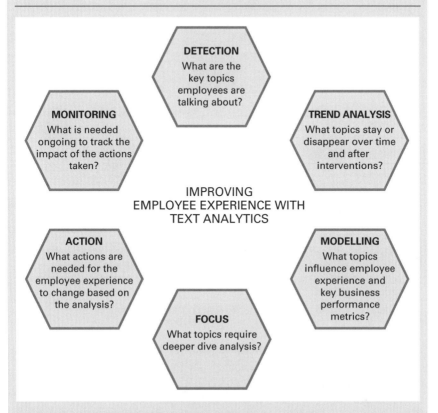

SOURCE Reproduced with kind permission of ABN AMRO, May 2020

The second is making recommendations simple to understand so that all functions involved can use them to improve their processes and practices.

Finally, that employee listening as a topic lends itself to using data visualization to its full potential. When communicating to many thousands of people, the old proverb that 'a picture is worth a thousand words' is crystallized. To do that, Patrick and his team use simple visuals to capture the insights and actions to be taken.

Combining the data of each pulse survey, the team are able to produce a visual such as the one shown in Figure 7.7.

The top-right quadrant (Celebrate) shows the highest Net Promoter Score combined with topics that ABN AMRO is perceived to be doing well at. The bottom-left quadrant (Focus area) demonstrates lower Net Promoter Score combined with topics that are recommendations for improvement.

Figure 7.7   Example of visualization for ABN AMRO pulse survey results

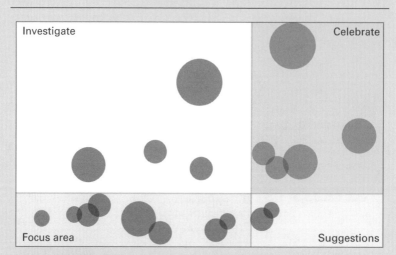

NOTE The x-axis represents the numeric recommendation score. The y-axis represents the 'top' versus 'tip' difference. Each bubble represents a single workforce topic (for example, management performance). The size of bubble indicates the relative number of text comments aggregated.

SOURCE Reproduced with kind permission of ABN AMRO, May 2020

The people analytics team and colleagues from the employee experience team regularly present these insights to the Executive Committee and senior management. Such is the impact of people analytics on employee experience at ABN AMRO. Most importantly, this work is discussed with all top business management teams as part of their decision making for improving the business.

Patrick concludes: 'All this together proves for us that our organization takes the voice of the employee seriously. Through focusing on the employee experience, the team provides insights to really help our people while also benefitting the bank.'

TOP TIP

Make text analysis a specialist skill in people analytics.

The Responsibility of people analytics to the 'Workforce as a Consumer of People Processes'

When aggregated, the 'employee of one' concept becomes very complex indeed. How do you understand, analyse and manage the whole spectrum of people processes – such as succession planning, learning and development, performance management and compensation – while making it 'feel' individual?

The key is to use technologies that give employees the opportunity to provide feedback. The various methods of gaining feedback are essentially a technique in gathering data – and these add new toolkits to the people analytics practitioner toolbox.

For example, as Diane Gherson, former Chief Human Resources Officer at IBM, explained in an episode of the Digital HR Leaders podcast as part of an effort to understand how employees felt about new ways of working prompted by the global pandemic, IBM held a company-wide jam and used people analytics to collect, analyse and communicate the insights (Green, 2020). As we will see in the case study, Performance management with data: FIS, later in this chapter, FIS used a similar crowd-sourced approach to overhaul its performance management system.

These examples outline how the gathering of data from the entire workforce is possible. They also demonstrate how the 'one size fits all' concept of the HR programme design of yesteryear, mentioned earlier in this chapter, can be replaced with more contemporary methods.

Once data is gathered and analysed, the insights can be used to 'personalize' outcomes to segments of the workforce, segment by segment. This way, different segments receive different variations of the same 'people process'.

Employees should also experience the outputs of people analytics as consumerized and personalized solutions or offerings. A good example is in the case study Scaling analytics for value: IBM (see Chapter 8), where Diane Gherson explains why 'offerings' are important: '… referring to our work as 'Offerings' instead of 'Programmes' fundamentally changed the way that the business and workforce received the work. 'Offerings' implies that someone is at the other end of your work, that each employee might have a valuable perspective on it, and your work is going to be of significant importance to them.'

The following case study, Performance management with data: FIS, provides an example of how the use of people data collected at the individual level and aggregated together with core HR provides the ability to reimagine an entire HR process in a new way. The key message from FIS is: *Use data to deliver business outcomes and redesign performance management.*

 CASE STUDY

Performance management with data: FIS

Many, many organizations have an ongoing conversation about the effectiveness of performance management and how it drives improved performance. This conversation has been growing louder in recent years with the likes of Deloitte (Cappelli and Tavis, 2016) and IBM (Gherson *et al*, 2019) writing publicly about changing their performance management system, not just to improve value but to engage employees themselves in what performance management should be. Fidelity National Information Services, Inc or 'FIS'[9] is a company that epitomizes the way that data can shape the development of performance management and make it modern, attractive and valuable.

Isabel Naidoo is Inclusion & Talent Lead at FIS, responsible for a team of over 200 people in Inclusion & Talent Centres of Excellence across the globe. Together the team manages people strategy, global learning, employee experience, inclusion and diversity, talent and career, workforce analytics and planning, and leads development and implementation of FIS's strategic talent agenda.

'My team have a mission: create an environment where the world's top talent can do the most fulfilling work of their career.'

At FIS, the HR organization is known as the People Office. This is representative of the approach that FIS takes to its workforce: it wishes to strive for a more personal touch in managing its human resources. This certainly comes across in the work that Isabel and her team have undertaken with analytics – even submerged in data, they never lose sight of the people at the source. This approach was central to the redesign of FIS's performance management system, following feedback from managers and employees that the then current approach needed to be more supportive of people, their engagement and their development. Isabel took steps to revise FIS's approach to performance management using data and personal insight from the people affected to redefine performance management.

The first step in this work was defining the project, the overall theme of the work and gaining sponsorship. Using research into best practices both outside the company and in particular inside the company, Isabel's team met with senior People Office leaders and managers. Finding an appetite for the work within the organization, the team quickly developed and launched a new performance management concept. They called it 'Performance365' after crowd-sourcing the name among their global colleagues. This enabled the project to be defined.

The next step of the work was the data analysis phase. The Performance365 project quickly became data-rich and it enabled FIS to create robust solutions and outcomes because of the data-driven insights. What makes this project truly special is the way it was built and continues to develop: Performance365 is built on a foundation made up of a myriad of data-gathering methods including statistical analysis of core data together with surveys, text, focus groups and a wide range of interviews. Each of these methods contributes a variety of insights, all feeding into the one project.

This approach to data-gathering is a far cry from 10 years ago when most HR teams would have just surveyed a couple of hundred people and taken their opinion as representative for the whole company!

'We wanted to use as much good data as possible,' Isabel explains, 'so that we could truly understand what employees were really asking for and deliver empirical evidence to executives. A pulse survey of a couple of focus groups was never going to reveal the full picture. We wanted Performance365 to be valuable and actually solve the problem!'

In the prior few years, FIS had invested heavily in its data infrastructure and people analytics technology. A combination of having Workday implemented with Visier as a people analytics technology on top, and Glint as an embedded engagement and pulsing tool provided them with the confidence to undertake this level of data gathering with confidence and ease. FIS is a tremendous example of understanding the value of data, wanting to apply that to HR as a function – and then actually getting the investments and implementing the required data resources and technology, as well as investing in experts. Many companies have the vision and talk about it, but don't actually do anything. FIS is a poster child for doing it and being able to use it to undertake a project like Performance365.

The third piece of the project was to engage employees in Performance365 through a co-design philosophy. The team connected with all parts of the business to gather feedback – using surveys, focus groups and interviews – frequently and on an ongoing basis, ensuring any insights from the data that were used to make design decisions were taken iteratively and collaboratively.

For the survey, the team analysed hundreds of employee and manager comments on the current management process. Areas of negative perception were isolated and consolidated, allowing the team to identify the main issues to address. In addition to the survey, the team conducted more than 50 1:1 interviews with employees from a variety of grades and countries, spread throughout the process.

Layering these methods meant that Isabel's team had a solid baseline of data and understanding, which could then be adjusted with real-time data gathered through interviews. More than 1,000 employees directly and indirectly influenced project design.

Step four in the project was creating the recommendations and using the data to tell the story. The first magical moments for the business came in late 2018 when, using all the data, the team could highlight some key business benefits.

'The first key insight we found was that resignation rates were lower in teams where employees collaborated with managers. The second key insight was that there are lower resignation rates when employees and managers meet regularly. So, we recommended managers should start collaborating with individual employees in very specific ways.'

One of the recommendations that FIS implemented was Quarterly Connect, an initiative that asked managers to meet with individual employees every quarter to discuss performance and career development. These meetings are structured and take place on specific days as guided by the recommendation.

Step five was implementing the recommendations. Because they were backed by such robust data that managers and employees had the confidence to do the Quarterly Connect meetings, they knew there was a benefit for both the individual, the team and FIS overall. But more importantly, they felt employees across the organization had collectively been listened to and involved in the redesign, and data was being used to deliver clarity.

'In a way,' Isabel ponders, 'managers and HR professionals knew all of this all along. It's been embedded in training for decades. But somehow only now that the data shows it and it was co-created with employees, we can implement these changes. It is fantastic! The analysis of people data is delivering benefits.' In 2020, Performance365 was proven to benefit both FIS

Figure 7.8 The FIS project methodology for people analytics

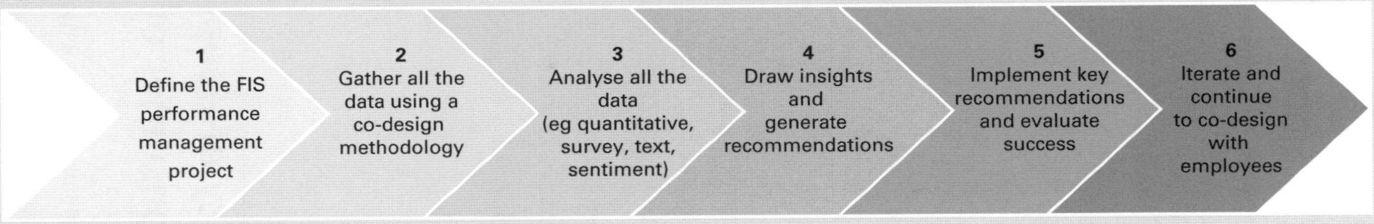

1
Define the FIS performance management project

2
Gather all the data using a co-design methodology

3
Analyse all the data (eg quantitative, survey, text, sentiment)

4
Draw insights and generate recommendations

5
Implement key recommendations and evaluate success

6
Iterate and continue to co-design with employees

SOURCE Reproduced with kind permission of FIS, August 2020

employees by providing frequent touchpoints for them to align on goals and focus their development, as well as the company through enhanced performance. Ninety-five per cent of colleagues took part in the first year of Quarterly Connects, and 93 per cent responded in a survey that they found the process helpful.

On reflection, Isabel and her team have learnt many things from this work. One of them is that they developed a project methodology for future large-scale enterprise projects (see Figure 7.8). Another learning is that engaging with so many people across the business in co-design has also benefitted the speed of implementation and acceptance.

'The people we interviewed and spoke with have formed a network of Performance365 champions. They are extraordinary! When we deploy a new process or recommendation, they get creative.' Some of the project's champions hosted internal talk shows and radio shows for their local offices, explaining the work and engaging employees on an individual, human level.

Isabel believes Performance365 has been a key moment for her team: 'It has been life-changing for us, really. Literally, in terms of what we're able to do as a function, and also having the colour and the dialogue with people to bring our work to life.'

TOP TIP

Use data intelligently to redesign HR programmes.

The Responsibility of people analytics to the 'Manager as a Consumer of People Data'

The third audience for people analytics focuses on the specialized group of employees that are responsible for managing other people. Managers need to provide direction, assistance, inspiration, motivation and clarity to individuals and the team. To do this effectively, they need to have access to data about each person, and collectively about the team. They should understand how the insights from that data help their team meet their performance objectives and therefore achieve company goals. Finally, managers should receive insights and recommendations to help them become more effective in their role and improve each of their team members' performance.

Managers have traditionally relied on HR business partners for support when requesting data and information about their teams. However, with the democratization of data delivered by people analytics, managers have an alternative option. They are able to extract insights and recommendations about their organization and the employees they manage through having access directly to relevant people data and information. A side benefit is that HR business partners can use the same data to drive decision making and strategic discussions in real time.

This is supported by a *Forbes* article (Marr, 2017). With regard to data democratization, the author outlines, 'It requires that we accompany the access with an easy way for people to understand the data so that they can use it to expedite decision making and uncover opportunities for an organization.'

An example of data democratization in action is provided in the case study, Scaling people analytics adoption: Merck KGaA in Chapter 9 (Culture). In that case study, Alexis Saussinan, Global Head of people analytics & Strategic Workforce Planning, knew that to implement a culture of analytics and empower HR and the business, the team 'needed to provide all HR colleagues and business leaders with transparent access to the company's people data'.

Having successfully democratized people data means that users can 'in real time, take stock, check on, adapt or develop new strategies as rapidly as business circumstances or people circumstances change'.

The ability for people analytics teams to democratize data for managers has increased exponentially in The Age of Innovation. This saw the emergence of new systems and platforms as described in Chapter 5 (Technology) that aggregate different sources of data into dashboards to provide powerful insights and visualizations for managers. Whether an organization chooses to 'buy' or 'build' such a system or platform, technology that aggregates, visualizes and democratizes people data, if done well, will deliver substantial impact.

As part of a 2018 McKinsey article, Ted Colbert, the then Chief Information Officer of Boeing, captures the challenge and benefits of democratizing data, namely ease of access, behavioural change, and value: 'You have to figure out how to really democratize the data-analytics capability, which means you have to have a platform through which people can easily access data. That helps people to believe in it and to deliver solutions that don't require an expensive data scientist. When people begin to believe in the data, it's a game changer: They begin to change their behaviours, based on a new understanding of all the richness trapped beneath the surface of our systems and processes' (Díaz, Rowshankish and Saleh, 2018).

As we progress further into The Age of Value, technology will make the democratization of data for managers even more accessible and easy to use. As Bernard Marr writes in his 2018 book, *Data-Driven HR*: 'Rather than HR professionals and managers throughout the company reading and interpreting data, advancements like natural language processing and chatbots mean it will be possible to have a conversation with your data analytics tools and ask questions like: "Who in my team may be about to leave the company?"'

The discussions about the democratization of data lead us to conclude that treating managers in the company as 'consumers' as well as 'stakeholders' is going to be a key responsibility for the people analytics team, and the human resources function more broadly, in the coming years.

The Responsibility of people analytics to the 'Executive as a Consumer of People Insights'

Executives are often viewed only as stakeholders (see Chapter 3 – Stakeholder Management). In fact, executives can assume many personas: employee, manager, executive, stakeholder and sponsor. This section of the chapter considers each persona from a new angle: as a 'consumer'.

Executives receive a lot of insights – some of them are for making decisions at that moment, based on insights from a single project or piece of work. Decisions are made, the insights used and 'the business changes'. However, sometimes it is different. The insights generated can be repeatable, and the process of using the insights can be consumed multiple times.

Consider this example. A project sponsor asks to consider what happened when a key executive – let's call them Executive A – left the company. Did they become a risk to the company? Will other employees also be at risk of leaving the company too? This scenario is a familiar one.

Let's assume that the insights did reveal that employees with certain demographic characteristics (let's say those that worked with Executive A for at least three years) did leave the company. So Executive A became a retention risk factor for associated employees (those with greater than three years tenure working with Executive A).

Now the same sponsor wants to know if this is true for all key executives who leave – so the study now looks at 100 more executives who resigned from the company in the last five years and the effect they had on other employees. The study concludes that employees who work with a departing executive for at least three years in the years immediately prior to the executive's departure – let's call these 'Key Employees' – do indeed have a higher propensity to leave.

The key now is to productize these insights. Every senior executive who manages other executives should have an 'offering' that allows them to identify Key Employees. The 'offering' could be an early-warning system to allow action to be taken when an employee becomes a Key Employee, ie reaches the three years mentioned above. The 'offering' would be rooted in the analytical algorithm plus prescribed actions and options for reducing the risk. All of this will happen proactively – and before a Key Employee 'leaves'. Of course, it is impossible to prevent every person from resigning from the company, but this example indicates how people analytics solutions can be 'productized' for executives if they are thought of as 'consumers'.

Other advice is to make solutions that fit with the consumers' – or in this case, the executives' – ways of working. For executives, we recommend a 'mobile-first' approach as most senior executives in the modern business world use mobile and tablet devices as their predominant digital device.

Furthermore, integrating several people analytics solutions into one interactive system can pay high dividends. Executives think about 'people'. They tend not to think about 'attrition', then 'succession planning', then 'reward', then 'training' and so on. In thinking about executives as consumers, consider how several advanced analytics solutions, plus reports and dashboards, can be integrated into one platform.

During our research, we found that this level of sophistication in people analytics is very rare. Indeed, over the last three years one of the only examples we could find is described in the following case study, Bring analytics to life: Santander Brasil, where they describe how they amalgamated several solutions into one application. Their key message: *Only create algorithms that the business can actually use.*

CASE STUDY

Bring analytics to life: Santander Brasil

Banco Santander[10] is one of the largest banking institutions in the world. It is a very big, global company, with more than 196,000 employees and presence in all global financial centres. As a financial services company, it has built up many acquisitions across mainly Latin America and North America. Banco Santander's Brazilian operation, Santander Brasil,[11] is a large organization in its own right: headquartered in São Paulo, Santander Brasil comprises more than 50,500 employees and nearly 4,000 branches.

In the world of people analytics, Santander Brasil has achieved something few other organizations worldwide have, to our knowledge. They have integrated multiple advanced people analytics algorithms into one platform that leaders can access and use to make decisions around retention, compensation and succession planning.

Often, people analytics doesn't deliver the value it deserves because the 'cool stuff' isn't readily able to be used by leaders to really answer the questions leaders ask, for example:

Who is most at risk in my team? Which five people would I replace that person with if they left tomorrow? Which executive alumni are soliciting people in my organization? How can I motivate them to stay? If I want to give someone a salary increase, how does that affect my compensation budget, and can I afford it? How does this compare with the external marketplace?

Many of these questions can be answered in isolation. To get detailed answers, HR specialists need to be brought in. In some cases, organizations never get to the answers because the data is just not organized well enough.

This is not the case at Santander Brasil. The leader behind the people analytics team is Head of HR Information and Analytics, Vinicios Augustos Bevilacqua Costa, based in São Paulo. We first met Vinicios at a 2019 workshop in Mexico City for all of Banco Santander's people analytics teams led by Luis Fernando Aránguez Montero, Head of Global HR Data Analytics, and Pere Torrens, Global Head of HR Culture and Strategy. Working closely with them and the people analytics teams across Banco Santander, we became impressed by the overall approach that Banco Santander took to using data and insights in running its business operations.

Vinicios's background is in financial risk management, and he looks at people analytics through the same business lens. He has an impressive skill set for people analytics and data science, which he combines with strong emotional intelligence and deep relationships with stakeholders. As a people analytics leader, Vinicios understands what it is that leaders want to know about people.

Vinicios and his team spent many months working on four algorithms that analysed attrition, recognition and compensation, networks and succession planning (see Figure 7.9). Each one provided real insights that could help leaders make people decisions. However, following the launch of the first algorithm, for attrition, Vinicios realized that the insights were only providing part of the people story. And, in their own way, the systems providing these algorithms were not intuitive enough to provide recommendations that allowed leaders to take actions. In short, Vinicios noticed that few leaders and HRBPs were accessing these four systems and using the analytical models.

Figure 7.9 HR topics where algorithms have been created for executive insight at Banco Santander Brasil

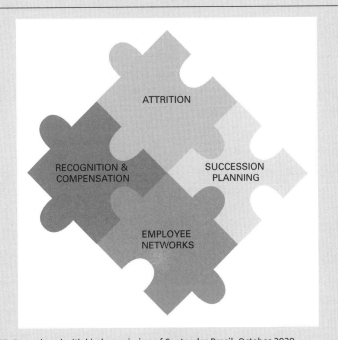

SOURCE Reproduced with kind permission of Santander Brasil, October 2020

'Some people knew they existed, sure, but no one used people analytics algorithms on a daily or even monthly basis,' Vinicios recalls. 'We had created these great tools, but we still had to do something to bring them to life for our leaders.'

Algorithms like those created by Vinicios's team are talked about in numerous companies. But no other company we have encountered has built its own system of four predictive solutions, interlinked and fully contextualized. 'We didn't need clever tools,' Vinicios reflects. 'When we thought about why HRBPs and leaders weren't using our analytics as we expected, we realized it was because each algorithm only addressed one specific problem.'

It took a matter of weeks for Vinicios and his team to build the 'Portal de Gestão RH' (HR Management Platform): a single dashboard pulling data from multiple systems to create a holistic, collective view of people data and the related business problems. Each of the four algorithms is displayed intuitively in the platform, in simple language and based on solid user experience principles.

Leaders can use the platform to drill down into specific regions, departments, demographics, diversity and individuals in their team, and view a full picture of performance, vulnerability, network and compensation. It is a glittering source of people-related information for Banco Santander executives, built by Banco Santander HR analysts.

Vinicios shared the technology at Banco Santander leadership roadshows to gain traction for the change management needed to embed this across the organization. The platform is intended for use by the top 800 leaders and all HRBPs at Santander Brasil.

He used real examples of insights to demonstrate the value of the platform. One example that stands out to us is how Vinicios used the platform to back-test the attrition model based on a leader who had left the organization a year ago: he found that of the top five people at risk of leaving with the leader 12 months previously, three of them had already left. The team could now identify the remaining people at risk with confidence and make decisions on those people.

Another great example was focused on the succession management of a particular role, forward projecting compensation decisions on each of those people and modelling the additional cost (so, the impact of compensation) for that team, plus the impact of compensation versus the external marketplace.

A third example showed users how they could look at leaders who had left and identify future talent leavers at risk in a prioritized order – and highlight each of those people on a performance–pay grid to identify the potential and most desired actions to be taken.

In this way, Vinicios presented the story of the platform through the eyes of an employee and leader. As part of the roadshow, leaders were encouraged to test the platform live, in a show-and-tell fashion.

'The platform impressed everyone. Each person who has seen it has had their own uses for it, many of which we hadn't even thought of,' Vinicios says. 'And we have used the roadshow to build credibility for the platform and HR Analytics team. We have also partnered with leaders to make it more useful to them. That is, after all, why we built it in the first place.'

An example of this partnership is an enhancement that was added in a later iteration of the platform – a predictive insights function. Vinicios explains, 'One leader described the platform as "a data candy store". They said that they didn't know where to start when it came to translating the data into actions. So, we built a recommendation function'.

The team's recommendation function works in two ways: first, following a request for more information, it can immediately suggest actions a leader should take, for example, 'whom should I promote?' and the platform produces a list of top candidates based on performance, skill set and flight risk. Second, the platform allows leaders to ask a question and view a predictive simulation of what will happen if they take a particular action.

Vinicios is well-equipped to bring people analytics algorithms to life for leaders: he is a data-driven business leader and a game changer. The HR Analytics team did not create this platform in response to a request from the business, nor did it ask for approval or take time to hunt for a sponsor. Vinicios empathized with the business, anticipated what leaders really required and leant on his experience in risk management to develop a genuinely useful analytics product. 'Looking at the business challenge of "how do we do work with more than 40,000 people all over Brazil?", it was clear how we needed to support leaders.'

In summary, bringing to life the real value of people analytics did not require Vinicios to buy super-cool technology from a third-party vendor or not even create the best statistical model. It's only essential to provide all HRBP and managers with the ability to quickly access the insights when they need them.

Looking back on the journey so far, he says the solution is obvious: 'It is when you are thinking like a business leader, combining that with an analytical mindset and implementation, that value can truly be delivered.' Vinicios's belief is to use data science and bring it alive in front of business leaders and HR business partners. Only then is decision making enabled. Having a supportive leader is also essential: 'This evolution was only possible because our HR Vice President, Vanessa Lobato, trusts our work, gives autonomy and constantly provokes us to be the leaders of the HR transformation.'

TOP TIP

Bring predictive models together as a complete jigsaw to enable executive decision making.

Summary

People analytics should benefit four groups of consumers in the organization through providing personalized workforce experiences: employees, managers, executives and the workforce as a whole. Things to consider when thinking about these audiences include:

- Aim to provide a 'fair exchange of value' whereby employees get personal benefit from sharing their data with the organization.
- Help HR colleagues define, measure and manage employee experience through taking a data-driven approach.
- Analyse and identify 'moments that matter' for employees.
- Provide insights that help individual employees and implement technologies that give a personalized experience.
- Create a digital ecosystem that continuously listens to the workforce, and design HR programmes with a human-centred approach.
- Democratize data to managers to help them understand their team and individual employees.
- Deliver advanced analytics solutions to executives as consumable, intuitive products that are easy to use.

References

Burrell, L and Gherson, D (2018) Co-creating the employee experience, *Harvard Business Review*, March – April. Available from: https://hbr.org/2018/03/co-creating-the-employee-experience (archived at https://perma.cc/8P4H-2WV4) [Last accessed 7 February 2021]

Cappelli, P and Tavis, A (2016) The performance management revolution, *Harvard Business Review*, October. Available from: https://hbr.org/2016/10/the-performance-management-revolution (archived at https://perma.cc/P7VC-CLPR) [Last accessed 7 February 2021]

Coolen, P, Veldkamp, J, Breugelmans, A and Korteman, S (2020) Visualizing the voice of the employee [Blog] LinkedIn, 25 March. Available from: https://www.linkedin.com/pulse/visualizing-voice-employee-patrick-coolen/ (archived at https://perma.cc/C7HJ-CDQY) [Last accessed 7 February 2021]

Díaz, A, Rowshankish, K and Saleh, T (2018) Why data culture matters, *McKinsey Quarterly*, 6 September. Available from: https://www.mckinsey.com/business-functions/mckinsey-analytics/our-insights/why-data-culture-matters (archived at https://perma.cc/AB7B-KRXM) [Last accessed 7 February 2021]

Ferrar, J, Styr, C and Ktena, A (2020) Delivering Value at Scale: A new operating model for people analytics [Report] Insight222 Research, 24 November. Available from: https://www.insight222.com/people-analytics-operating-model-research (archived at https://perma.cc/ZW6J-HK7C) [Last accessed 7 February 2021]

Gherson, D, Hancock, B, Tavis, A and Ryder, A (2019) Make it personal: lessons From IBM on reinventing performance management [Webinar] *MIT Sloan Management Review*, 17 April. Available from: https://sloanreview.mit.edu/video/webinar-lessons-from-ibm-on-reinventing-performance-management/ (archived at https://perma.cc/TFC7-TF7X) [Last accessed 7 February 2021]

Green, D (2020) How IBM is reinventing HR with AI and people analytics, with Diane Gherson [Podcast] Digital HR Leaders, 8 September. Available from: https://www.myhrfuture.com/digital-hr-leaders-podcast/2020/9/8/how-ibm-is-reinventing-hr-with-ai-and-people-analytics (archived at https://perma.cc/2QHT-NDW9) [Last accessed 7 February 2021]

Hinssen, P (2018) What HR can learn from marketing about employee experience, *Forbes*, 12 September. Available from: https://www.forbes.com/sites/peterhinssen/2018/09/12/what-hr-can-learn-from-marketing-about-employee-experience/?sh=4247df184bef (archived at https://perma.cc/YW82-MRHQ) [Last accessed 7 February 2021]

Hougaard, R, Carter, J and Hogan, K (2019) How Microsoft builds a sense of community among 144,000 employees, *Harvard Business Review*, July–August. Available from: https://hbr.org/2019/08/how-microsoft-builds-a-sense-of-community-among-144000-employees (archived at https://perma.cc/Y44K-R2RR) [Last accessed 7 February 2021]

Howell, D (2020) The customer of one: how personalisation is the key to long term profitability, Silicon, 21 October. Available from: https://www.silicon.co.uk/data-storage/business-intelligence/the-customer-of-one-how-personalisation-is-the-key-to-long-term-profitability-348281?cmpredirect (archived at https://perma.cc/8TZM-3HKG) [Last accessed 7 February 2021]

KennedyFitch (2019) Employee Experience 2020: Global Report & Case Studies [Report] EX Leaders Network, KennedyFitch. Available from: https://www.exleadersnetwork.com/wp-content/uploads/2019/12/EX-2020-Report-by-EX-Leaders-Network.pdf (archived at https://perma.cc/M987-B7C2) [Last accessed 7 February 2021]

Levy, M (2020) Why employee experience will be your #1 priority, LinkedIn Talent Solutions. Available from: https://business.linkedin.com/talent-solutions/resources/talent-management/employee-experience (archived at https://perma.cc/98KN-ZS6V) [Last accessed 7 February 2021]

LinkedIn (2020) Global Talent Trends 2020 [Report] LinkedIn Talent Solutions. Available from: https://business.linkedin.com/talent-solutions/recruiting-tips/global-talent-trends-2020 (archived at https://perma.cc/XM4E-7549) [Last accessed 7 February 2021]

Marr, B (2017) What is data democratization? A super simple explanation and the key pros and cons, Forbes, 24 July. Available from: https://www.forbes.com/sites/bernardmarr/2017/07/24/what-is-data-democratization-a-super-simple-explanation-and-the-key-pros-and-cons/?sh=2cd0a2486013 (archived at https://perma.cc/F6G6-34U3) [Last accessed 7 February 2021]

Marr, B (2018) Data-Driven HR: How to use analytics and metrics to drive performance, Kogan Page, London

Morgan, B (2018) How Amazon has reorganized around artificial intelligence and machine learning, Forbes, 16 July. Available from: https://www.forbes.com/sites/blakemorgan/2018/07/16/how-amazon-has-re-organized-around-artificial-intelligence-and-machine-learning/?sh=12520f1c7361 (archived at https://perma.cc/WJR4-LA6B) [Last accessed 7 February 2021]

Morgan, J (2016) The Global Head of Employee Experience at Airbnb on why they got rid of human resources, Forbes, 1 February. Available from: https://www.forbes.com/sites/jacobmorgan/2016/02/01/global-head-employee-experience-airbnb-rid-of-human-resources/?sh=57c4991b7c4e (archived at https://perma.cc/NU6D-65AX) [Last accessed 7 February 2021]

Sexton-Brown, E (2018) Employee experience at ABN AMRO [Blog] HRD Connect, 18 May. Available from: https://www.hrdconnect.com/2018/05/18/interview-frank-van-den-brink-hr-director-employee-experience-abn-amro/ (archived at https://perma.cc/S62Q-QDY6) [Last accessed 7 February 2021]

Shook, E, Knickrehm, M and Sage-Gavin, E (2019) Decoding organizational DNA: Trust, data and unlocking value in the digital workplace [Report] Accenture. Available from: https://www.accenture.com/gb-en/insights/future-workforce/workforce-data-organizational-dna (archived at https://perma.cc/N2K8-5NX2) [Last accessed 7 February 2021]

Smith, D and Cantrell, S M (2015) Managing Your People as a Workforce of One, [Report] Accenture Strategy

TI People (2019) 3… 2… 1… On The Launchpad: From Strategy to Execution – The State of Employee Experience 2019 Research Report [Report]. Available from: https://www.ti-people.com/what-is-the-state-of-ex-in-2019 (archived at https://perma.cc/V4J8-ZFH4) [Last accessed 7 February 2021]

World Economic Forum (2019) HR 4.0: Shaping People Strategies in the Fourth Industrial Revolution [Report] 11 December. Available from: https://www.weforum.org/reports/hr4-0-shaping-people-strategies-in-the-fourth-industrial-revolution (archived at https://perma.cc/6KKM-QRLT) [Last accessed 7 February 2021]

Notes

1 See Glossary: Fair exchange of value. In general, this refers to the exchange of two things of equal *value* as the basis for a reasonable and honest trade. In the context of people analytics, this describes the personal benefit employees receive from analytics in exchange for sharing their data with the organization to enable analytical work to occur.

2 See Glossary: Trust Dividend. The impact of workforce trust on financial performance when it comes to the use of employees' data. Most notably used by Accenture in the 2019 study, Decoding Organizational Data: Trust, data and unlocking value in the digital workplace.

3 See Glossary: Big Brother. Originating from George Orwell's novel *Nineteen Eighty-Four*, to signify the theme of continuous oppressive surveillance. This led to its widespread use today to indicate a person, organization or government exercising total control and surveillance over people's lives.

4 'Move the needle' is a business expression to indicate an acceleration in progress. The metaphor being that the needle on a speedometer (odometer) moves only when the accelerator is pressed in a vehicle.

5 ABN AMRO Bank N.V. is a Dutch bank with more than 17,000 employees (see https://www.abnamro.com/en/about-abnamro/profile/who-we-are/purpose-and-strategy/index.html (archived at https://perma.cc/3PZ5-MNHR), last accessed 7 February 2021).

6 See https://www.abnamro.com/en/about-abnamro/profile/who-we-are/purpose-and-strategy/index.html (archived at https://perma.cc/D3YT-U8HK), last accessed 7 February 2021.

7 See Glossary: Stratified sampling. A process that involves dividing the population of interest into smaller groups, called strata. Samples are then pulled from these strata, and analysis is performed to enable inferences about the greater population of interest.

8 OrganizationView GmbH is based in St Moritz, Switzerland and was founded in 2010 (see https://www.workometry.com/ (archived at https://perma.cc/PP96-5G2W), last accessed 7 February 2021).

9 FIS is a US financial services and technology products provider that serves 90 per cent of the 50 largest banks and 90 per cent of top 20 private equity firms. Its more than 57,000 employees handle over 75 billion transactions across the world totalling an average of US$ 9 trillion each year (see https://www.fisglobal.com/about-us (archived at https://perma.cc/Y8F8-9BRP), last accessed 7 February 2021).

10 Banco Santander, doing business as Santander Group, is a Spanish multinational financial services company and one of the largest banking institutions in the world. Founded in 1857, it operates in 10 main markets and consists of more than 196,000 employees in 2021 (see https://www.santander.com/en/about-us/key-facts-and-figures (archived at https://perma.cc/F8J4-SRSC), last accessed 7 February 2021).

11 Santander Brasil's approximately 43,000 employees serve more than 48.3 million customers throughout Brazil, as the country's only scaled international bank (see https://www.santander.com/en/about-us/where-we-are/santander-brasil (archived at https://perma.cc/XDE7-K44S), last accessed 7 February 2021).

Business Outcomes

08

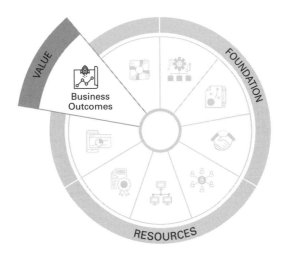

In this chapter, we discuss the most important aspects of people analytics: the real outcomes it delivers to the organization, and how to use a value chain to provide the right approach, mindset and structure for success.

DISCOVER...

- the essential elements of the People Analytics Value Chain;
- a five-step methodology for driving business outcomes;
- why working with finance is key to creating impact.

WITH INSIGHTS FROM...

- MetLife, Inc., on securing investment for people analytics;
- Nestlé S.A., on speaking the language of the business;
- IBM, on scaling for value with advanced analytics and technologies.

Overview

> **BUSINESS OUTCOMES**
>
> Business Outcomes, as one of the Nine Dimensions, describes the rationale and techniques that lead to delivering outcomes as a result of people analytics activity. These outcomes are actionable insights and recommendations, financial value and tangible business improvement across the enterprise.

There are many examples of how people analytics delivers significant financial value to companies' top and bottom lines, some of which are described in this book. Work that leads to a clear return on investment excites senior business executives. It also provides the climate to elevate the function and create more investment.

Nevertheless, as many of our case studies testify, not every people analytics project is about financial return. As we discussed in Part One (The case for people analytics), there are four broad categories of outcomes where people analytics creates impact and delivers results (see Figure 8.1).

Generating insights that inform decision making is often cited as the basis of all people analytics work. Beyond insight, however, is something far more powerful. As Piyush Mathur, Global Head, Enterprise Functions Talent Management and Insights at Johnson & Johnson, perfectly captures in a Digital HR Leaders podcast (Green, 2020): 'Insight without outcome is simply overhead.' Realizing measurable outcomes from people analytics avoids accusations of 'analytics for the sake of analytics', creates value for organizations and their workforces, demonstrates why analytics matters and builds the case for increased investment.

Taking a 'business-first' approach

This book advocates for an 'outside-in' approach to people analytics, with a focus on working directly with business executives to solve the key challenges confronting the organization. During our many years in the field working with and studying organizations, and the time spent writing and researching this book, we have observed that advanced organizations have a business-first approach to people analytics.

Figure 8.1 Four outcomes of people analytics

Workforce experiences

Employee experiences
Data democratization to managers
Insights for executives
Entire workforce improvements

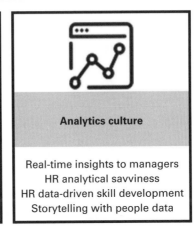

Analytics culture

Real-time insights to managers
HR analytical savviness
HR data-driven skill development
Storytelling with people data

Business performance

Financial impact
Managing risk & compliance
Revenue and market share growth
CEO Skills conundrum

Societal benefits

Organizational inclusion
Workforce equality
Gender parity improvements
Wellness & mental awareness

We believe that business and strategy topics – such as sales effectiveness, business strategy execution, risk and compliance, crisis management and culture – are becoming more common focus areas for people analytics teams.

Research conducted with 60 global organizations (Ferrar, Styr and Ktena, 2020) confirmed our belief (see Figure 8.2).

In these companies, topics of a business and strategy nature are seen as more important than traditional HR topics such as retention, talent management and talent acquisition. Business and strategy are considered the area that adds the most value, above other important business focus areas like employee experience and well-being, strategic workforce planning and employee productivity.

Figure 8.2 The top areas where people analytics adds value

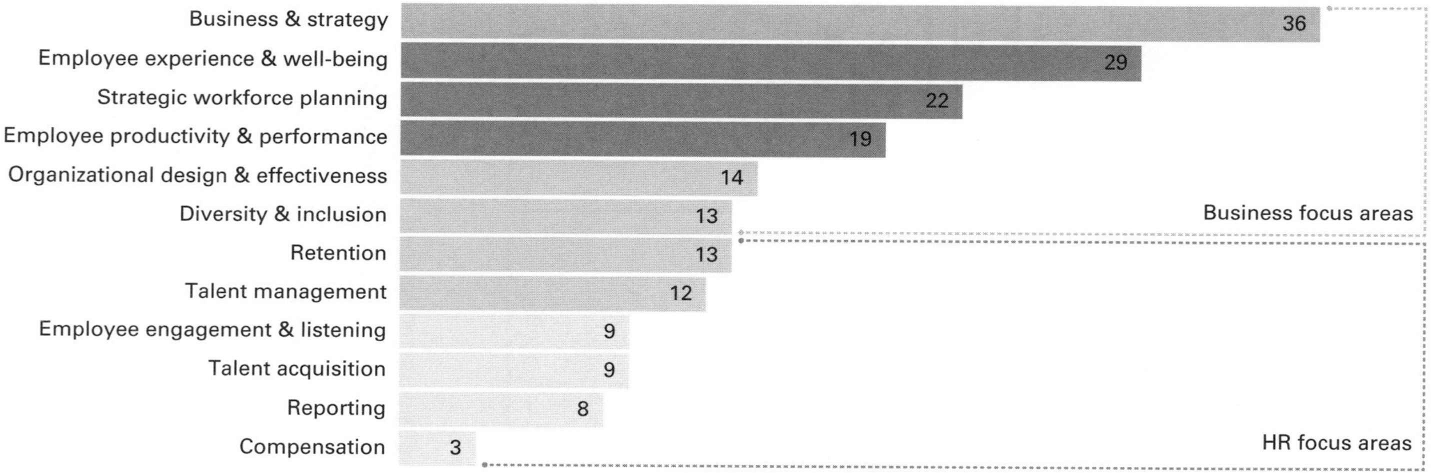

Business & strategy — 36
Employee experience & well-being — 29
Strategic workforce planning — 22
Employee productivity & performance — 19
Organizational design & effectiveness — 14
Diversity & inclusion — 13
Retention — 13
Talent management — 12
Employee engagement & listening — 9
Talent acquisition — 9
Reporting — 8
Compensation — 3

Business focus areas

HR focus areas

SOURCE Ferrar, Styr and Ktena (2020)

The results of this part of the research confirmed our belief that people analytics teams in large global businesses are now becoming more business focused. Specifically, they are aligned with organizational topics that were often seen as being well outside of HR's responsibility.

The People Analytics Value Chain

Successfully transitioning towards a more business-centric approach has enabled people analytics to become increasingly important to companies. It is not easy to transform people analytics to an outside-in approach. In some ways, it is simpler to start with a 'blank sheet of paper' – a fresh approach.

We recommend the People Analytics Value Chain, shown in Figure 8.3, as our model for delivering business outcomes. This is a model for The Age of Value, discussed in Part One (The case for people analytics). It is also the model that defines the operating model for people analytics outlined in Chapter 4 (Skills).

The People Analytics Value Chain is underpinned by a single principle: Value eats analysis for breakfast![1]

In other words, client drivers – business strategy, stakeholder challenges, and people and HR strategy – are the input; and measurable business outcomes such as commercial value, employee experience and organizational change are the output. The people analytics function is responsible for this entire process.

Figure 8.3   People Analytics Value Chain

SOURCE Ferrar, Styr and Ktena (2020)

In practice, the People Analytics Value Chain means that instead of pondering staple questions such as, 'what's my attrition rate?', the people analytics function examines more business-leading questions such as 'what people factors will improve my business performance?' and 'which roles in my organization deliver the most value?'

This outside-in approach empowers the function to focus on business challenges and generate business value; enhance the workforce experience and benefit the wider society. It will deliver outcomes that are more helpful and create more impact for the organization.

How to drive business outcomes

Throughout this book, we have presented case studies highlighting the benefit of an outside-in approach to people analytics and the business outcomes that can subsequently be enjoyed. This is particularly evident in the three cases from MetLife, Nestlé and IBM included hereafter in this chapter.

While each case is different, the people analytics functions behind them all took the approach to ensure business outcomes were the goal, and all activities were aimed at delivering that goal. Reflecting on this, we can identify five steps that people analytics functions take. These form an easy guide for others to remember: Five steps for business outcomes, shown in Figure 8.4 and described in detail below.

Step 1: Align work to strategy

Step 2: Validate likely impact and value

Step 3: Share insights and recommendations

Step 4: Deliver solutions at scale

Step 5: Quantify outcomes

Figure 8.4   Five steps for business outcomes

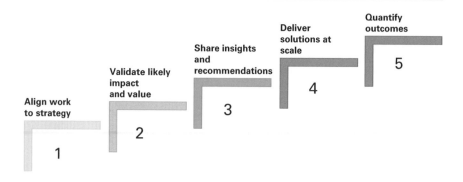

Step 1: Align work to strategy

It is necessary to align people analytics with the most important business challenges facing the company. As discussed in Chapter 2 (Methodology), the process of criteria-based prioritization provides a basis for selecting the people analytics work that leads to the highest value. These are determined in Chapter 2 as either 'Quick Wins' or 'Big Bets'. The essence of prioritization is to align with the answer to the key question: 'What is the potential business value?' Answering this involves asking stakeholders the right questions to uncover the topics and opportunities that will reveal the greatest value. This is also discussed in Chapter 3 (Stakeholder Management).

Consider the business outcomes needed before committing to work. One way to do this was discussed in *The Power of People* (Guenole, Ferrar and Feinzig, 2017). The Seven Forces of Demand model (see Figure 8.5) identifies common areas of business demands that are drivers for people analytics. Some of these business drivers align more naturally with business strategy and operations, including the drive for competitive edge (or advantage), regulatory concerns, operational efficiency and cost pressure.

Understanding business challenges means that focused outcomes are more likely to be delivered. To do this, work with relevant stakeholders to frame the business questions that are needed to be answered and build the hypotheses needed to test for each of them.

Figure 8.5 Seven Forces of Demand

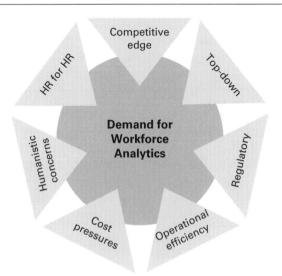

SOURCE Guenole, Ferrar and Feinzig (2017)

Step 2: Validate likely impact and value

After prioritizing people analytics work, it is time to re-engage stakeholders to define the scope of the work, create any investment case needed and collaborate with finance to measure outcomes. One technique to set an analytics project up for success is the Focus-Impact-Value Model outlined in Chapter 2 (Methodology) and summarized below:

- **Focus** – Define the scope of the project, secure a project sponsor, agree on the budget and define realistic time frames.

- **Impact** – Determine the impact of the project on each of the seven stakeholder groups and establish the extent of their involvement in the work.

- **Value** – Assess and define the anticipated value of the project.

Consider the example of assessing the potential financial value of an analytics project. Working with finance will speed up completion of this step and provide the validation required to drive subsequent discussions with other stakeholders and the project sponsor. Typically this includes agreement on how to measure outcomes in terms of revenue or cost optimization, as well as how to model it, for example, with return on investment (ROI), net present value (NPV) or internal rate of return (IRR).

This case study – Securing investment: MetLife, shows a perfect example of how to work with the finance function to co-develop an investment case. The partnership created between the people analytics team and the finance team was based on one strong principle: *Use the language of finance.*

 **CASE STUDY**

Securing investment: MetLife

Laura Shubert leads the Global Workforce Analytics business at US insurer, MetLife.[2] The team provides insights about the workforce that enable human resources and business leaders to make informed, fact-based people decisions, and its work products range across the full spectrum of analytics from complex analyses and modelling to general reporting. Laura's success is underpinned by her ability to secure investment when needed.

Laura's team undertook a significant initiative in 2020: a two-pronged approach to workforce management that involved building capabilities in strategic workforce planning (SWP) and creating an internal career marketplace. This kind of work needed an incremental budget if it was going to come to fruition and add value to the business and employees.

Before entering human resources, Laura spent 15 years working in financial planning and analysis, fund administration, and mergers and acquisitions.

'My experience means I know how to talk to finance about money,' Laura says. 'And the key things to remember are simple: Involve financial analysts at an early stage of the work, and always translate HR's actions into business outcomes.'

Laura followed her own advice when it came to the SWP and internal career marketplace. She scheduled a meeting with finance colleagues to take place in the initial planning stages of the work, and assembled a MetLife-focused financial analysis of the initiative.

You don't necessarily need a formal background in finance to do any of this, Laura advises. In fact, in this case, she started with collating general business information – all of it that was readily available and in existence. First, Laura scoured publicly available business information online. In one press release, Laura found supporting information for a statement she recalled back in 2016 when MetLife's Chief Executive Officer announced that the company would cut its run rate by $1 billion by the end of 2019 (Scism, 2016). Laura used this and similar information to examine voluntary attrition, career development and data around employee growth versus employee hiring. Thinking deeply about this information helped Laura to develop her understanding of what the work would entail. Her research also provided a solid foundation for a conversation with the business.

Putting pen to paper, Laura was very straightforward. She asked for the investment the team needed for the initiative: a technology vendor, advisory services from external consultants and an increased headcount. 'One thing I learnt over the years is don't ask for less than what you need,' Laura comments. 'Be bold. How can you assess the full investment of something if you aren't clear about the entire cost at the beginning? Don't start work on the back foot.'

Laura intended to frame the proposal in a way business executives would understand, using financial language. She also needed to formally request support for the initiative from finance. Having given some thought to what questions the financial analysts would have for Workforce Analytics, Laura's team conducted a financial analysis of the work and its value to MetLife. The team knew from its research that MetLife does not typically model work in terms of return on investment (ROI); it uses the internal rate of return (IRR) measured over five years. So, Laura presented the case in terms of IRR. By doing so, she was cementing the credibility of her team and its work and – more importantly – communicating in a language that people across MetLife understood.

Everything clicked together neatly when the discussions began. HR and MetLife's financial experts collaborated to validate the models to calculate the investment and potential value of the initiative. Everyone was invited to share their expertise and perspective on the work. Laura was delighted: 'While they were running the numbers, finance actually suggested to Workforce Analytics that we should make things less conservative. The finance team even gave us ideas for how to maximize the value of the work!' Laura believes the discussions went so well for two reasons. First, she took lots of informed people into the room, including data people. 'I didn't want our people in the room to be unable to answer a question, so bringing in people who really understood the work meant that finance could probe and understand everything about the initiative. There was no hidden black box. We welcomed every question because we understood that the finance professionals were doing their job.' The second reason, says Laura, was the team's approach to the discussions: 'We were determined to build relationships with the finance team. That would take time and several iterations of the models and plans. We understood what finance might want from us, and we were prepared to work together.'

It paid off. Workforce Analytics got the green light for both the SWP and reskilling career marketplace work when the work was presented at an executive operating committee meeting. At that meeting, it was clear that the senior-most executives for both HR and finance were in sync – not just on the topic but on the analysis that had been done. Finance was a loyal partner; the potential business value of the work had been thoroughly understood and tested, and every penny of the investment was accounted for and labelled.

Figure 8.6 Open your black box[3] to finance: Laura Shubert's approach for working with finance colleagues

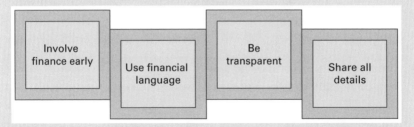

| Involve finance early | Use financial language | Be transparent | Share all details |

SOURCE Reproduced with kind permission of MetLife, October 2020

When the COVID-19 pandemic hit, work on these projects intensified. 'The impact of the pandemic clarified the business case,' Laura explains, 'and we were able to respond accordingly because the investment was sound, the analysis was agreed, and we could account for every dollar spent. Because we had done all this research and modelling, and worked with finance from the outset, it made any scrutiny easier and the journey smoother.'

MetLife's Workforce Analytics team secured investment by making a clear request, analysing the impact and using the language of finance. Laura's key takeaways from the experience (shown in Figure 8.6) apply to all HR professionals looking to secure budget.

'Involve finance in what you are trying to achieve from the outset of the project; use financial language and make sure you understand terminology and definitions; when it comes to presenting the financial model, share all the detail and be open about the methods used to build it and your assumptions behind it. And finally, don't be secretive or hold anything back about your work. Open your black box.'

'We took these steps carefully and thoughtfully. Now Workforce Analytics is – sustainably – making a difference to our employees and the business.'

TOP TIP

Make friends with colleagues in the finance team and learn their language and terminology.

Step 3: Share insights and recommendations

The third step to drive business outcomes (see Figure 8.4) is to ensure that the work provides insights and recommendations that can be realistically actioned by the business.

Key points to note are:

- **Reveal insights** – The people analytics team needs to identify insights from their analyses to help prove or disprove the hypotheses being tested. Moreover, it should not be assumed that project sponsors or stakeholders will be able to derive insights for themselves. Perhaps more importantly, if data and analyses are presented without insights, executives and project sponsors may draw their own conclusions to best fit their objectives, preconceptions or biases.

- **Determine recommendations** – While insights are interesting, only recommendations will help improve the business. Either by providing them themselves or by working together with stakeholders, people analytics teams need to provide clear recommendations designed to drive decisions and create an impetus for change.

    The key to determining recommendations is to always be mindful of the original business question from stakeholders and the potential impact and value as the analyses are undertaken. In doing so, it is recommended to start thinking about how to 'get your point across'.

- **Get your point across** – This is the acid test for any analytics project. Can insights and recommendations be delivered to project sponsors and stakeholders so they take action? Effective storytelling, carefully considered visualizations and using the right language all improve the success rate of people analytics work.

Speaking the correct language of the business requires understanding the business as well as the project sponsor and stakeholders involved. Learning to frame insights and recommendations in business, rather than HR language, is a skill worth learning.

We saw a prime example of this in the previous case study from MetLife. The next case study, from Nestlé, also highlights the importance of speaking the language of the business. It demonstrates that not every piece of analytics work should be distilled in purely financial terms. The key message of this case study is: *Sometimes, switch from framing the story financially to the language of the specific business unit.*

 CASE STUDY

Speak the language of the business: Nestlé

Nespresso[4] is a valuable part of Nestlé's[5] coffee business. Its boutiques offer exciting experiences to consumers through expert advice and guided coffee tastings. Their staff of smartly dressed coffee specialists select slender, colourful sleeves of coffee capsules and place them into stylish shopping bags for customers. The Nespresso brand is impressive in all aspects. So too is their appreciation of people analytics. Global Head of People Analytics at Nestlé, Jordan Pettman, has been involved with developing the analytical approach across Nestlé and in particular for the Nespresso business for several years.

It started with an attempt to connect HR data and HR activity to boutique performance. In 2019, the HR team hypothesized that completion of a particular Nespresso training course led to the commercial success of a boutique. However, the analyses disproved the hypothesis. Completion of the course made no real difference to boutique performance.

The Nespresso leadership were still very interested and came up with multiple other hypotheses. Through working with the stakeholders and using his previous experience as a consultant, Jordan clarified the hypotheses down to a small, prioritized list. The team launched comprehensive analyses into staff and manager turnover, training, diversity and engagement.

With full support from the HR and business leadership teams in Nespresso, Jordan's team of data scientists and analysts found some compelling insights. The tenure and engagement of employees had a small influence on boutique performance. However, the voluntary termination rate of managers had a much greater impact. The insight that caught the attention of leaders was that voluntary termination rates of boutique managers were strongly related to boutique sales performance. The analysis showed that if the business could decrease the voluntary termination rate of managers by 5 per cent or more, the business would see a positive impact on boutique sales performance.

'All of our findings were quantified in financial terms,' Jordan recalls. 'We didn't get the "wow!" reaction from the wider business we had hoped for. So, we evolved this approach and brought it closer to the overall business language. We started telling the story in terms of the number of Nespresso coffee capsules sold – a metric that every single person in the Nespresso business understands, from finance to marketing and manufacturing.'

The project was a great success. First, the team managed to successfully identify vital insights even after disproving the first hypothesis; second, it translated the insight into the language of the business, which engaged stakeholders; and finally, manager training recommendations were quickly deployed to boutiques around the globe, which led to business improvement. People analytics had proven its worth.

Jordan exclaims: 'The buy-in from employees and leaders means that people analytics has been invited to continue to add business value for years to come! It was a case of success breeding success. Once leaders understood the value people analytics could add, every unit wanted it! It's an exciting place to be in.'

In June 2020, when Valerie Robert joined as Global Head of HR for Nespresso, Jordan was one of the first people she contacted. As a business leader with HR expertise, when she heard the story of how people analytics had contributed to the commercial success of boutiques the previous year, Valerie knew that it could be an important part of developing the business further still.

One of the first topics Jordan and Valerie discussed was Nespresso's ecosystem of culture and behaviour. Specifically, they considered the impact of culture and behaviour on boutique performance and how they could measure it.

'My team and I had seen evidence that people analytics is a problem-solving machine,' Valerie explains. 'There was a precedent of good partnering between Jordan's global Nestlé team and Nespresso, and there was proof of how we could connect people-data-driven insights to meaningful value.'

Very shortly after her arrival, Valerie and Jordan started work on the culture topic. In August 2020, they set out with an iterative approach. The combined effort saw Nespresso HR gather feedback from eight virtual focus groups and a quantitative survey of 1,300 people (a 10 per cent representative portion of the workforce) in three languages, with inclusive polling and prioritization technology embedded. With an emphasis on iteration and speed as opposed to precision, it took as little as 90 seconds to gather 3,000 votes.

Once the feedback had been analysed, Valerie and Jordan's teams presented their findings to stakeholders. Taking a similar approach to the first project, Jordan looked to translate everything into business performance to engage people throughout the agile process.

As a senior HR professional, Valerie is inspired by analytics. Partnering with people analytics on this work revealed a few lessons, which she passes on to her colleagues:

Don't wait for perfect data:

- Make sure you have enough data, and that it is credible.

- Be prepared that some outcomes might not be positive.

- An iterative approach to providing insights is helpful to get the management team engaged progressively.

- The right time to do people analytics is when the business needs the analysis – don't wait for the 'perfect' time.

The success of people analytics at Nespresso is replicable elsewhere, says Jordan. 'Leaders didn't believe in us at first because we had no established credibility. Our work with Nespresso opened doors throughout the business. One of the most important things we have learnt is to look beyond leaders' pet projects and instead to go out and find the meaningful work, where you attract the best stakeholders and spokespeople and advocates.'

Jordan concludes: 'All people analytics projects aren't going to "save the business!" Sometimes you have to accept that some projects and their return on investment will be small. But that's okay. Building trust within the business will allow you to work on much more important things once you have established credibility.'

TOP TIP

Analytics is a progressive activity; work iteratively, amending questions as stakeholder input develops, and tell the story as meaningfully as possible.

Step 4: Deliver solutions at scale

The fourth step to driving business outcomes (Figure 8.4) focuses on realizing the value through scaling and productizing analytical solutions.

As well as focusing on the People Analytics Value Chain (Figure 8.3) to maintain an outside-in perspective, a new way of working for people analytics also depends on productizing services and adopting a service-centric delivery model.

As explained in the report, Delivering Value at Scale: A new operating model for people analytics (Ferrar, Styr and Ktena, 2020): 'People analytics functions often experience a tipping point. They shift from trying to find projects, to a tipping point when they don't know how to get all of the proposed projects completed. The times before and after the tipping point are both critical, and require different areas of focus: before, the team is focused on building credibility, capability and infrastructure and after, the function must scale the most valuable and important analytics solutions quickly.'

For example, as soon as a people analytics project is proven to deliver value, it needs to be quickly converted into a product delivered across the relevant parts of the organization. This requires productizing the solution. The skills required to do this have been discussed in Chapter 4 (Skills).

The case study below, Scaling analytics for value: IBM, is a prime example of how to scale and productize analytics by harnessing technology and developing analytics skills and capability across the entire HR function. Embedding people analytics across the organization requires creating a data-driven culture across HR, as discussed in Chapter 9 (Culture).

Step 5: Quantify outcomes

Surprisingly, many companies that invest in building people analytics functions do not quantify the business outcomes of their work. Indeed, some do not evaluate projects and don't even consider determining their return on value to the organization. This greatly limits the potential, stymies investment and risks placing people analytics in the bottom drawer.

However, companies that do quantify outcomes prove they deliver the value they set out to achieve, and provide benefits to the workforce and employees themselves, and often simultaneously improve their credibility with stakeholders. An example of a company like this is IBM.

Finally, it is important to communicate the success of people analytics – both internally and externally. From an internal perspective, it creates momentum, drives demand, increases investment and improves scale. From an external perspective, it can help attract and retain analytics talent and provide a positive brand image for the organization. At a minimum, the people analytics leader gains credibility for their function.

In the case study that follows, the value of people analytics work is assessed in partnership with finance professionals. This methodology has enabled IBM to achieve impressive results. The message of this case study is: *Gain credibility through proving the financial and commercial benefit of people analytics.*

 CASE STUDY

Scaling analytics for value: IBM

Human Resources at IBM[6] is rightly recognized as a pioneer in using people analytics to deliver business value. Much of this is due to its advancement of people analytics to include artificial intelligence (AI) technologies.

IBM has over 20 years of structured people data, and a formal people analytics function developed since the late 2000s. This enduring commitment to the discipline of people analytics has delivered millions of dollars to the business and improved the experience of hundreds of thousands of employees worldwide. None of this would have been possible without a business-first approach, a deep understanding of the financial value of people analytics and the enhancement of people analytics with AI.

The leaders of this success include Diane Gherson, Chief Human Resources Officer and Senior Vice President from June 2013 to September 2020, Nickle LaMoreaux, former Vice President of Human Resources and now Chief Human Resources Officer, and Anshul Sheopuri, Vice President and Chief Technology Officer for Data, AI & Offering Strategy, and IBM Distinguished Engineer.

The first move towards a formal people analytics function began in 2010, with a single team that provided reporting and insights across the global organization of 170-plus countries. This equipped global leadership with data and metrics from across the business in a consistent fashion with universal definitions. By early 2013, people analytics had undertaken some advanced studies and started implementing more complex technologies such as employee listening.

However, from an employee experience perspective, individual employees still had to stitch together front-end solutions for themselves. For example, as a new hire joining the company, you would use one system for your benefits, another to order your security badge, and yet another to activate your company devices.

'Every one of those processes might have been efficient, but the experience was poor,' Diane recalls. When Diane first became the CHRO, she focused on people management through the lens of the employee experience rather than the lens of HR policies and processes. 'The purpose of human resources is to benefit humans, so we started with a strategy that was able to be measured according to human experience.' As such, the performance and impact of IBM's HR offerings began to be measured by Net Promoter Score (NPS) in 2013.

Diane's second point of action was to reframe how HR served the business. 'It may sound like semantics,' she smiles, 'but referring to our work as "Offerings" instead of "Programs" fundamentally changed the way that the business and workforce received the work. "Offerings" implies that someone is at the other end of your work, that each employee might have a valuable perspective on it, and your work is going to be of significant importance to them.'

HR also worked to provide substantial benefits to the business. The people analytics team set out to work on key business challenges. One of those challenges was understanding how to attract and retain the skills needed for the business's future success as it was transforming. Another challenge was to manage pockets of attrition in existing business-critical functions.

It took a series of iterative projects over three years in collaboration with IBM's Watson Analytics[7] team, to refine a predictive algorithm that now has a 95 per cent degree of accuracy for skills and retention. Within three years of implementation, the team enhanced the proactive retention offering with artificial intelligence technologies (AI), so that it became smarter. This led to the analytics solutions learning from each individual employee instance of retention in real-time. IBM's use of cutting-edge AI in the context of advanced people analytics as outlined by then Chief Executive Officer Ginni Rometty, in 2019 secured dozens of crucial skill sets for the business – and saved IBM $300 million.[8]

This data-driven approach to tackling business problems created other opportunities for the people analytics team. The business's appetite increased, and the team started to look at how to scale people analytics across the organization. This strategy is further emphasized by the team's relationship with two key functions, finance and IT.

First, with finance, at the initiation stage, the value of all people analytics work is assessed in partnership with financial experts. 'To this day, every offering begins by finding out what is important to the business, quantifying the potential value and aligning our efforts with that,' says Anshul. 'These principles have ensured that the team have continued to conduct analyses that matter and improve the employee experience.'

Second, working with IT colleagues meant the team had access to their experience of using technology and an Agile project management approach, which were integral to being able to deliver and scale offerings to employees. Being a technology company, IBM also had the opportunity to use some of its suite of AI capabilities, Watson, to enhance its other offerings, following the success of the proactive retention initiative. The pace of implementation of AI has accelerated to the extent that most organizations now have easy access to these advanced technologies. This low bar of entry for developers allows people analytics to be infused with machine learning as a means to improve prediction and scale offerings rapidly across a broad workforce.

One offering Diane is particularly proud of is Your Learning,[9] which provides recommendations in a personal format to employees on their development by pulling data together on skills, workforce plans, and content and career options. In keeping with Diane's experience-led philosophy, the platform is measured with appropriate metrics, in this case, NPS and user behaviour.

In October 2020, Your Learning achieved a stellar NPS of 58 out of 100, 35,000 people – almost 10 per cent of IBM's total workforce – sign in to the platform every single day, and 98 per cent of the business actively use the platform every quarter. Financially, the platform has resulted in deep granularity and transparency and has been critical to retaining employees and skill sets. Diane also credits Your Learning as a contributing factor to IBM's status as one of the top companies to work for in the world (Stoller, 2020).

Reflecting on these experiences, Diane suggests four action points leaders should use to align the business interests with HR through the use of people analytics and technology.

The first of these points is to understand the business strategy fully. 'I started out in consulting, so I spent years listening to the business and probing the strategy until I fully understood how HR could support it. Skipping that step is the first big pitfall,' she notes.

The second point is to be prepared to cancel work and change direction. Diane cites a recent personal favourite project as evidence of how significant this pitfall can be. 'The business needed a skills and career development offering. The MyCareerAdvisor (MYCA) platform was conceptualized to help reframe HR from a compliance perspective, reinvent workflow and ensure managers made good decisions,' she explains. 'But it had a poor NPS. There was no getting around the fact that people simply weren't going to use it.' Diane scrapped MYCA herself.

While breaking the platform into parts, the team realized that the work could still be useful: it was, after all, designed with a business need in mind. The components most aligned with IBM's skills and career development goal were reworked, and feedback was integrated into a new initiative: the successful aforementioned Your Learning platform. Because the goal was business focused, and the financial metrics were relevant, the team knew how to build an offering that would fit with the culture and needs of the company and individuals.

The third point is to enable HR practitioners to be analytically savvy to realize business outcomes. The first education in analytics delivered to HR practitioners was as early as 2012 when over 600 HRBPs undertook a course in basic analytics. By October 2020, 6,000 members of IBM's HR organization had received in-depth analytical skills education, including how to use trusted AI solutions and data responsibly and ethically. This formed the basis of HR's Code of Conduct.

Diane's fourth and final point is powerful: the true purpose of people analytics is to benefit the business and its employees, concurrently. 'The role of people analytics in a company is to add value to the business – not to lower costs. It should always be about opportunity, not compliance.'

Diane's successor, Nickle, who transitioned into the role of Chief Human Resources Officer of IBM in September 2020, shares this purpose for analytics: 'Successfully using AI as part of our people analytics offerings enables employees to be great leaders, ensures teams develop the skills needed for market agility, and gives the business competitive advantage.'

It is thanks to IBM and its suite of AI technologies that the people analytics field has expanded. Other companies are inspired by what IBM does to scale and increase the value of people analytics to the business and its employees.

TOP TIP

Always start with the business strategy.

Summary

The most important responsibility of people analytics is to deliver outcomes that improve business performance, support strategy and manage risk. Some important steps to take when focusing on outcomes include:

- Take a value-chain approach to people analytics focused on client drivers as inputs and measurable business outcomes as the outputs.

- Orient all activities involved in people analytics work on delivering quantifiable outcomes.

- Work closely with finance and agree at the outset how the outcomes will be measured.

- Learn to be a storyteller; get to know each audience and the language that will compel them to take action.

- Look to scale analytics across the enterprise. This is when value is fully realized. Don't limit analytics to experiments, projects or pilots.

References

Ferrar, J (2017) The power of people (article 3 of 7) [Blog] LinkedIn, 24 May. Available from: https://www.linkedin.com/pulse/power-people-article-3-7-jonathan-ferrar/ (archived at https://perma.cc/NY6J-8YHJ) [Last accessed 29 January 2021]

Ferrar, J, Styr, C and Ktena, A (2020) Delivering Value at Scale: A new operating model for people analytics [Report] Insight222 Research, 24 November. Available from: https://www.insight222.com/people-analytics-operating-model-research (archived at https://perma.cc/5MYJ-KC6B) [Last accessed 7 February 2021]

Green, D (2020) How J&J uses people analytics to drive business outcomes, with Piyush Mathur [Podcast] Digital HR Leaders, 10 March. Available from: https://www.myhrfuture.com/digital-hr-leaders-podcast/2020/3/10/how-johnson-and-johnson-uses-people-analytics-to-drive-business-outcomes (archived at https://perma.cc/NMW2-DRGA) [Last accessed 7 February 2021]

Guenole, N, Ferrar, J and Feinzig, S (2017) *The Power of People: Learn how successful organizations use workforce analytics to improve business performance*, Pearson, London

Scism, L (2016) MetLife to cut costs by \$1 billion through 2019, *Wall Street Journal*, 4 August. Available from: https://www.wsj.com/articles/metlife-to-cut-costs-by-1-billion-through-2019-1470320096 (archived at https://perma.cc/Y7LW-Z8BH) [Last accessed 7 February 2021]

Stoller, K (2020) The world's best employers, *Forbes*, 15 October. Available from: https://www.forbes.com/consent/?toURL=https://www.forbes.com/lists/worlds-best-employers/#9e995ed1e0ca (archived at https://perma.cc/2L5F-CMHM) [Last accessed 7 February 2021]

Notes

1 A little play on words, inspired by the 'Culture eats strategy for breakfast' quote attributed to renowned management thinker, Peter Drucker. The idea is that the value derived from statistical analysis – not the analysis itself – is essential.

2 MetLife, Inc. is among the largest global providers of insurance, annuities and employee benefit programmes with 90 million customers in more than 60 countries and serving more than 90 of the top 100 FORTUNE 500® companies in the United States. MetLife employs 49,000 employees across five regions (see https://www.metlife.com/about-us/corporate-profile/global-locations/ (archived at https://perma.cc/VN2H-DAEP); https://s23.q4cdn.com/579645270/files/doc_financials/2019/ar/2019_Annual_Report.PDF (archived at https://perma.cc/SJE4-WFBN), last accessed 7 February 2021).

3 According to *The Oxford Dictionary*, a 'black box' is a complex system or device whose internal workings are hidden or not readily understood.

4 Nestlé Nespresso S.A. (Nespresso) is an operating unit of the Nestlé Group, based in Lausanne, Switzerland, and the pioneer and reference for highest-quality portioned coffee (see: https://www.nestle.com/investors/annual-report (archived at https://perma.cc/UZU2-DUK2), last accessed 7 February 2021).

5   Nestlé S.A. is the world's largest food and beverage company. Incorporating more than 2,000 brands, Nestlé is present in 187 countries and home to 352,000 employees (see https://www.nestle.com/investors/annual-report (archived at https://perma.cc/56MB-5YMD), last accessed 7 February 2021).

6   IBM (International Business Machines Corporation) is a US technology company with a workforce of more than 360,000 people across 172 countries (see https://www.ibm.com/uk-en/about (archived at https://perma.cc/J7YT-GTPS), last accessed 7 February 2021).

7   Watson Analytics is a suite of AI capabilities hosted on cloud technology. When applied to HR purposes, it greatly accelerated IBM's people analytics journey (see https://www.ibm.com/watson (archived at https://perma.cc/6SST-854L), last accessed 7 February 2021).

8   Ginni Rometty, Chief Executive Officer of IBM 2011–2020, announced the results at the Work Talent and Human Resources Summit, New York City, NY, USA in 2019.

9   IBM Your Learning (see https://yourlearning.ibm.com/about/ (archived at https://perma.cc/QA3N-A97U), last accessed 7 February 2021).

Culture

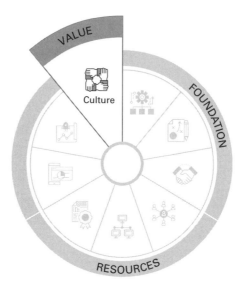

09

In this chapter, we discuss how to build a data-driven culture across the human resources function and the wider enterprise by developing an analytical mind-set and involving HR experts in people analytics solutions and activities.

DISCOVER...

- the skills needed for the future HR professional;
- how to create the right mindset for analytics;
- ways to get HR professionals involved in analytics.

WITH INSIGHTS FROM...

- Merck KGaA, on the adoption of a culture of people analytics across the enterprise;
- Rabobank, on how to engage and enable HR to kick-start a data-driven culture;
- PepsiCo, on building collaboration between global and local teams.

Overview

> **CULTURE**
>
> Culture, as one of the Nine Dimensions, is focused on building analytically willing and savvy people across the human resources function. It considers the skills and mindset needed for the future HR professional and how these can be developed and instilled to provide a basis for innovation, curiosity and delivering value to the organization.

According to Aon's 2019 Intangible Assets Financial Statement Impact Comparison Report, in little more than 40 years, intangible assets evolved into a major consideration for investors. By the end of 2018, those intangible assets comprised 84 per cent of all enterprise value on the S&P 500, a massive increase from just 17 per cent in 1975. Intangible assets include intellectual property, brand, data and – of course – people, networks and relationships.

People, the networks they create and the culture of the organization are increasingly important. McKinsey & Co outlines that a culture of data matters, too; its 2018 report notes that the emergence of data analytics as an omnipresent reality of modern organizational life means that a healthy data culture is becoming increasingly important (Díaz, Rowshankish and Saleh, 2018).

It is also important, therefore, for people analytics. The need for the chief human resources officer to create a culture of data across the entire human resources function is imperative. But the question is this: Is HR – as a function – ready for analytics?

Guenole and Feinzig (2018) discuss how to develop a data-savvy HR department in a *Harvard Business Review* article. The authors summarize three types of people that coexist in HR: the analytically savvy, the analytically willing and the analytically resistant.

In addition, research by Insight222 undertaken in 2019 found that the more deeply people analytics is embedded in the culture of the HR organization, the less resistant HR professionals are to using it (Green, 2019). Additional research[1] concludes that a lack of capability in people analytics skills leads to low self-efficacy and confidence. As a result, HR professionals find it hard to embrace a data-driven culture.

However, it's important not to confuse a lack of knowledge with a lack of motivation. In its study, Insight222 disproved the myth that HR professionals with low levels of analytical skill and knowledge are resistant to people analytics. As shown in Figure 9.1, over 80 per cent of HR professionals strongly agree that people analytics drives business value and a similar number believe that people analytics is good for their career.

Unfortunately, only two-thirds of those surveyed believe they are capable of having conversations about analytics, and significantly fewer are confident about using analytics without guidance.

The messages are clear: develop skills and build confidence. The motivation and belief among HR professionals are already there.

In summary, it is clear that building a culture of people analytics across the entire human resources function requires four elements.

Figure 9.1 Key takeaways from a survey of HR leaders and practitioners

82% of HR professionals agree that people analytics drives business value		41% of HR professionals believe they are capable of having conversations about data
...and ...	...but ...	...and ...
84% of HR professionals believe people analytics is important for their career		23% of HR professionals are comfortable using people analytics without guidance

SOURCE Reproduced with kind permission of Insight222, November 2019

Figure 9.2 The Culture Pyramid

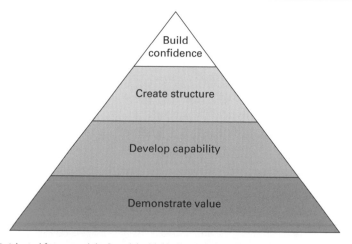

Build confidence

Create structure

Develop capability

Demonstrate value

SOURCE Adapted from an original model with kind permission of Kirsten Levermore, February 2021

These four elements are layered as The Culture Pyramid (see Figure 9.2). Each level requires the prior level as a building block. And each of the four levels is needed to build a pervasive and enduring data-driven culture across the entire human resources function. The four elements are:

- Demonstrate **value**: Create a platform of belief in analytics through communicating and demonstrating the value of people analytics itself.
- Develop **capability**: Invest in education and learning to develop HR professionals in skills needed for the future.
- Create **structure**: Develop tools and activities that will engage people in analytics at all levels across the breadth of the HR function.
- Build **confidence**: Encourage a mindset shift to a data-driven way of working.

We have discussed in Chapter 8 (Business Outcomes) how value is delivered from people analytics. Therefore we will not discuss this in detail here, except to say that it is the responsibility of the chief human resources officer together with the people analytics leader to instil and affirm the value of people analytics at every opportunity. At the same time, a data-driven culture is created and reinforced.

Developing a culture in HR is complex. Before we consider the skills needed for HR professionals in the future, we outline how one company focused its energy on building a data-driven culture in HR. The case study, Scaling people analytics adoption: Merck KGaA, demonstrates how it requires persistence. Its key message is: *Scaling people analytics and creating a data-driven culture in HR requires a multi-year approach.*

 CASE STUDY

Scaling people analytics adoption: Merck KGaA

What the Global Head of People Analytics & Strategic Workforce Planning of Merck KGaA[2] ('Merck') Alexis Saussinan and his team have achieved is an impressive example of implementing a culture of analytics across HR and the business.

Over a period of four years, with a clearly articulated vision and multi-year road map up front, people analytics is now a part of the day-to-day approach in HR and is a top priority of the Global HR Strategy 2022.

With over 70 per cent of the Merck HR organization actively using its global people analytics platform, this allows HR professionals to embed data into their conversations with business executives to enable strategic decision making.

Accomplishments like this don't happen overnight, Alexis explains to us on a call. '2015 marked the very beginning of people analytics in our business,' Alexis recalls. 'Merck had a small team of just three people working in people analytics. I joined to lead and develop the team in 2016. My task was to build a culture of analytics across HR for Merck.'

Alexis epitomizes international business: being French and brought up in Europe, now living in Singapore and having worked across the US, Europe and Asia in business, marketing, sales and HR roles, he has a strong appreciation for building global teams and delivering a vision that inspires people from a variety of cultures. This background certainly helped Alexis to deliver on this HR transformation.

By 2020, Alexis's team had more than tripled in size and established people analytics and strategic workforce planning as a central component of Merck's global HR ethos. Furthermore ('and we have the data to measure this,' adds Alexis), people analytics is at the centre of strategic people decision making and discussion at board level, executive committee level and throughout Merck.

Under Alexis's leadership, the team ascertained there were a number of things it would have to do in order to make this transformation come to life:

- Establish a clear vision.
- Clarify the understanding of business challenges.
- Harness the technology to scale the adoption of analytics.
- Secure stakeholder buy-in.
- Use reverse marketing rather than direct marketing.
- Deliver quantifiable business impact.

In 2016, Alexis's first goal was to clarify the vision: 'to create a culture of analytics across HR'. To achieve this vision, the team knew it had to standardize and integrate business processes and generate a single, accessible and global view of more than 350 million people-data points ('and growing every day!') that could be easily understood by the HR and business populations.

Guided by this vision, Alexis and his team worked with strategic HR business partners (HRBPs) to approach senior executives and invited them to share their most important business challenges. 'Introducing people analytics into business practice is like leading a horse to water,' says Alexis. 'You can present it to people, but whether they will engage with it and use it is a different problem. Building credentials to show management by actually doing work and delivering visible impact was a natural next step.'

Demonstrating how people analytics could deliver value to the business became a cornerstone of Merck's strategy for scaling the work across the organization. One example is shown here:

A business leader was searching for a successor with a specific profile for a key position. The people analytics team and HRBPs were able to connect them with another business leader in a different part of the organization who had a high-potential person (HiPo) with this exact profile looking for a next career step, because data highlighted a solution existed for this problem. Armed with this data, their two respective HRBPs found they could create a solution to solve the business leaders' challenge, by moving one HiPo from one part of the organization to another. Previously, without this analytical view and access to the data, those types of interactions would only happen by chance, and if the two HRBPs happened to know each other. 'Data, discussions, mobility, opportunity – done,' Alexis comments.

This type of relatively simple situation was one of many small building blocks that showed how analytics could solve business and people challenges. For this type of simple scenario, the team worked – but how could it scale its impact to the entire enterprise?

The people analytics team was limited in size and could cope with small projects. Scaling solutions as wide as Group level would necessitate big steps. The team needed to work on strategic projects and to enable the whole Merck community of HR professionals to access and interpret the data.

Scaling people analytics was essential, and the team moved to the next stage of embedding analytics and technology across the enterprise. The team implemented its first version of the global people analytics platform.

Truly enabling the HR community meant that Merck needed to provide all HR colleagues and business leaders with transparent access to the company's people data. To facilitate this, the team worked closely with relevant data privacy teams and works councils. 'They were always very supportive – and our transparent and strategic relationship with them means that we are able to deliver impact across the entire business while safeguarding Merck's very strong ethics and data privacy standards at all times.'

This has resulted in the situation that today, people analytics enables Merck HR colleagues to be extremely agile. They can, in real time, take stock, check on, adapt or develop new strategies as rapidly as business circumstances or people circumstances change. At Merck, there is 'no business plan without a people plan', and people analytics underpins this.

'Merck HR strategic people consultants are powerhouses,' says Alexis. 'Easy access to all of the organization's data means that they can support business leaders strategically. My team helps our HR colleagues translate business objectives into people strategies and arms them with numbers that they can refer to and share with the business on the app and track over time on a live basis.'

As the business started to recognize the value of people analytics, the team established credibility and HR colleagues' appetite increased, Merck found they needed to engage even more with senior business stakeholders, continuously. Doing this across a global enterprise was challenging using traditional methods employed by HR and Internal Communications. So, they looked for alternative ways to secure stakeholder buy-in (see Figure 9.3).

The cornerstone of this three-pronged approach was the use of reverse marketing (where the customer seeks the supplier rather than the supplier's marketers seeking the customer): the team promoted people analytics in such a way that senior leaders and the HR community would use it organically (via the platform) to answer their everyday questions.

To do this, the team spent the early months of 2017 reviewing and segmenting its target audience, developing detailed personas and user journeys for business managers. 'We switched gears from promoting people analytics as a tool to integrating people analytics seamlessly into "customer journeys",' Alexis explains. Pushing personas – as opposed to the technology – resulted in highly personalized, relevant solutions and bite-sized insights called 'Did You Knows', which helped grow adoption exponentially in just a few months.

For example, Merck's business leaders typically start planning for the following year between July and October – so the people analytics team pushed them bite-size 'Did You Know' insights explaining how people analytics could help them with these people plans, highlighting concerns such as

Figure 9.3 Merck KGaA People Analytics' three-pronged strategy for promoting the potential of people analytics

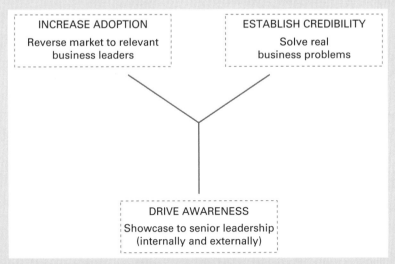

SOURCE Reproduced with kind permission of Merck KGaA, July 2020

capability requirement, possible organizational set-up optimizations, evolution and anticipated attrition risks.

The persona approach worked: facilitating discussion and opening doors between the business, HRBPs and the people analytics team meant that the adoption curve within HR grew nine-fold in only six months. By the end of 2017, almost half of Merck HR professionals were using the people analytics platform on a regular basis.

Simultaneously, in 2017 the team was invited to present the global people analytics capabilities at Merck's Global Executive Committee (GEC) event, which welcomes approximately 200 of the organization's most senior global leaders to meet annually and discuss corporate strategy and results. Sandwiched between a new drug in development, a cutting-edge research and development process, a sophisticated humanoid robot and an interactive VR headset, Alexis and the people analytics team showcased Merck's people analytics capabilities and examples of impact – and won the award for the Most Visited Booth! Of all of the amazing initiatives and projects shown at the GEC event, global leaders were most interested in people analytics.

It was the turning point for people analytics at Merck. Since 2017, the team has increased adoption within HR and has demonstrated the power of people data to senior executives.

Today, the team is dedicated to implementing its strategic people analytics road map. Its three focus areas include the continuous development of people analytics capabilities at Merck, the accelerated leverage of people analytics to drive strategic workforce planning to help shape the future of work, and to prepare for the future with advanced people analytics and machine learning. For example, the team is increasingly solving business challenges such as piloting text analytics to infer potential employee skills and drive development of future capabilities. It is also using organizational network analysis to identify critical science talent in acquired companies and how to effectively transition and retain them into Merck. Furthermore, it is working with their Diversity & Inclusion teams to show how specific team diversity profiles drive maximum innovation.

'At this point, everybody in the firm knows what "people analytics" is,' Alexis concludes. 'Not everybody uses it,' he offers, humbly, 'but everybody can say what it is and what it is not. And everybody knows the benefits it adds to the business.'

'It's been a long journey, and it is not over. We still have a long way to go, but HR at Merck has certainly become data-driven.'

TOP TIP

Developing a culture of analytics requires a clear vision and persistence – be in it for the long haul.

Building capability in analytics across HR

With the value of people analytics demonstrated, it is important to build capability in data-driven skills to improve the analytical-savviness of HR professionals generally. While Chapter 4 (Skills) focuses on the skills required for the people analytics team itself, this section focuses on the skills needed for HR professionals more generally to help them in their quest to become more data-driven.

Figure 9.4   Nine Skills for the Future HR Professional

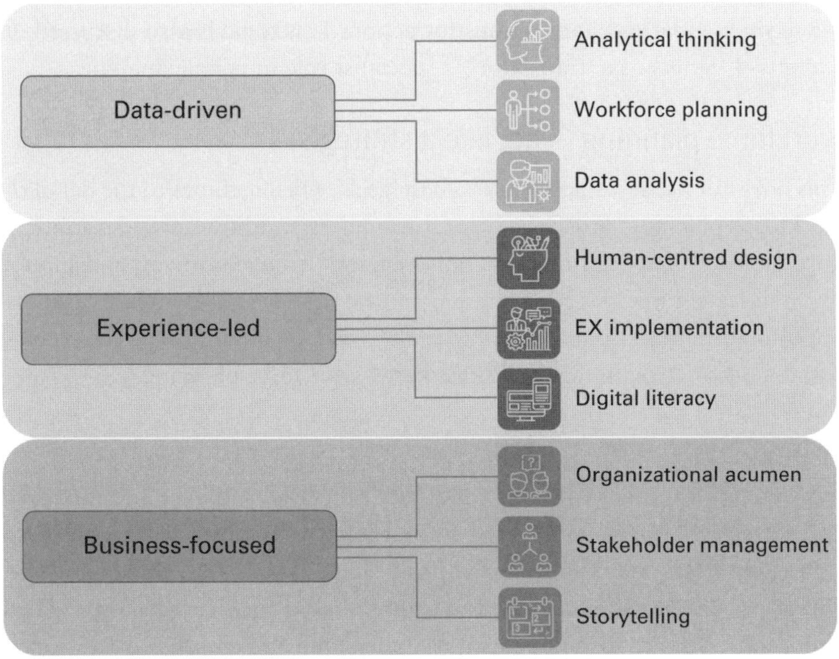

Data-driven
- Analytical thinking
- Workforce planning
- Data analysis

Experience-led
- Human-centred design
- EX implementation
- Digital literacy

Business-focused
- Organizational acumen
- Stakeholder management
- Storytelling

SOURCE Reproduced with kind permission of Insight222, February 2021

Work by Insight222 in 2021 clarified skills required by HR professionals for the future in The Age of Value. Figure 9.4 shows those nine skills across three categories: business-focused skills, data-driven skills and experience-led skills.

Data-driven skills

There are three key skills, above all others, that are particularly important when considering data-driven skills required by the HR professional: analytical thinking, workforce planning and data analysis.

Analytical thinking – 'think like an analyst'

For the HR professional in general, analytical thinking requires the capability to frame business problems into questions and hypotheses through conversations with business leaders. Then, partnering with data analysts and consultants in the people analytics team to translate requests into solutions, information and insights. And finally, understanding how to translate quantitative information back to a business stakeholder, so they understand the recommendations and options for action. This topic is also discussed in Chapter 4 (Skills) as a 'translator', a specialist role in people analytics.

Workforce planning – 'act like a strategist'

This does not mean it's necessary to be a 'geek' when it comes to the detail of workforce planning. Still, it is helpful to understand how business strategy impacts workforce decisions, and how demand (from executives) and supply (from the talent market, both internal and external) of skills impact business opportunities. It is also important to understand the difference between cost-based workforce planning[3] and skills-based workforce planning.[4]

Data analysis – 'be a scientist'

Individuals and teams with this capability can gather, analyse and interpret data to provide insights to support business needs and deliver business value. Important attributes are the basic skills of statistics, trends and the ability to use MS Excel[5] and dashboarding tools to visualize data. Philosophically, it is also important to understand and embrace data science in all things, at all times.

Experience-led skills

There are three key skills in this category. These enable HR professionals to understand technology in a contemporary world and its application to 'employees'. It considers human-centred design, employee experience (EX) implementation and digital literacy.

Human-centred design – 'think like an employee'

These skills enable HR professionals to consider employee experience (EX) from the employee's viewpoint as a consumer. It includes learning design techniques, agile methods of co-creation and collaboration, and the techniques for collecting people data to measure 'touchpoints' and 'moments that matter'. These topics are also discussed in Chapter 7 (Workforce Experiences) and Chapter 6 (Data) related to emerging data sources such as text.

EX implementation – 'act like a marketeer'

These skills require partnering with business leaders to shape and realize new solutions that will improve the employee experience. Also key is to learn marketing processes and concepts, such as consumerization, personalization and digitization. These concepts are discussed in some detail in Chapter 7 (Workforce Experiences).

Digital literacy – 'be a technologist'

Digital literacy should go beyond the grounding of different types of data provided in Chapter 6 (Data) or university and executive education courses and other books. It is essential to have knowledge of the potential for artificial intelligence (AI) and robotic process automation (RPA) at work and how it can be applied in HR to, for example, improve service delivery. From our experience, the best way to do this is to stay up to date on technological advancements, how they are impacting the workforce and how to better use digital tools to support employees.

Business-focused skills

There are three key skills we highlight for HR professionals in the future: organizational acumen, stakeholder management and storytelling. We will consider each of these in turn.

Organizational acumen – 'think like an executive'

This includes understanding the organization's vision and strategy and how they align with HR programmes and initiatives. Individuals with strong organizational acumen have political awareness and astuteness that enables them to interpret organizational dynamics and influence across teams – vital when introducing new concepts and solutions. Finally, organizational acumen also implies an individual can learn and thrive in a constantly changing environment and deal with ambiguity.

Stakeholder management – 'act like a diplomat'

Chapter 3 (Stakeholder Management) outlines this topic as it relates to the people analytics team itself. Here, we consider this as it relates to HR professionals more generally – although the concept of engaging stakeholders is the same. The required skills include the ability to partner with business leaders to understand their perspectives, concerns and challenges, identify and build relationships across the organization to support the adoption of HR programmes and initiatives, and motivate and engage stakeholders by building trust and credibility.

Storytelling – 'be a narrator'

This capability is essential in translating analytics into comprehensible insights and actionable recommendations, which should be tailored for each audience. Being a storyteller, with data, is becoming an important part of every business-facing HR professional's toolkit. Three qualities are required for successful storytelling in people analytics: numerical literacy, creativity and an ability to connect different pieces of information into a single coherent story that resonates with stakeholders and is tailored for each audience. For more on storytelling with data and other communication skills, see Chapter 4 (Skills) or study the book, *Storytelling with Data* by Cole Nussbaumer Knaflic (2015).

Skills in practice

There are hundreds of resources for developing these nine skills outlined above. Resources such as those from myHRfuture.com[6] offer a plethora of opportunities to learn in a contemporary way, using a combination of 'bite-sized' training modules through media such as video, podcast and articles.

The best way to learn the complex and new skills listed above for an entire human resources function is to involve HR professionals in co-creation and collaborative projects. This will allow professionals to learn skills while working on real business challenges. One example of this is showcased in the next case study, Engage and enable HR to kick-start a data-driven culture: Rabobank. As we will see, Rabobank's success is underpinned by a strong principle, which is that only when you 'experience' do you 'get it'. The key message of this case study is: *Create a data-driven culture by empowering HR teams with actionable data and insights.*

 CASE STUDY

Engage and enable HR to kick-start a data-driven culture: Rabobank

Dutch farmers have worked together for more than a century. It is on this foundation that cooperative bank, Rabobank,[7] stands and thrives. With a value system rooted in collaboration and sustainability, and a vision that is still deeply connected to society and enabling people, Rabobank is rapidly evolving into a human–digital bank that helps customers via a blend of digital tools and in-branch services. Rabobank puts its mission 'Growing a Better World Together', into practice through local initiatives and has members rather than shareholders. Rabobank took collaboration to a new level when it brought its decentralized system into a more centralized cooperative structure in the mid-2010s.

Chief Human Resources Officer Janine Vos has always believed in the statement: 'happy people, happy customers'. This vision, together with Rabobank's cooperative approach, provided a great foundation for people analytics.

Tertia Wiedenhof is the People Analytics & Insights Product Owner at Rabobank. The first questions she asked herself and the team were, 'What is a happy person?' and 'How can a happy person deliver value to the customers?'

'Using data and insights to the benefit of our employees and teams has been my focus since I started in HR,' Tertia reflects during a conversation about people analytics and its impact on the business in 2020. 'And now, with the support of my leader and access to the data, researchers and scientists, I can truly bring this to life at Rabobank.'

Both Janine and Tertia are champions of data-driven HR. Tertia herself has a strong HR information system (HRIS) background, so she has deep insight into the benefits of a tech-powered HR, but with a human touch: 'We believe that great HR should be high-tech, high-touch. For me, that means using data, but combining this with your experience and intuition And, when combined with easily accessible and innovative technology, we know that HR can also improve the employee experience at speed and scale, and across all levels.'

By 2018 Tertia and her colleagues were regularly demonstrating the value of analytics to HR managers, business partners and other HR professionals. The people analytics team developed an extensive, interactive programme on data-driven HR, proving the value of data to HR professionals. And it seems to have worked, as HR business partners (HRBPs) and other HR professionals are now more and more able to go out to the business and use data appropriately to make informed decisions that create value.

With the target audience in mind, all Tertia needed was one brilliant initiative to bring everyone together and prove how valuable people data could be. Watching her colleagues work and operate in the wider world provided the inspiration: as external circumstances rapidly changed and the ways of work shifted underfoot, increasingly complex work was completed by teams, rather than individual people. It was a revelation. 'Too often, HR is focused on the individual,' Tertia exclaims. 'But collaboration and teamwork are the essential ingredients in the modern workforce.' The people analytics team considered how it could deliver results to collaborating teams that would support decision making.

At the same moment, Rabobank as a whole was transitioning to Agile frameworks. 'Embracing Agile means facilitating very fast collaboration, so our project would not only help individuals, but also had real business relevance.' This was critical to the adoption (and appreciation) of the work.

This organizational change provided Tertia and her team with the opportunity to launch the collaboration analytics project. The HR function became the first Rabobank department to pilot the project, while at the same time again experiencing the value of data-driven insights.

With help from a privacy committee and works council, the people analytics team launched a minimum viable product (MVP) in September of 2019. Fed with anonymized calendar metadata and team survey data (see Figure 9.5), passive network and survey data analyses were conducted on four HR teams with a minimum of eight people. Concise, actionable insights were reported back to the teams at the team level.

Participating teams responded to the initiative within weeks: being able to track their style of collaboration allowed them to know when and where to interact and intervene. Examples include insights on where collaboration with certain departments lagged behind; or when action was taken to improve psychological safety within the team. It boosted teams becoming more self-steering and enabled them to improve on delivering customer value.

Another significant benefit emerged: 'Insights based on teams rather than on individuals accelerates the team dialogue on diversity and inclusion and being yourself at work,' Tertia explains, noting that it was the quick, actionable insights that led to immediate results that really got teams excited about people analytics. By mid-2020, the project had been rolled out across all of HR: 25 teams, 450 people.

Figure 9.5 Collaboration data was collected from calendars and team surveys of high-performing team traits at Rabobank

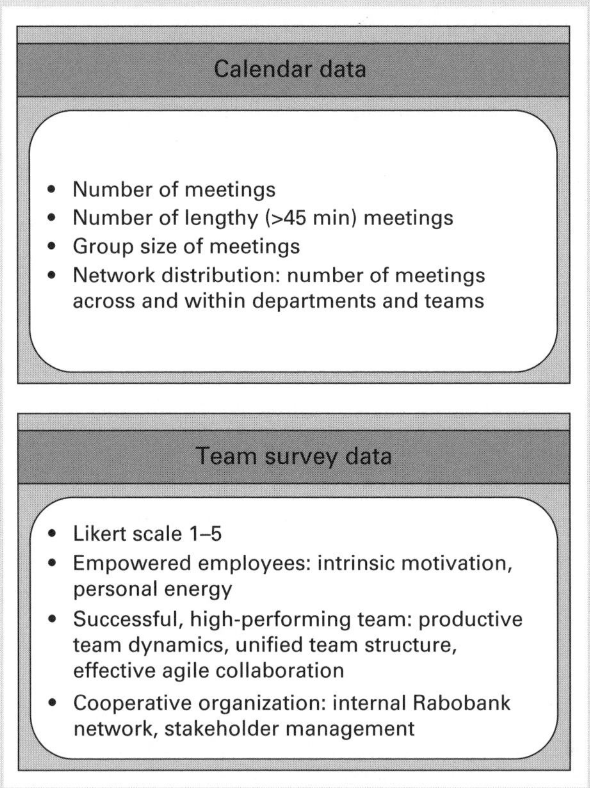

Calendar data

- Number of meetings
- Number of lengthy (>45 min) meetings
- Group size of meetings
- Network distribution: number of meetings across and within departments and teams

Team survey data

- Likert scale 1–5
- Empowered employees: intrinsic motivation, personal energy
- Successful, high-performing team: productive team dynamics, unified team structure, effective agile collaboration
- Cooperative organization: internal Rabobank network, stakeholder management

SOURCE Reproduced with kind permission of Rabobank, September 2020

Evolving an aggregated view helped HR to establish new practices underpinned with data across its teams. Implementation of the recommendations has been trickier: 'Managers really do need to let go of control in an agile organization,' Tertia notes. 'Empowering teams with data and information, rather than managers, boosts team autonomy, but is something people need to get used to.' Nevertheless, Tertia and her colleagues have persevered, communicating extensively and meeting with HR managers and employees to explain benefits. Of course, having a great data-driven leader in Janine helps (sponsorship is key!).

The blossoming data-driven culture was put to the test when the global COVID-19 pandemic changed the working practice in Rabobank – and everywhere – almost overnight. 'We knew we had to discover new insights immediately to help the bank respond.'

With the buy-in Tertia and her colleagues had achieved over the previous year, they were able to mobilize new analytics very quickly. In less than five days, the people analytics team designed, developed and deployed employee listening surveys on support and employee needs during COVID-19. They struck a healthy balance between sending information and surveys to employees, listening to what they said and making fast improvements based on employee feedback, as they explained in an enlightening article (Keunen, Wiedenhof and Wiertz, 2020).

Employees were eager to give feedback – and leaders were ready to listen to the insights that people analytics provided. 'People were open with us, and as a result, we revealed a number of insights that helped Rabobank respond to the enforced "work from home" shift that gripped the nation and most of the working world. They even gave us glimpses of what we should keep doing in the future, and the kind of support people needed.'

Between the work done during the crisis and the collaboration initiative, Tertia believes that people analytics is accepted across Rabobank: 'HR is getting the message out into the bank via HR business partners and people who have benefitted themselves from our work. They only have to say, "We are building a product to empower teams," or "We are helping you help our customers," and share their own experiences, and employees are interested.'

It's a good lesson from marketing: people are often more passionate and constructive when they have experienced the product for themselves! 'Empowered HR teams have become the best advocate and proponent for a data-driven culture we could ask for.'

TOP TIP

Develop simple MVPs of analytics solutions for colleagues.

Create structures and build confidence

Delivering value through a culture of people analytics means convincing HR – in particular, HRBPs – to think differently. In The Culture Pyramid (see Figure 9.2) shown earlier in this chapter, we outline four elements, the first two of which are 'demonstrate value' and 'develop capability'. Both of these have been discussed throughout this book and in this chapter. We will now consider the last two; 'create structures' and 'build confidence'.

In doing this, we contemplate the enablement of global and local teams and the creation of psychologically safe environments.

A word about both global and local teams

Constructing organizational structures that enable global and local teams to work seamlessly together is complicated. Both have key roles and responsibilities in the organization. In our experience and through research undertaken by Insight222 in 2020, we found that the majority of people analytics teams, almost two-thirds of 60 global companies, operate in an organization that has a highly centralized structure. And in all of those companies, the people analytics team resides in the global reporting structure, even if the people themselves might be physically located in many locations.

The key is that when the people analytics team help to build a data-driven culture across the organization, they must think carefully about the local and country-based HR professionals. The case study below, Build globally, enable locally: PepsiCo, is a good example of how it has been conducted effectively.

Psychological safety

The final topic on culture is about helping the entire human resources function feel safe when learning and building analytics and digital skills. As we have outlined throughout this book, it can be challenging to support HR to be analytically savvy, create impact and deliver value. Nevertheless, as we've also outlined, the benefits of doing so are immense, as evidenced in many of the case studies and in Part One (The case for people analytics).

To succeed and build the future data-driven culture and convert this opportunity into business outcomes requires a lot of hard work and confidence to succeed. And to do this, the topic of psychological safety is paramount.

As defined most clearly by William Kahn in 1990, psychological safety is 'being able to show and employ one's self without fear of negative consequences of self-image, status or career'. In terms of how the brain learns and integrates skills (shown simply in Figure 9.6), psychological safety is the crucial nurturing environment required for the evolution of learning from conscious incompetence right up to mastery.

Figure 9.6   The four stages of competence

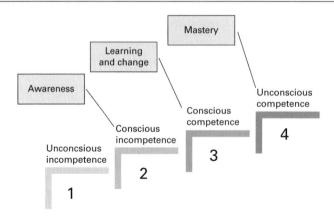

SOURCE Evolution Culture (2019)

It is helpful for the chief human resources officer to allow failure without significant consequences. This is referred to casually as 'fail fast'. Embracing a 'fail fast' mentality – it's not just words – is a way of working that fosters innovation.

To help all HR professionals succeed in a digital and data-rich environment, when their general competence may be low, the need for psychological safety is very real. If further inspiration on the role of psychological safety is required, we recommend reading one of the best-known examples of a people analytics project – Google's Project Aristotle (re:Work, 2016).

This study, which is profiled in an extensive article in *The New York Times Magazine* (Duhigg, 2016), sought to answer the research question: 'What makes a team effective at Google?' The people analytics team eventually found that the top dynamic of an effective team was psychological safety. Specifically, team members felt safe to take risks and be vulnerable in front of each other. This learning can certainly be applied in efforts to support HR professionals acquire the skills outlined in this chapter.

The final case study in this chapter is Build globally, enable locally: PepsiCo. It provides a great example of how people analytics teams can use a strong centralized knowledge structure to enable local adaptation, ownership and people analytics culture to deliver real value across a global workforce. Their key message is: *When broken into bite-size pieces with practical toolkits, people analytics enables a culture of do-ability at the local level.*

 **CASE STUDY**

Build globally, enable locally: PepsiCo

PepsiCo's Jason Narlock video calls from a rented refuge by a lake in Minnesota during the middle of the 2020 coronavirus crisis. Even when in isolation (like a large proportion of the working world), he explains his excitement as Senior Director of Global People Analytics. 'It's busy!' Jason starts. 'But in many ways, this is what people analytics professionals live for; we are being asked to step up and provide the data that will help take care of our workforce and preserve the business.'

'The PepsiCo team is passionate about enabling people and business units, so, as chaotic as this time is, we have the framework in place to thrive.'

One facet of this framework is the food and beverage company's approach and implementation of long-term strategic workforce planning (SWP).

PepsiCo[8] is structured in sectors: divided by category (such as beverages and foods) in the US, and by geography outside the US. Business strategy is similarly structured, with each market tailoring its strategy to its particular needs and remaining locally focused.

PepsiCo's People Analytics Center of Excellence (the Center) first received a request for a long-term SWP in 2012. The market that requested the SWP was rapidly emerging and in need of support with recruitment and skills: where could the local HR team find skills, and how could they acquire them in line with the local market's business strategy?

'Sector teams play a vital role in the rollout and evolution of PepsiCo's SWP approach,' Jason explains.

'The role of the Center is to be a thought leader and provider of toolkits using cutting-edge technology and ideas. In parallel, sector people analytics teams add value by building additional tools and processes that facilitate local activation.'

The traditional purpose of SWP has been to get the right people with the right skills in the right place at the right time. Determining what all of these 'rights' are, obtaining buy-in, and achieving that future state in the right way is a common challenge. PepsiCo set out to create a modern version of this clichéd approach.

PepsiCo set out to understand the market's business strategy, including formal strategic planning documents and interviews with the senior executive team. The first iteration of its new approach to SWP was documented in an article for SHRM, *People + Strategy* (Tarulli and DeLuca, 2019).

At the time that article was published, Jason was a local recipient of that toolkit and framework in his capacity as People Analytics Director for Latin America. Now promoted to the global leadership role, Jason aims to expand the remit of SWP while not losing the strong development over the last few years: 'The Center partnered very closely with sectors. It was never a case of "we're coming in to do it for you". The Center quickly realized that by enabling the sector's autonomy to implement SWP in a locally relevant manner, you drive maximum buy-in as well as practical toolkits and tracking mechanisms that are actually used.'

One other aspect that made the project successful was that it was built around the partnership of a people analytics group (both Center and sector teams), local HR business partners and senior business executives in the market. The Center terms this partnership, 'the triumvirate'.

PepsiCo's Lead Data Scientist for Europe and a former sector People Analytics leader for Europe, Philip Miles, recalls: 'The triumvirate is crucial to the SWP product.'

'Working with local HRBPs and business is critical to translate the business strategy into the largest people challenges. Some trends will be similar across the whole organization, but the key to success is to address those talent pain points that will achieve local sponsorship and ownership.' The Europe sector acted as 'the team in the middle', helping business leaders with a clear line of sight of their strategic business goals understand the talent issues of the moment, and enabling HR to see the long-term business value.

Each local SWP project took six months or longer, although recently sectors such as Europe have streamlined this process down to three months. The investment in time is due to the complexity of gathering all the data and aligning it to dynamic business markets. In an effort to keep the process simple and the team focused on the outcome, as well as being easily actionable for the local team, a modern PepsiCo SWP consists of three core components among others: Talent flows, external data and prediction models (see Figure 9.7).

Figure 9.7 Three core components of a PepsiCo SWP

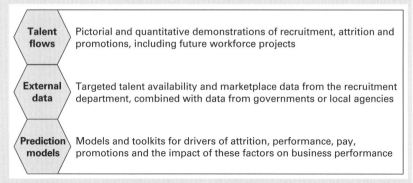

Talent flows	Pictorial and quantitative demonstrations of recruitment, attrition and promotions, including future workforce projects
External data	Targeted talent availability and marketplace data from the recruitment department, combined with data from governments or local agencies
Prediction models	Models and toolkits for drivers of attrition, performance, pay, promotions and the impact of these factors on business performance

SOURCE Reproduced with kind permission of PepsiCo, August 2020

Having initially developed SWP as a global framework in partnership with the business, sector teams then implemented it, refined it and brought it to life, augmenting it with local market talent data as well as models that were appropriate for their individual sector.

'Ultimately, the local teams know their own market and implementation tactics better than the Center does,' Jason explains. This was not the end of the work, however (see Figure 9.8).

The Center gains feedback from sectors regularly to enhance the global framework. Teams work together via hackathons or sprints to refine models and improve the entire SWP process. 'In this way,' says Philip, 'the Center acts as a connector, and the relevant sector acts as an implementer, developer and innovator simultaneously.'

The Center quickly deployed the global SWP framework into new sectors that needed assistance. Today, PepsiCo operations in rapidly emerging countries such as Brazil, Mexico, China, India, Russia and Turkey, and in developed countries including Spain, the UK and other countries in Western Europe, have successfully implemented strategic workforce planning.

Asked what he learnt as both a sector leader and now the global leader, Jason pauses, to consider the vast landscape ahead of him.

'One thing we learnt is sponsorship from very senior leaders, both business executives and local HR leaders. It is crucial to have their support to drive sustainable implementation of strategic workforce plans. When we have this support, we get traction. When we don't, the plan stalls.'

Figure 9.8 PepsiCo Center of Excellence strategic workforce planning stages

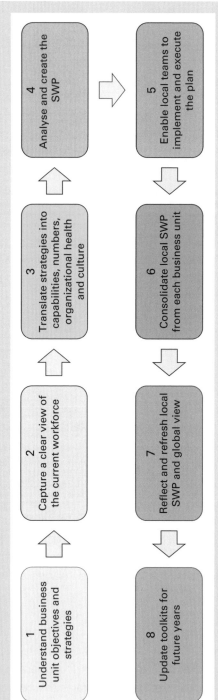

1 Understand business unit objectives and strategies

2 Capture a clear view of the current workforce

3 Translate strategies into capabilities, numbers, organizational health and culture

4 Analyse and create the SWP

5 Enable local teams to implement and execute the plan

6 Consolidate local SWP from each business unit

7 Reflect and refresh local SWP and global view

8 Update toolkits for future years

Today, PepsiCo's strategic workforce plans continue to attract the attention of the Chief Human Resources Officers and General Managers across sectors. It is the harmony between the Center and the sector that gives the people analytics team the edge.

> **TOP TIP**
>
> Build globally, enable and evolve locally – don't 'throw it over the fence'.

Summary

If an organization wants to realize sustainable and long-term value for people analytics, then it has to create a data-driven culture across the entire human resources function. These are some of the steps the chief human resources officer and head of people analytics can take together to achieve this:

- Create a platform of belief in analytics through communicating and demonstrating the value of people analytics itself.
- Invest in education and learning to develop HR professionals in skills needed for the future.
- Develop tools and activities that will engage people in analytics at all levels across the breadth of the HR function.
- Allow HR professionals to learn skills while working on real business challenges.
- Encourage a mindset shift to a data-driven way of working and reinforce it through clear and consistent communications.

References

Aon (2019) 2019 Intangible Assets Financial Statement Impact Comparison Report [Report] Available from: https://www.aon.com/getmedia/60fbb49a-c7a5-4027-ba98-0553b29dc89f/Ponemon-Report-V24.aspx (archived at https://perma.cc/V8Q7-WRZR) [Last accessed 7 February 2021]

Díaz, A, Rowshankish, K and Saleh, T (2018) Why data culture matters, *McKinsey Quarterly*, 6 September. Available from: https://www.mckinsey.com/business-functions/mckinsey-analytics/our-insights/why-data-culture-matters (archived at https://perma.cc/27T3-BEXY) [Last accessed 7 February 2021]

Duhigg, C (2016) What Google learned from its quest to build the perfect team, *The New York Times Magazine*, 25 February. Available from: https://www.nytimes.com/2016/02/28/magazine/what-google-learned-from-its-quest-to-build-the-perfect-team.html (archived at https://perma.cc/9H6R-97GH) [Last accessed 7 February 2021]

Evolution Culture (2019) 4 Stages of competence [Blog] 11 November. Available from: https://www.evolutionculture.co.uk/4-stages-of-competence/ (archived at https://perma.cc/7UJW-5YHQ) [Last accessed 7 February 2021]

Green, D (2019) Six factors for the adoption of people analytics [Blog] myHRfuture, 28 June. Available from: https://www.myhrfuture.com/blog/2019/6/28/six-factors-influencing-the- adoption-of-people-analytics (archived at https://perma.cc/Z368-ZF7F) [Last accessed 7 February 2021]

Guenole, N and Feinzig, S L (2018) How to develop a data-savvy HR department, *Harvard Business Review*, 11 October. Available from: https://hbr.org/2018/10/how-to-develop-a-data-savvy-hr-department (archived at https://perma.cc/ECG8-GF8U) [Last accessed 7 February 2021]

Kahn, W A (1990) Psychological conditions of personal engagement and disengagement at work, *Academy of Management Journal*, 33 (4), pp 692–724

Keunen, A, Wiedenhof, T and Wiertz, M (2020) How Rabobank uses continuous listening to understand employee sentiment during COVID-19 [Blog] myHRfuture, 13 May. Available from: https://www.myhrfuture.com/blog/2020/5/12/how-rabobank-uses-continuous-listening-to-understand-employee-sentiment-during-covid-19 (archived at https://perma.cc/5D8J-TVS8) [Last accessed 7 February 2021]

Nussbaumer Knaflic, C (2015) *Storytelling with Data: A data visualization guide for business professionals*, Wiley, New York, NY

re:Work (2016) Guide: Understand team effectiveness [Online] Available from: https://rework.withgoogle.com/print/guides/5721312655835136/ (archived at https://perma.cc/3TCC-M7XY) [Last accessed 7 February 2021]

Tarulli, B and DeLuca, D (2019) Evolving the strategic workforce planning strategy at PepsiCo, SHRM Executive Network, *People + Strategy*, Fall. Available from: www.hrps.org/resources/people-strategy-journal/Fall2019/Pages/tarulli-deluca-feature.aspx (archived at https://perma.cc/Z3GJ-RFEU) [Last accessed 3 April 2020]

Notes

1 This research was undertaken by Eleni Zarkada as part of her MSc in International Human Resources Management at University of Edinburgh Business School. Her thesis, *Reasons why some HR professionals are resistant to People Analytics and how they can build their People Analytics expertise* was sponsored by Insight222 Limited. Eleni was awarded a distinction for her MSc. The authors would like to thank her again for the dedication she showed in 2019 in conducting this research.

2 Merck KGaA is a German multinational science and technology company headquartered in Darmstadt, Germany. Its majority owners are still the descendants of the founder. Founded in 1668, it has more than 56,000 employees across 66 countries as of 2020 (see https://www.merckgroup.com/en/company.html (archived at https://perma.cc/G633-TG4U), last accessed 7 February 2021).

3 See Glossary: Cost-based workforce planning. The activities of workforce planning, whether strategic, operational or tactical, that focus on the cost of labour and its associated impact on an organization.

4 See Glossary: Skills-based workforce planning. The activities of workforce planning, whether strategic, operational or tactical, that focus on the skills of labour required in the future to deliver organizational outcomes.

5 MS Excel is a spreadsheet application. It features calculation, graphing tools, pivot tables and a macro programming language called Visual Basic for Applications. It is a product of Microsoft Corporation and one of the most fundamental tools for any progressive business professional to master.

6 myHRfuture is a learning platform for HR professionals. It provides over 800 pieces of content related to the topics of analytics, digital and the 'future of work'.

7 Rabobank is a Dutch multinational banking and financial services company headquartered in Utrecht, Netherlands. It is a global leader in food and agriculture financing and sustainability-oriented banking (see https://www.rabobank.com/en/about-rabobank/profile/index.html (archived at https://perma.cc/63QB-NKQ3), last accessed 7 February 2021).

8 PepsiCo is a US multinational food, snack and beverage corporation founded in 1898 and headquartered in Purchase, New York. In 2018 it had an annual revenue of more than $64 billion and a workforce of more than 260,000 people (see https://www.pepsico.com/about/about-the-company (archived at https://perma.cc/L2VV-HYZ4), last accessed 7 February 2021).

PART THREE
The next steps for people analytics

Transforming people analytics

What should I do next?

Whenever we talk with business executives, human resources leaders or people analytics practitioners and discuss the Nine Dimensions outlined in this book, we are always asked this question: What should I do next?

Whether the company is making its first inroads into people analytics, is well established or is a pioneer, leaders and executives are keen to understand what they should do to deliver more value and create impact. In reality, this means that they want to focus on the next steps.

The Nine Dimensions model offers a plethora of opportunities, and to some, the number of options available could seem quite daunting. In this situation, with any organization, a deep diagnosis of the current state of people analytics would certainly be sensible. This is something that we have undertaken numerous times to help organizations get started with the next steps. Consequently, what we see is that invariably many people want to get to the 'quick fix' with their questions:

- What are the next actions I should take?
- What are the main topics to consider?
- How can I create more value?
- What additional impact can we make using people analytics?
- What should I focus on in the next year?

Our advice is to adopt a 'business-first' approach (see Figure 10.1) with the following three actions:

1 Connect with business stakeholders.
2 Prioritize to find 'Quick Wins' and 'Big Bets'.
3 Define the ambition of people analytics.

Figure 10.1 Adopt a 'business-first' approach with three steps

Adopt a 'business-first' approach

1. Connect with business stakeholders
Engage with business leaders and executives from across your organization. Understand their business. Learn about their priorities. Listen to what their goals, opportunities and challenges are. Discuss what people analytics can do to help them achieve their goals.

2. Prioritize to find 'Quick Wins' and 'Big Bets'
Build a prioritization model that is dynamic and flexible. Define criteria. Engage stakeholders, especially human resources executives as the model, and the criteria, are developed. Look for high-impact 'Quick Wins' and 'Big Bets'.

3. Define the ambition of people analytics
Understand the ambition of the people analytics team. Engage a range of stakeholders and analytics experts in defining the ambition. Set a clear goal and mission, and create a brand for the function.

Let's discuss each of these, in turn, and highlight the most important aspects to boost confidence for each step.

Connect with business stakeholders

If there is only one action for a people analytics leader to undertake – this is it.

Above everything else, listen to and talk with business stakeholders. Whatever level of experience, and whatever the ambition, listening to business executives will be extremely valuable.

We talk about the types of stakeholders in Chapter 3 (Stakeholder Management) and the general process of mapping stakeholders and approaching them. We recommend starting with business leaders above all other stakeholders.

These are the people who are accountable for delivering the primary goals of the business. They understand the marketplace and are aware of the customer, competition, opportunities, sales, marketing, research, development, product innovation, finance, compliance and people. The closer a business executive is to what a company produces, sells or delivers, the better they will understand how to convert the corporate strategy into business operations.

Business executives are the people who think most about how to improve their company's performance – and these are the people who will be thinking about what they can do to improve their team's performance too. They will provide a real understanding of the business and what is needed in both the short and long term. They will be willing to explore and talk about their challenges, opportunities, beliefs and opinions of what needs to be done to improve their business operations. They will, in short, help the people analytics leader to understand 'what keeps them awake at night!'

Here are some examples of topics that we have come across during our research:

- Productivity: 'How can we improve the productivity of my development staff? I have over 2,000 people, and they are involved in compliance-related activity and other business process topics every week. We could turn their attention more to product development while becoming more efficient in other business activities such as compliance. I'd like to understand what we could do.'

- Market competitiveness: 'I would like to get ahead of the market by diverting a portion of my hiring budget to future-focused skills, rather than using all my hiring budget just to replace people who have left this year. If we could work out the most important skills needed in the future and what skills exist in our core markets, maybe we could predict the amount of budget to focus on hiring for the future, with confidence.'

- Culture: 'How can we understand what people think about the company, in real time, to allow us to make micro-adjustments daily, weekly and monthly, to move towards the new culture we need to compete in future years?'

- Real estate: 'How has the pandemic changed our approach to remote working? Which of our offices are needed in the next five years, based on home-working patterns, cost of office space, skills available in the marketplace and our customer demographics, based on our product life cycles and new product launches? Let's look at our real estate through multiple lenses rather than just through a financial lens.'

- Sales: 'What is the perfect profile of our sales associates, based on skills, behaviours and relationships, rather than just sales territory strategies and incentive plans? How can we use this to improve our customer conversion, share of wallet and customer retention rates?'

Once business executives are engaged, it's important to reprioritize the people analytics agenda.

One conversation relating to this, in particular, is included in the case study, Business stakeholders are critical for success: Syngenta, in Chapter 3 (Stakeholder Management). In the case study, we learn how Madhura Chakrabarti used conversations with business stakeholders to significantly develop her people analytics road map, alongside input she had gained previously from her other, mostly HR, stakeholders. When Madhura presented the road map to the HR leadership team (HRLT), she found that the team agreed with the new ideas and topics from the business stakeholders. She gained the HRLT's buy-in for the strategy and these priority topics, and they were consequently very excited to invest in the people analytics function.

The people analytics road map was focused on the business agenda, with input from both business leaders and HR executives. This made Madhura's journey going forward a lot smoother as she built the function. As she advises in the case study: 'Be courageous when talking with senior executives.'

This message is clear – build plans based on what the business requires and needs. Engaging with business stakeholders is the most important part of the next steps for transforming people analytics.

Prioritize to find 'Quick Wins' and 'Big Bets'

With a portfolio of many projects and constant new requests from human resources executives, it is no surprise that many people analytics leaders are reluctant to speak with more stakeholders – especially business stakeholders they don't know. They fear that it will increase expectations and mean they risk delivering even less. Worse still, they fear that they may damage the reputation of the people analytics function by overpromising and underdelivering. Some also fear their own credibility will be damaged.

Our advice is to meet with those stakeholders and gather inputs for important projects. To do this, people analytics leaders will need to be skilful at prioritizing the options. We have laid out the techniques for prioritization in Chapter 2 (Methodology), which describes a solid approach to criteria-based prioritization.

Furthermore, we suggest involving stakeholders in the process of prioritization. We have seen that prioritization fails to meet expectations when a prioritized list is delivered as a 'fait accompli'.

We notice that it is very tempting – and even more so for a leader with an analytical background – to manage prioritization without involving others.

It is an interesting exercise, one that can be undertaken with a spreadsheet and a curious mind. In simple terms, building a prioritization matrix is a reasonably straightforward analytical activity.

However, doing this without involving stakeholders is a mistake. Every executive will claim that the criteria are flawed and that their idea, their project or their work is still the most important.

At large multinational banks, global pharmaceutical companies, Fortune 100 technology firms and dozens of other companies, the answer is the same: Make the prioritization methodology available to everyone to inspect and discuss. Make it transparent.

We remember one large European company, where the chief human resources officer didn't like 'their' project being labelled as a Pet Project like those described in Chapter 2 (Methodology). They just did not want to accept it. So, the people analytics leader was left with no option but to take on a full plate of significant work, and also reluctantly take this extra lower-impact project. It was hard to do everything, but it was even harder to motivate the team to do the work, knowing that this particular 'CHRO project' was complex and of lower potential value than other work. The problem lay in not being open and transparent about the prioritization process, up front.

In one other global technology organization, the prioritization process – including selecting the correct criteria and sharing these with senior executives and other stakeholders – took three months. But it was worth it. The HRLT, in particular, were engaged and 'bought in' to the process. They started making suggestions for how to make the process of prioritization dynamic. How could they use it on an ongoing basis to check the validity of existing work through a project's life cycle and ensure that new requests for work were treated with the same rigour of prioritization? All of this made the people analytics leader more confident when asking for investment to deliver the 'agreed upon priorities'.

With all this attention on the process of prioritization, we are often asked: Why place such a high focus on it? And why undertake it in such a precise and rigorous manner?

Our response is that it creates three simultaneous advantages for the people analytics leader:

1 It provides the most objective way to select the highest-impact work.

2 It delivers the most effective vehicle to create an investment case for skills, technology or data.

3 It allows a productive evidence-based conversation for low-value 'Trivial Endeavours' or 'Pet Projects' to be deprioritized.

Prioritization, when conducted well, is an important way for the people analytics function to gain credibility, make an impact and deliver high-value work that will be meaningful to the organization overall.

Define the ambition of people analytics

As Marcus Aurelius is quoted as having said: 'A man's worth is no greater than his ambitions.'

It is true of the people analytics team, too. Defining the ambition of the team is an important step to determine the level of desire. In our work with people analytics and human resources teams, we find that those who have clear ambitions for analytics deliver more value.

The ambition should be distilled from conversations about 'desire' in particular from the following: the chief human resources officer, the people analytics leader, the HR leadership team and key members of the people analytics team. All other stakeholders typically are either 'internal clients' (such as business leaders) or enablers of success (such as technology and finance teams).

As part of the ambition, we recommend cementing the ambition of people analytics with a clear brand and mission, which were addressed in Chapter 1 (Governance) and the case study, Credibility begins with a clear brand: Trimble. Defining the ambition and then realizing that ambition means even a relatively small people analytics team can provide significant value to their organization.

Finally, we advocate for communicating the ambition, goals and, in particular, ethical standards for people data (see the case study, Ethics, ethics, ethics: Lloyds Banking Group in Chapter 1 – Governance) broadly. This should be communicated to stakeholders including business executives, managers, employees and colleagues in other functions.

Lastly, communicate! Enlist the support and sponsorship of the CHRO to communicate the mission of people analytics broadly across the human resources function globally. Provide the team with momentum by making the ambition widely known.

This creates a solid platform for communicating the success of projects as they materialize to generate benefits that can be enjoyed by the entire workforce.

In summary, when asked the question 'What should I do next?' we believe the most important steps are to engage business stakeholders, provide transparency in prioritization and communicate the ambition for people analytics. The rest is just 'work'.

 **CASE STUDY**

Transformation in practice: Allstate

The Allstate Corporation[1] (Allstate) has been undertaking people analytics for a long time, and in 2019, the HR organization decided it had been underutilized: People Analytics would have to transform and step into the light.

Of all the companies that we researched and worked with while writing this book, Allstate is the best example of a team that seized the opportunity for transformation and aligned that transformation with business strategy to such an effect that they were able to make a significant change in a short time. Their story is one that will be helpful to many others.

Know why you are transforming

When you think about an insurance company and all of the pricing, the modelling and the analytical capability required to simply run the business, it's extraordinary. Allstate has a long history of using data and CEO Tom Wilson 'believes he is not running an insurance company per se, but a data and technology company' (Morgan, 2019).

The question is: how does that capability translate and take root across the rest of the business, especially in a particularly people-centric human resources function? In 2019, Jesse Moquin, Strategic Workforce Planning Director, Rudy Gezik, Workforce Insights Director and their teams asked exactly this question.

At the time, Allstate had an established complement of people analytics staples: an engagement survey, some links to stakeholders, decent reporting, skilled HRBPs and strategic workforce planning. Allstate even had some employees dedicated full time to people analytics. It was a company like many others: it was 'doing people analytics', but the function was underutilized. There was a real need for change and more significant business impact.

Jesse and Rudy can't point to a single moment that triggered a 'we need to do people analytics better!' transformation. There was no epiphany. Allstate as a business was performing well; there was no particular burning platform. But there were some obvious signs that change was needed: its data-driven CEO wanted employees to be treated as well as customers, and HR leadership had invested heavily in digital transformation, data, technology and people analytics.

'The clients that we serve are all Allstate business clients, and they expect us to be as business-driven and data-driven as they are,' says Rudy.

'We all knew how important it was that HR should become more data-driven and that people analytics should deliver more value. Everyone was trying, but something just wasn't clicking,' Jesse reflects. 'We couldn't put our finger on one specific reason why, we had just reached a ceiling in terms of impact.'

However, Carrie Blair's arrival as Executive Vice President and Chief Human Resources Officer solidified the focus needed. In the latter months of 2019, it became clear that Carrie and her HR leadership team wanted to transform HR and realize the data-driven vision for HR as a strategic business partner. This was reinforced on 19 December 2019 when Allstate announced a new strategic direction called the Transformative Growth Plan (Allstate Newsroom, 2019).

A phased approach to transformation

HR leadership initially wanted to start with a new operating model to deliver impact quickly through a reorganized team. However, Jesse and Rudy wanted to take a deeper approach and look end-to-end at the entire people analytics opportunity.

To do this, they decided to understand the business strategy first. They worked with Carrie, the rest of the HR leadership team and a range of senior stakeholders from across the business to then understand HR's role in Allstate's transformation. Putting this up front was key to interpreting the 'whys': why should we do people analytics, why is data important, why does people analytics exist within Allstate, why should we bother?

One person in the HR leadership team, in particular, was instrumental in helping drive the direction. Christy Harris, Senior Vice President of Talent Management, Employee Experience and Inclusive Diversity, had a passion for talent development and using data. For the next several months, Christy helped guide the process of the transformation of the people analytics function.

'We took on a phased approach under the guidance of external experts,' Christy explains. 'They brought a depth of knowledge of people analytics specifically, which allowed us to think through the transformation more holistically.'

The second phase of the transformation saw the team meet with stakeholders – lots of them – systematically. Using a stakeholder map similar to that shown in Chapter 3 (Stakeholder Management), the team

Figure 10.2 A phased approach to transformation at Allstate

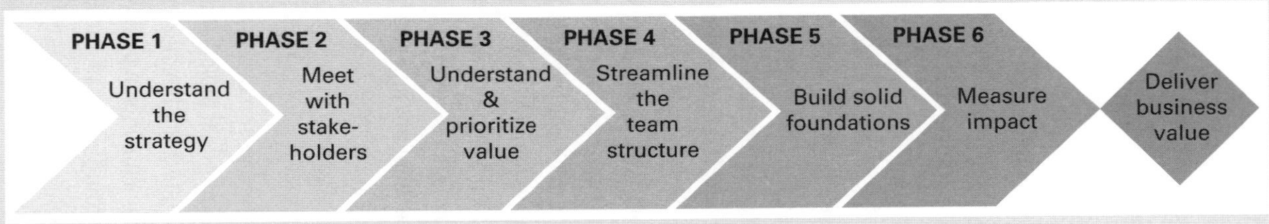

PHASE 1	PHASE 2	PHASE 3	PHASE 4	PHASE 5	PHASE 6
Understand the strategy	Meet with stake-holders	Understand & prioritize value	Streamline the team structure	Build solid foundations	Measure impact

Deliver business value

SOURCE Reproduced with kind permission of Allstate, October 2020

coordinated efforts to discuss challenges, problems and what each stakeholder wanted to achieve. Although it had already met with stakeholders before, the team decided they would meet again. Only one rule applied: 'This time, these conversations would not be about HR or people analytics,' Jesse explains. 'We wanted these discussions to be entirely focused on the stakeholders' business – fact-finding, listening and building trust. If we were going to understand how we could have an impact on their business, we needed to understand their business.' This outside-in approach led to a different understanding of stakeholders. 'We felt we had changed the narrative and could start to change how people analytics could deliver value to Allstate, better.'

The third phase of Allstate's transformation was a change in the understanding of value. The leaders decided to shift the culture of people analytics to be more outcomes-driven, not inputs-driven.

Jesse and Rudy realized they needed to focus on an effective method for prioritizing work and all the requests that they received into the various teams that made up what was to become the new people analytics team at Allstate.

'It's really easy to fall into the trap of being led by requests from the business and thinking that fast responses to ad-hoc projects are what's really going to make people think you are of value,' Jesse reflects. 'But we realized that if we were going to think "outcomes, business value, financial value", we needed to develop a rigorous way of assessing work coming in.' The team undertook a prioritization exercise to establish its approach to incoming work, data and technology, and established a complexity-impact model similar to that shown in Figure 2.2 over four weeks. This model was then presented to and discussed with the various stakeholders, including at an important meeting with the HR leadership team in March 2020.

The meeting was important because it was a moment where the focus moved to the most business-critical topics and what was needed to analyse these topics. It resulted in a business case being completed, which led to incremental investments in people analytics.

In the next phase – the fourth – Jesse and Rudy were able to properly implement an operating model that reflected the new goals. Up to this point, the people analytics function had been carried out by three teams that reported into three different leaders across Allstate: People Science, Workforce Insights and Strategic Workforce Planning (see Figure 10.3).

Each team was formed in a different period for different reasons and had different objectives. Yet they were all broadly trying to achieve the same goal: to use analytics and insights to guide leaders to make better people decisions. 'It was a case of great people doing great work, but all individually,' Rudy recalls. 'If we could row in the same direction, imagine how much more we would be able to accomplish.'

The leaders of the three teams plus critical technology leaders met for the first time in November 2019, on a chilly but sunny day in Illinois. Thereafter they met every week for several months. Inside the meeting room, the group of people who had rarely met came together and rallied around a single mission. Surrounded by flipcharts and passionate conversation, with sunlight flooding through the window, it was almost as though it was providing the energy for the change in momentum. 'When we realized the special things we could do as one team, one force, that was when we really got excited,' Jesse remembers.

It took several months to design the future people analytics function that would cater for the business needs and individual skill sets, but by the middle of 2020, the leaders formed one people analytics mission, strategy and road map – and their teams merged into one function.

Figure 10.3   Three siloed teams joined together into one unified front

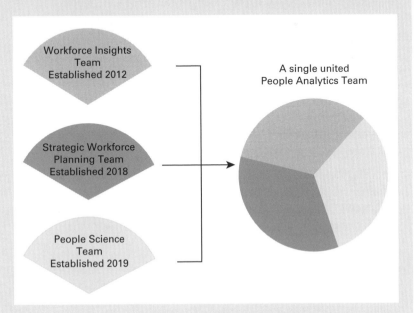

SOURCE Reproduced with kind permission of Allstate, October 2020

The fifth phase required the leaders to establish the foundations required to deliver real business value with people analytics. Many of the structural components that the team focused on are explored in this book, such as the governance structures and ethics charter described in Chapter 1 (Governance). The team partnered with people across enterprise analytics, legal, IT, finance and marketing to create its structures, ensuring alignment to the Transformative Growth Plan.

Finally, with its understanding of strategy, focus on business value, solid foundations and ability to prioritize and map outcomes, the team could start thinking about measuring return on investment (ROI) and impact. Jesse and Rudy remember this – differentiating between scorecards, metrics and actual impact – as the hardest part. 'Analytics reveals loads of cool stuff, but we had to be focused on the outcomes we were trying to drive and the business value we were trying to create,' Rudy explains.

'Ultimately, we are trying to use people analytics in a more intentional way. We want people analytics to be more valuable, more scalable and used further up the decision-making process than ever before,' says Jesse. This kind of shift hasn't been easy; the organization was not accustomed to using the function of people analytics at a strategic level. But in Allstate, having HR leadership declare people analytics a priority made a difference to linking to the business strategy more closely. In an effort to contribute to the Transformative Growth Plan, the team collaborated with finance to determine the value and financial benefits of analytics work. They knew they had to change from an organization based on people and processes into one based on business outcomes. And this is how people analytics is now set up to deliver increased value at Allstate.

Allstate is a prime example of a people analytics function in transformation. It was already delivering value, but it has ascended to a higher level of business impact. With the hard work of everyone in HR, it has unified three teams into a people analytics force, combining all of the strengths to deliver against a business-first, long-term strategy. It has established a range of robust structures on which to operate, including a clear leadership structure, a governance board of business executives, productive relationships with stakeholders and a charter for the ethical use of people data. It has also seen the team align around a new mission to deliver increased value through people analytics.

All of these moves have resulted in the function attracting more funding in internal investment and new people, including a full-time dedicated people analytics leader reporting directly to the CHRO, Carrie. James Gallman is that person.

'Joining an organization with such a great history of using data to make commercial decisions is so exciting,' James says. 'And it's fantastic to see that people analytics is already transforming, so we can focus on translating people data into business value.'

Everyone involved in people analytics at Allstate has a shared mission and clear strategic goals. They know they need to prove value on an ongoing basis, project by project, but they now have all the foundations and are confident they are structured in a way to achieve this.

References

Allstate Newsroom (2019) Allstate Announces Transformative Growth Plan [Press release] Available from: https://www.allstatenewsroom.com/news/allstate-announces-transformative-growth-plan/ (archived at https://perma.cc/QC94-GJKT) [Last accessed 7 February 2021]

Morgan, B (2019) Allstate is now a data and technology company – my CES interview with CEO Tom Wilson, Forbes, 10 January. Available from: https://www.forbes.com/sites/blakemorgan/2019/01/10/allstate-is-now-a-data-and-technology-company-my-ces-interview-with-ceo-tom-wilson/?sh=bf540a7665fe (archived at https://perma.cc/KA4F-84H8) [Last accessed 25 March 2021]

Note

1　The Allstate Corporation is a US-based insurance company headquartered in Northfield Township, Illinois, since 1967. Founded in 1931 as part of Sears, Roebuck and Co., it was spun off in 1993. Today the company offers 113 million proprietary policies through multiple brands and distribution channels, including auto, home and life insurance (see https://www.allstate.com/about.aspx?intcid=ILC-OurStory-141201:AllstateOverview (archived at https://perma.cc/6BGK-E7JM), last accessed 7 February 2021).

Epilogue: the future of people analytics

The case for people analytics is clear. Throughout this book, we have presented how people analytics can provide immense value to organizations and their workforces. Indeed, the work undertaken by people analytics teams has contributed millions of dollars to the top and bottom lines of a growing multitude of companies.

Therefore, it is not surprising that people analytics as a discipline continues to expand in importance, both in human resources and across the business world. It has significant room to grow. With a long and promising future, and much yet still to be discovered about its contribution to the human resources profession, predictions abound about how it will shape the future of business.

We have identified four themes that will drive the continued growth of people analytics and the value it provides to an increasingly diverse group of stakeholders, far beyond HR, in the coming years.

These themes are:

- The human experience of work.
- The CEO skills conundrum.
- Investor demands.
- Improving society.

The human experience of work

As discussed in Chapter 7 (Workforce Experiences), over the past decade, employee expectation for consumer-grade experiences at work that are meaningful, deeply personalized and digital has increased dramatically. Indeed, by the start of 2020, employee experience (EX) was recognized by HR professionals themselves as the top trend changing the way that organizations attract and retain talent (LinkedIn, 2020).

As data and analytics helped drive the growth of customer experience in the marketing function, so are people data and analytics key enablers in developing EX in the HR function.

Since providing recommendations for EX requires data to monitor employee 'touchpoints' and 'moments that matter', the people analytics function is hugely important. In essence, it's not possible to measure, personalize and improve the employee experience without analytics. When coupled with people analytics, employee experience can drive significant value for the business as well as the workforce.

While EX as an initiative may have been born in human resources, it now transcends the whole business, with TI People's 2019 study concluding that 35 out of 36 critical employee touchpoints are owned by business functions other than HR (Jacobs, 2019). Therefore, to manage EX effectively, HR has to deploy people analytics and engage and involve line managers in concert with other functions such as IT, real estate, procurement, compliance and finance.

For human resources as a function, the shift from the 'one-size fits all' programmes of the past to a focus on delivering individual, personalized and relevant experiences to employees will enable human resources to become a strategic powerhouse (Smith and Cantrell, 2015). It will transform HR from being an arbiter of processes to a creator of offerings and experiences.

The CEO skills conundrum

Three-quarters of CEOs are concerned about the availability of key skills and how this could constrain them from acquiring, developing and retaining the talent they need to drive growth (Stubbings and Sethi, 2020). By 2025, it is estimated that 50 per cent of all employees will need to be reskilled with 97 million new jobs emerging and 85 million being displaced by a shift in labour between humans and machines (World Economic Forum, 2020).

The global pandemic further exacerbated this seismic disruption. Consequently, the increased pressure on organizations from remote work and dramatically reorganized supply chains further complicated the skills challenge beyond any scenario plan. According to Gartner (2020), this skills conundrum is the top priority for human resources leaders in The Age of Value.

People analytics teams are at the heart of the shift in focus from jobs to a much deeper analysis of skills, which is reshaping workforce planning and bringing skills, learning and careers together. In the research for this book, we discovered that almost all global people analytics organizations want to build a skills-based approach to workforce planning. But only a quarter of the companies we researched were actively doing so.

In organizations that have shifted towards a skills-based approach for workforce planning, people analytics teams are increasingly involved in inferring and creating value from employee skills data (McKinnon & Wornoo, 2020). Companies including IBM[1] (Bailie, 2020; Green, 2020), Unilever (Fleming, 2019), Schneider Electric (Anderson, 2020) and Johnson & Johnson (Hoffman and Kofford, 2020) are building cultures with a significant emphasis on skills. To achieve this, they have brought together HR programmes such as learning, career development and internal mobility, with skills data and technology that enables personalization and creates a thriving internal marketplace for talent (Gantcheva et al, 2020).

We expect this focus on analysing skills data to drive the personalization of learning and the development of talent marketplaces to be a primary focus for people analytics teams in the years ahead. If this is done well, it will go a long way towards solving the skills conundrum.

Investor demands

Boards of directors and company investors increasingly ask complex questions that end up on the people analytics leader's desk. Questions such as 'what is the value of our company's workforce?' and 'what is the return on investment on talent?' are inherently complex. People analytics has the opportunity to help investors and boards of directors transform human capital from only an intangible asset to one that can be measured.

A series of events have combined to create this momentum, as noted in David McCann's 2019 article 'Disclosing vital data about a company's workforce will soon be the norm'. A notable milestone came in December 2018, when the International Standards Organization (ISO) published their first set of human capital metrics standards (ISO 30414) (ISO, 2018; Naden, 2019), highlighting that with workforce costs making up to 70 per cent of an organization's expenditure: 'effective human resources (HR) strategies can have a positive impact on organizational performance.'

A second example pointing towards the widespread public disclosure by organizations of information relating to human capital came in August 2020, when the US Securities and Exchange Commission (SEC) mandated human capital disclosure by all companies selling securities in the United States (Vance, 2020). This rule came into effect from 9 November 2020.

It is not just regulators, compliance institutions or standards bodies that are driving the change either; companies are reassessing their purpose in the context of having a broader set of stakeholders. In August 2019, the Business Roundtable group of 180 of the largest organizations in the United States of America issued a statement redefining its purpose from a sole focus on shareholders to one that serves all stakeholders – consumers, employees, suppliers and communities – as well as shareholders (Business Roundtable, 2019).

These landmark shifts and the growing realization of the pivotal role an organization's people play in business success, which has only been accelerated by the crises of 2020, means that in the 2020s and beyond, all publicly listed companies will likely need to report on aspects of human capital that have previously not been necessary. The ramifications of this are numerous and will spark heightened interest from boards and investors about the value of people data, provide public information that will help differentiate companies, increase the discussion around privacy and security related to personal data, and further raise the people analytics team's profile and work.

Improving society

Additional regulations are coming into effect that are supporting societal topics such as equality. These currently manifest as, for example, statutory gender pay gap reporting in countries such as the United Kingdom, where companies with 250 employees or more are required to disclose data relating to gender pay (GOV.UK, 2020).

The rise of people analytics has coincided with an increasing expectation from employees and the broader population on companies to address topics around diversity, equality and inclusion that go beyond merely reporting numbers, statistics and trends. A growing number of companies such as Microsoft (McIntyre, 2020), PwC (Ryan *et al*, 2020),

Netflix (Myers, 2021), and Target (2020) publish annual diversity and inclusion reports that provide transparency around representation and the initiatives each company takes in these areas.

People analytics functions are increasingly becoming involved in these broader societal topics. For example, organizations have taken a pronounced interest in mental well-being in response to isolation and home-working driven by the global pandemic. The societal drive for equality has been significantly heightened by political activism and movements such as MeToo and Black Lives Matter that bring to the forefront the issues of sexual harassment and racial injustice, respectively.

People analytics can rise to these challenges because of the tools that are available. For example, teams can now measure homophily[2] with organizational network analysis technology (Arena, 2019). This allows organizations to address 'inclusion' as a bigger topic than what has typically been done in reporting 'diversity' to meet regulatory standards or legal compliance.

It is inspiring to see businesses, the human resources function and people analytics teams rise to these most critical and global missions, which extend beyond adding value directly to the organization.

The future of the function

The four themes discussed above are getting more attention from business leaders and chief human resources officers and are helping shape people analytics functions. Together they highlight the extent and magnitude of the work of people analytics teams.

The themes also provoke thinking around what this means for the future of the function of people analytics and its relationship and proximity to human resources. Business leaders and CHROs are now asking the following questions:

- Should the people analytics function report directly into the CHRO?

  In leading organizations, the answer is already 'yes'. Over the course of the research for this book, it has become clear that the people analytics function must have access to the CHRO to deliver value. However, this group constituted only a fifth of companies we researched during 2020 as part of writing this book. Reporting into the CHRO or, where that is not possible, having access to the CHRO, is imperative to delivering value from people analytics.

- Should the people analytics function report into an enterprise analytics function, and not into human resources at all?

Currently, this is the case only in very few companies. Our hypothesis for why this is the case is that the big topics are not just human resources topics. As outlined earlier in this chapter, these big themes extend far beyond the function and responsibilities of human resources. Thus a collaborative effort with multiple parts of the business is required to solve them. Having people analytics embedded in a broader enterprise analytics function may be key to this.

- If the entire HR function becomes data literate, will a defined people analytics function be needed at all?

As future HR professionals become more analytically savvy and data literate due to the importance of analytics at graduate and postgraduate levels, it calls into question whether quantitative and qualitative analytics will become a core function of every HR professional. If so, it changes the skill set of the entire human resources function itself, and in this scenario, it is highly likely that a specific people analytics function will not be needed at all except in the most complex and advanced activities when using super-advanced statistical analysis and cognitive computing technologies.

These questions lead us to wonder: What do leaders of this profession think is going to happen? Where is the future of people analytics?

In considering this, we talked to several expert leaders in people analytics functions around the world. Given its innovative culture, we consider Uber and its Global People Analytics Leader, RJ Milnor, as a case study of how the future of people analytics may develop.

 CASE STUDY

The future of people analytics: Uber

Uber Technologies, Inc ('Uber')[3] continues to revolutionize the taxi industry in more than 10,000 cities worldwide. It is one of the 'titans of the technology sector thanks to its much-needed disruption of the taxi sector since 2009, two years after the arrival of the iPhone' (Dans, 2019). Uber's Global People Analytics Leader, RJ Milnor, began his career in investment banking, where he discovered the impact of talent on profitability and shareholder return. RJ has since spent almost two decades using data-driven strategies to improve and measure organizational performance and delivered value through people data at companies including McKesson and Chevron.

'My team delivers business impact through Uber's people. We do this by providing the data-driven insights, research and products that ignite opportunity, improve productivity and increase engagement and well-being across the company. We have a dual mandate to drive better outcomes for the business and employees by leveraging people and other types of data.

I'm continually thinking about how to use data to innovate at Uber and, to do this, how the people analytics field itself must change and develop in the future. One question always floats to the surface: what will become of people analytics?

I don't mean what work we will do – there is always something! – but rather, where will the people analytics skill set and purpose evolve in the wider business? Will "people analytics" become HR? Will all HR professionals understand HR data and analytics so well that one day HR "is" people analytics? Will "people analytics" remain a separate centre of excellence within HR? Or do we merge with an enterprise analytics organization and leave HR altogether?

The people analytics field must broaden its view. We have to use data beyond just people or HR data in order to deliver actionable insights and recommendations that enable both our business and our employees to succeed. If we think about workforce planning and location strategy and budget planning; all these things come together. People analytics at its best isn't just about HR data. It's really integrating all types of data in a way that benefits the business and therefore benefits our employees in a more holistic way. It's a dual mandate: people analytics drives the business forward and helps our employees continually excel and reach their full potential.

HR professionals will undoubtedly become more analytical. The future of the whole HR function is rooted in data. Considering the exponential growth in the availability of data, computing power and accessibility to more advanced statistical analysis, HR must embrace data to stay relevant.

So many of my conversations today are about building the HR function to be more data and digitally literate. There's often an assumption that the people analytics team stays within its own silo, developing its own staff surrounded by walls of high-tech and data. But that is a mistake. In practice, people analytics practitioners have a responsibility to engage deeply with our HR functions, educate them about data and technology, and build analytical acumen across our teams. A data mindset in HR is no longer a competitive differentiator, it's quickly becoming table stakes. Our HR colleagues require these data and analytical skills to interpret the work of people analytics and extend our solutions into the business.

Undertaking this dual mandate has been central to how we at Uber have delivered, and plan to deliver, value. For example, in workforce planning, we have facilitated collaboration between Learning and Development and the workforce planning teams by providing them with a common currency and language around skills for the organization, enabling their work with data, analytics and technology, and helping them learn these skills at the same time.

Historical evidence over the last 20 years certainly points to the notion that executives who bring data and analytics have become more influential in driving organizational strategy. Irrespective of how the discipline of people analytics develops, one of our most critical roles over the next few years is to help the business unlock even greater value by providing HR executives with a more data-driven voice.

To bring this to life at Uber, we are focusing on big-ticket topics such as productivity at the employee and team levels, the well-being of all of our people, and the inclusion needed in our workforce, community and society that will enable our company and people to succeed. As a leader of people analytics, this is the work that really "gets us out of bed": it's big, it's complex, it's innovative, it's disruptive. More than anything, it is purposeful.

Though the innovations and structures that will define our field are yet to emerge, our mandate is clear: people analytics exists to deliver value.'

References

Anderson, B (2020) 6 Tactics Schneider Electric used to amp up internal mobility [Blog] LinkedIn Talent Solutions, 26 May. Available from: https://business. linkedin.com/talent-solutions/blog/internal-mobility/2020/schneider-electric-internal-mobility (archived at https://perma.cc/2RLY-JZ2Q) [Last accessed 7 February 2021]

Arena, M (2019) Diversity at the core of the network, HR Exchange Network, 18 September. Available from: https://www.hrexchangenetwork.com/people-analytics/columns/diversity-at-the-core-of-the-network (archived at https:// perma.cc/79RG-622U) [Last accessed 7 February 2021]

Bailie, I (2020) How does IBM use AI and analytics to measure employee skillsets? myHRfuture, 17 September. Available from: https://www.myhrfuture.com/ blog/2020/9/17/how-does-ibm-use-ai-and-analytics-to-measure-employee-skillsets (archived at https://perma.cc/KZX4-YT3X) [Last accessed 7 February 2021]

Business Roundtable (2019) Business Roundtable redefines the purpose of a corporation to promote 'an economy that serves all Americans' [Blog] 19 August. Available from: https://www.businessroundtable.org/business-roundtable-redefines-the-purpose-of-a-corporation-to-promote-an-economy-that-serves-all-americans (archived at https://perma.cc/2P7Y-NGFS) [Last accessed 7 February 2021]

Dans, E (2019) There are tech companies and then there are uber-tech companies…, *Forbes*, 12 April. Available from: https://www.forbes.com/sites/enriquedans/2019/04/12/there-are-tech-companies-and-then-there-are-uber-tech-companies/?sh=61471d3d4be6 (archived at https://perma.cc/TVU7-KKJ2) [Last accessed 7 February 2021]

Fleming, M (2019) How Unilever is using AI to 'democratise' upskilling and future-proof its employees, *Marketing Week*, 27 June. Available from: https://www.marketingweek.com/how-unilever-is-using-ai-to-democratise-upskilling-and-future-proof-its-employees/ (archived at https://perma.cc/5C6B-STA3) [Last accessed 7 February 2021]

Gantcheva, I, Jones, R, Kearns-Manolatos, D, Schwartz, J, Lee, L and Rawat, M (2020) Activating the internal talent marketplace, Deloitte Insights, 18 September. Available from: https://www2.deloitte.com/us/en/insights/focus/technology-and-the-future-of-work/internal-talent-marketplace.html/ (archived at https://perma.cc/4PVU-LYB5) [Last accessed 7 February 2021]

Gartner (2020) Top 5 Priorities for HR Leaders in 2021 [Report] Available from: https://emtemp.gcom.cloud/ngw/globalassets/en/human-resources/documents/trends/top-priorities-for-hr-leaders-2021.pdf (archived at https://perma.cc/DC59-KHP2) [Last accessed 7 February 2021]

GOV.UK (2020) Gender pay gap reporting, 14 December 2020. Available from: https://www.gov.uk/government/collections/gender-pay-gap-reporting (archived at https://perma.cc/32EB-YL87) [Last accessed 7 February 2021]

Green, D (2020) How IBM is reinventing HR with AI and people analytics, with Diane Gherson, former Chief HR Officer at IBM [Podcast] Digital HR Leaders, 8 September. Available from: https://www.myhrfuture.com/digital-hr-leaders-podcast/2020/9/8/how-ibm-is-reinventing-hr-with-ai-and-people-analytics (archived at https://perma.cc/3BJN-BZKJ) [Last accessed 7 February 2021]

Hoffman, M and Kofford, C (2020) How we're applying data science to unlock human potential [Blog] Johnson & Johnson, 4 March. Available from: https://www.careers.jnj.com/careers/how-were-applying-data-science-to-unlock-human-potential (archived at https://perma.cc/443X-AN5B) [Last accessed 7 February 2021]

ISO (2018) ISO 30414:2018 Human resource management – guidelines for internal and external human capital reporting, ISO, 1 December. Available from: https://www.iso.org/standard/69338.html (archived at https://perma.cc/E6TF-6AMK) [Last accessed 7 February 2021]

Jacobs, V (2019) The state of employee experience 2019 [Blog] TI People, 5 December. Available at: https://www.ti-people.com/what-is-the-state-of-ex-in-2019 (archived at https://perma.cc/7W2T-CKJK) [Last accessed 7 February 2021]

LinkedIn (2020) Global Talent Trends 2020 [Report] Available at: https://business. linkedin.com/talent-solutions/recruiting-tips/global-talent-trends-2020 (archived at https://perma.cc/F57L-6KGD) [Last accessed 7 February 2021]

McCann, D (2019) Human capital's big reveal, *CFO Magazine*, September 11. Available from: https://www.cfo.com/human-capital-careers/2019/09/human-capitals-big-reveal/ (archived at https://perma.cc/C6A3-DLXE) [Last accessed 7 February 2021]

McIntyre, L (2020) Microsoft's 2020 Diversity and Inclusion Report [Report] Available from: https://query.prod.cms.rt.microsoft.com/cms/api/am/binary/RE4H2f8 (archived at https://perma.cc/98MH-JBMF) [Last accessed 7 February 2021]

McKinnon, A and Wornoo, M (2020) The value of measuring employee skill data, myHRfuture, 25 November. Available from: https://www.myhrfuture.com/ blog/2020/11/24/the-value-of-measuring-employee-skill-data (archived at https://perma.cc/6K49-DW52) [Last accessed 7 February 2021]

Myers, V (2021) Inclusion Takes Root at Netflix: Our First Report [Report] Available from: https://about.netflix.com/en/news/netflix-inclusion-report-2021 (archived at https://perma.cc/L5GM-38LH) [Last accessed 7 February 2021]

Naden, C (2019) New ISO International Standard for human capital reporting, ISO, 15 January. Available from: https://www.iso.org/news/ref2357.html (archived at https://perma.cc/YB4S-24UY) [Last accessed 7 February 2021]

Ryan, T, Schuyler, S and Fenlon, M (2020) Building on a culture of belonging: 2020 PwC Diversity & Inclusion Transparency Report [Report] Available from: https://www. pwc.com/us/en/about-us/diversity/assets/diversity-inclusion-transparency-report.pdf (archived at https://perma.cc/P3JP-VLHT) [Last accessed 7 February 2021]

Smith, D and Cantrell, S M (2015) Managing Your People as a Workforce of One [Report] Accenture Strategy

Stubbings, C and Sethi, B (2020) Upskilling: Building confidence in an uncertain world [Report] Available from: https://www.pwc.com/gx/en/ceo-agenda/ ceosurvey/2020/trends/talent.html (archived at https://perma.cc/X6QE-AKHA) [Last accessed 7 February 2021]

Target (2020) Workforce Diversity: Composition of governance bodies and employees as of fiscal year end 2019 [Report] Available at: https://corporate. target.com/_media/TargetCorp/csr/pdf/Target-Workforce-Diversity-Report_FY2019.pdf (archived at https://perma.cc/Y3SS-5F3C) [Last accessed 7 February 2021]

Vance, D (2020) The SEC just mandated human capital disclosure: what does this mean for you? [Blog] ChiefLearningOfficer.com, 5 November. Available from: https://www.chieflearningofficer.com/2020/11/05/the-sec-just-mandated-human-capital-disclosure-what-does-this-mean-for-you/ (archived at https://perma.cc/ MUU4-FZPH) [Last accessed 7 February 2021]

World Economic Forum (2020) The Future of Jobs Report 2020 [Report] Available from: https://www.weforum.org/reports/the-future-of-jobs-report-2020 (archived at https://perma.cc/RWK5-PXFW) [Last accessed 7 February 2021]

Notes

1 Scaling analytics for value: IBM, case study, Chapter 8 (Business Outcomes)
2 See Glossary: Homophily. The tendency for people to seek out or be attracted to those who are similar to themselves. Often used in analytics related to investigating diversity and inclusion topics.
3 Founded in March 2009, Uber Technologies, Inc, commonly known as Uber, is a US company offering vehicles for hire, food delivery, package delivery, couriers, freight transportation, and electric bicycle and motorized scooter rental. Uber's 91 million monthly active platform consumers are served by almost 4 million drivers and 22,000 employees across 63 countries (see https://www.uber.com/en-GB/newsroom/company-info/ (archived at https://perma.cc/PP9S-2WA8), last accessed 7 February 2021).

Concluding remarks

People analytics is 'coming of age'.[1]

Over the last few decades, the field has transcended from focusing on topics such as employee engagement, with a handful of behavioural psychologists analysing data in a department within HR, to be central to the handling of the worst global pandemic in a century, helping chief executive officers and chief human resources officers manage complex decisions every day of every week.

It has progressed through The Ages of Discovery, Realization and Innovation to emerge in The Age of Value – ready to deliver outcomes to the workforce, human resources function, business stakeholders and society.

In The Age of Value, organizations, human resources functions, the CHROs who lead those functions and business executives, in general, would be well advised to learn how workforce data can deliver the value that has been quantified by many – including Shook, Knickrehm and Sage-Gavin (2019), who estimated the additional value from untapped workforce data to be US $3.1 trillion.

Once value from people analytics is accepted and delivered – at scale, repeatedly, across the business as a whole, globally – then people analytics will move into The Age of Excellence. The people analytics leader in every organization will need to use their skills to unlock this potential to get there.

Leaders who take a 'business-first' approach and work with a range of stakeholders across key functions and directly with business executives will ensure people analytics activities are aligned to the most critical topics across the enterprise. In any organization, once this happens, value is unlocked and everyone wins.

Employees and workers benefit. The company realizes value. The human resources function itself becomes more data literate. And wider society benefits.

Throughout this book, we have discussed and summarized 'Nine Dimensions' to attain excellence. By focusing on each of these, the function and activities of people analytics deliver value and become an asset to the company and the employees, workers and customers that it serves.

Figure 10.4   DRIVE: Five Ages of People Analytics

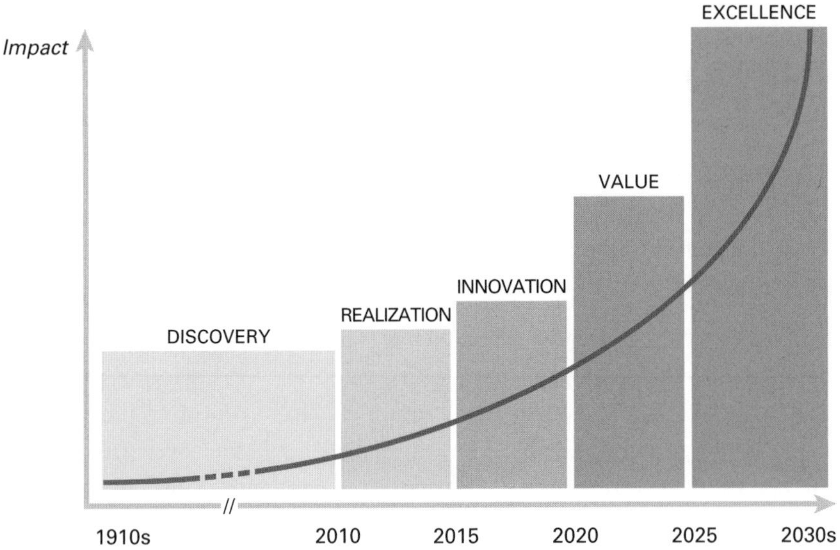

When the full power of people analytics is embedded in the fabric of the organization from the board of directors down, and when it is part of the culture of all human resources work, that is when we will achieve 'Excellence in People Analytics'.

Reference

Shook, Knickrehm and Sage-Gavin (2019) Decoding Organizational DNA: Trust, data and unlocking value in the digital workplace [Report] Accenture. Available from: https://www.accenture.com/gb-en/insights/future-workforce/workforce-data-organizational-dna (archived at https://perma.cc/V625-TN79) [Last accessed 7 February 2021]

Note

1   'Coming of age' is a term used to describe the transition between childhood and adulthood.

GLOSSARY

active (data collection) Collection of people data through 'active' mechanisms such as surveys and wearables. It is active because the employee is involved in order for the data to be collected. The opposite of active data collection is passive data collection.

advanced analytics Sophisticated analytical methods and tools that enable organizations to derive deep insights from data, make predictions and formulate recommendations. Sometimes this includes artificial intelligence, machine learning and cognitive computing.

Agile A collection of software and project development techniques and approaches under which solutions evolve through the collaborative effort of cross-functional teams and their end users.

algorithm A step-by-step set of rules to follow in calculations to meet analytical objectives such as prediction or classification.

analytics dashboards Dashboards that are derived through the use of analytics methodologies. In the context of people analytics, this refers to Second Wave systems (see Chapter 5 – Technology). See also **dashboards**.

application programming interface (API) A set of definitions, protocols and tools for building software applications, and for allowing software components from different sources to communicate with each other.

artificial intelligence (AI) The programming of machines to perform specific tasks normally requiring human intelligence, such as visual and speech recognition, decision making and language translation.

Big Bet A project that is of high impact and high complexity (see **Complexity-Impact Matrix**).

Big Brother Originating from George Orwell's novel *Nineteen Eighty-Four*, to signify the theme of continuous oppressive surveillance. This has led to its widespread use today to indicate a person, organization or government exercising total control and surveillance over people's lives.

Big Data Datasets of structured and unstructured information that are so large and complex that they cannot be adequately processed and analysed with traditional data tools and applications.

board of people analytics A steering group that meets to provide direction and enablement for the people analytics function.

burning platform Term used to describe the process of helping people see the consequences of not changing. By sparking just enough concern about what happens if the status quo remains the same, people begin to embrace change.

business acumen A keenness and agility in understanding, interpreting and dealing with business situations.

causality The effect of one variable on another (cause and effect). Two variables have a causal relationship if changes in one variable produce changes in the other.

centre of excellence (CoE) A team or entity that provides leadership, best practices, research, support and training for a focus area. Often refers to functions in human resources with expertise in specialist areas such as learning, talent acquisition, reward, etc.

change management The process, tools and techniques to manage the people side of change to achieve a required business outcome.

Chartered Institute for Personnel and Development (CIPD) A professional body for human resources and people development that has a worldwide community of members committed to championing better work and working lives. It is headquartered in London, United Kingdom.

chatbot An application that simulates and processes human conversation, either via voice or text, creating the impression for the user that communication is happening with a real person.

chief analytics officer The most senior person in an organization responsible for all analytics across the enterprise. Sometimes combined with the role of chief data officer.

chief data officer (CDO) The most senior person in an organization (or function) responsible for overseeing all aspects of the strategies, policies, governance and management of data. Sometimes combined with the role of chief analytics officer.

chief executive officer (CEO) The most senior person in an organization responsible for the overall business strategy, operations and performance.

chief financial officer (CFO) The most senior person in an organization responsible for overseeing all aspects of financial and risk management.

chief human resources officer (CHRO) The most senior person in an organization responsible for overseeing all aspects of the strategies, policies, practices and operations of human resource management.

chief people officer Another term for the chief human resources officer.

chief privacy officer The most senior person in an organization responsible for data privacy. See also **data privacy** and **data privacy officer**.

cloud computing A type of internet-based technology in which different services (such as servers, storage and applications) are delivered to an organization's or an individual's computers and devices through the internet.

cognitive computing Systems that understand, learn and reason as they interact with humans, using natural language to mimic the way the human brain works and enhance human performance.

Complexity-Impact Matrix A model to assess and prioritize people analytics work according to its relative complexity and impact. Used and reproduced with kind permission from the authors of *The Power of People: Learn how successful organizations use workforce analytics to improve business performance* (Pearson, 2017). The Complexity-Impact Matrix is the copyright of Nigel Guenole, Jonathan Ferrar and Sheri Feinzig.

consumerization of HR A term referring to employees' expectations that technology experiences at work will be personalized and similar to technology experiences as consumers.

core HR In the context of people analytics, this refers to First Wave systems (see Chapter 5 – Technology). See also **core human resources system**.

core human resources system Software that stores and manages employee information, such as payroll and benefits data, within a central database and system of record.

correlation (Pearson product-moment correlation.) A statistical measure that indicates the extent to which two variables are related. A positive correlation indicates that, as one variable increases, the other increases as well. For a negative correlation, as one variable increases, the other decreases.

cost-based workforce planning The activities of workforce planning, whether strategic, operational or tactical, that focus on the cost of labour and its associated impact on an organization. An alternative to '**skills-based workforce planning**'.

C-suite executives The most senior-level executives in an organization who typically have 'chief' in their role title, which implies that the person is the most senior person for a specific function or business. For example, the chief human resources officer (CHRO).

customer experience (CX) The term for the experience that customers have of a company's products and services. These include handling goods, using physical products, interacting with an organization's workforce in the receipt of services and interacting with digital platforms, such as the company's website. Measuring CX helps companies to assess if they are meeting their customers' expectations.

customer Net Promoter Score (cNPS) See **Net Promoter Score (NPS)**.

cybersecurity Technologies, processes, policies and activities to protect systems, such as applications, networks, devices, programs and data from being hacked, attacked, damaged or accessed in an unauthorized manner.

dashboard Organizes, stores and displays information about a series of topics using formats and visuals that are easy to interpret for the user.

data (plural); **datum** (singular) Facts, information and statistics collected together for reference or analysis.

data aggregation The process of collecting data from multiple systems and consolidating it in a summary form, often in readiness for statistical analysis or visualization.

data analysis A process of inspecting, cleaning, transforming and modelling data with the goal of discovering insights, drawing conclusions and informing decision making.

data analyst A person whose job is to collect and study data to reveal meaningful patterns and insights.

database A collection of information that is organized so that it can be easily accessed, managed and updated.

data democratization The process of making data and insights accessible to a much wider group of people across an organization who will benefit from its usage. The terms are interchangeable with the 'democratization of data'.

data ethics The fundamental legal and moral principles of right and wrong that govern the collection, storage, use and dissemination of data in analytics.

data governance The overall management of the availability, usability, integrity and security of the data employed in an organization.

data lake A centralized repository that allows the storage of structured and unstructured data at scale, without having to first structure the data into any order or pre-described format.

data management A set of disciplines and frameworks used to provide structure to the organization, processing, storage and usage of data within the parameters of policy and regulation.

data owner An individual or team who determines who has the right to access, edit, use and disseminate data.

data privacy The legal, political and ethical issues surrounding the collection, organization, processing, storage and usage of data, and especially the expectations of what information is shared with whom. In the context of people analytics, this is focused on the data related to employees and workers.

data privacy officer The person in an organization responsible for data privacy. The most senior person with this role in an organization is known as the chief privacy officer.

data science A field of expertise that combines scientific and statistical methods, processes and algorithms to extract insights from vast amounts of data.

data scientist A person whose job it is to perform statistical analysis, data mining and retrieval processes on a large amount of data to identify trends and other relevant information.

data security The practice of protecting valuable and sensitive data.

data standards Agreed and consistently applied definitions and protocols for managing data.

data steward A person responsible for managing data content, quality standards and controls within an organization or function.

data stewardship The process of managing data content, quality standards and controls within an organization or function.

data storage The methods and technologies used to collect and retain digital information.

data visualization The representation of quantitative information in a pictorial or graphic format so that an audience can easily grasp difficult concepts or patterns.

data warehouse A central repository of integrated data from one or more sources, storing current and historical data in one single place. A data warehouse is often formatted such that data is stored using predefined structures and protocols.

democratization of data See **data democratization.**

descriptive analytics A branch of analytics focused on gathering and summarizing data with the purpose of identifying historical trends and insights, as well as providing current data.

digital human resources The transformation of HR services and processes typically through the use of social, mobile, analytics and cloud technologies.

downstream systems Systems that receive and are dependent on data from other systems.

DRIVE: Five Ages of People Analytics A model developed by the authors of this book to describe the history and future of people analytics in five stages: The Age of Discovery (1910s–2010), The Age of Realization (2010–2015), The Age of Innovation (2015–2020), The Age of Value (2020–2025) and The Age of Excellence (2025 onwards). DRIVE: Five Ages of People Analytics is the copyright of Jonathan Ferrar and David Green.

Eight Step Model for Purposeful Analytics A model for designing and delivering people analytics projects at every level. Used and reproduced with kind permission from the authors of *The Power of People: Learn how successful organizations use workforce analytics to improve business performance* (Pearson, 2017). The Eight Step Model for Purposeful Analytics is the copyright of Nigel Guenole, Jonathan Ferrar and Sheri Feinzig.

emotional intelligence (EQ) The ability to be aware of, control and evaluate one's own and other people's emotions.

employee engagement The strength of the mental and emotional commitment an employee has towards the organization they work for. This is often measured through the use of employee engagement surveys, the practice of which has been in place in various forms for several decades.

employee experience (EX) The term for the experience that employees have of working in an organization. Measuring EX helps an organization assess if they are meeting their employees' expectations.

employee listening Obtaining valuable feedback, in the form of qualitative and quantitative data, from employees on important topics and 'moments that matter' with the goal of understanding and improving the employee experience.

In people analytics, this involves very advanced analytical techniques to collect and analyse the data on a continuous basis in real time.

employee Net Promoter Score (eNPS) An employee loyalty metric based on Net Promoter Score (see **Net Promoter Score**). In the context of the employee, eNPS usually refers to an organization asking their staff one question: Would you recommend [name of company] as a great place to work?

encryption The process of converting information into a particular form so that it can only be read by certain people.

enterprise analytics The function of analytics that supports business strategies and actions across an organization.

ethics charter A specific document that provides transparency on how people-related data is collected, analysed, managed, secured and used to protect employees and the organization.

fair exchange of value In general, this refers to the exchange of two things of equal value as the basis for a reasonable and honest trade. In the context of people analytics, this describes the personal benefit employees receive from analytics in exchange for sharing their data with the organization to enable analytical work to occur.

First Wave Technology adoption in people analytics focused on Core HR systems. See Chapter 5 – Technology.

Focus-Impact-Value Model A model describing how to undertake people analytics work targeted on delivering business outcomes. The Focus-Impact-Value Model is the copyright of Jonathan Ferrar and David Green.

fully loaded The costs of an employee that include the direct costs of a person (that is their salary, other compensation and benefits) plus standard incremental costs. The finance function usually has a calculation for these incremental costs that includes such items as real estate occupancy, IT costs and cost for headquarters staff.

homophily The tendency for people to seek out or be attracted to those who are similar to themselves. Often used in analytics related to investigating diversity and inclusion topics.

human resources business partners (HRBP) HR professionals who work closely with an organization's senior leaders to develop an agenda for managing people that supports the overall aims of the organization. These are usually generalists and do not normally specialize in any subfunction of HR.

human resources leadership team (HRLT) The most senior-level executive team in a human resources function, typically consisting of direct reports of the chief human resources officer.

hypothesis A proposed explanation in the form of a testable and falsifiable statement often informed by observations and previous research.

insight A deep and clear understanding derived from analysis.

Insight222 Nine Dimensions for Excellence in People Analytics® The model described in this book with the nine dimensions of Governance, Methodology, Stakeholder Management, Skills, Technology, Data, Workforce Experiences, Business Outcomes and Culture. This model is a registered trademark of Insight222 Limited, a company registered in England and Wales with registration number 10926588.

Insight222 Operating Model for People Analytics A model that outlines the structure and roles required for high-impact people analytics work. The model is the intellectual property and a trademark of Insight222 Limited, a company registered in England and Wales with registration number 10926588.

intangible asset An asset that is not physical in nature. Examples include software, franchises, patents and copyrights. Human capital is usually regarded as an intangible asset.

internal rate of return (IRR) A metric used in financial analysis to estimate the profitability of potential investments.

International Organization for Standardization (ISO) An independent, non-governmental international organization which, through its members, brings together experts from across the world to develop International Standards across a multitude of industries and specialisms. It is headquartered in Geneva, Switzerland.

ISO 30414 International Organization for Standardization publication 'Human resource management – Guidelines for internal and external human capital reporting'. The first ISO set of human capital metrics standards, published in 2018.

key performance indicators (KPIs) A variable or metric against which the success of a function or business is judged.

labour market data See **talent market data.**

Likert scale rating system A psychometric scale designed to measure people's attitudes, opinions or perceptions. Appears commonly in questionnaires as questions requiring answers such as 'strongly agree', 'agree', 'neutral', and so on. It was devised in 1932 by Rensis Likert.

machine learning A field of artificial intelligence (AI) focused on developing applications that automatically and continually learn from data, improving their performance over time without being programmed to do this.

master data The core, consistent and uniform data about a business that is essential to its operations. Employee records are an example of master data.

maturity model A step-by-step tool that helps people assess the current effectiveness of a person or group and outlines what capabilities are required to move sequentially to the next level in the model.

metadata Data about other data, for example, the date a digital asset was created or the file type.

metrics Facts and figures representing the effectiveness of business processes that organizations track and monitor to assess the state of the company.

minimum viable product (MVP) A version of a product or solution with enough functionality to be useful and for users to provide feedback for the next iteration.

mission statement A description of an organization or function's business, its objectives and its approach to achieving those objectives.

moments that matter These are the moments that impact an employee's experience of working for a company most significantly throughout each day and their entire tenure. Individual moments can cause an employee to make decisions about the way they work, or even in extreme cases, whether they stay or leave an organization.

natural language processing (NLP) A branch of artificial intelligence, computer science and linguistics that helps computers understand, interpret and manipulate human language.

net present value (NPV) A metric used in financial analysis to measure the difference between the present value of cash inflows and the present value of cash outflows over a period of time.

Net Promoter Score (NPS) A customer loyalty metric developed by Fred Reichheld, Bain & Company, and Satmetrix Systems, Inc, first introduced in Reichheld's 2003 *Harvard Business Review* article 'One number you need to grow'.

network analysis See **organizational network analysis (ONA)**.

Nine Dimensions A shortened term for the 'Insight222 Nine Dimensions for Excellence in People Analytics®'.

Nine Skills for the Future HR Professional A model that outlines nine required skills that human resources professionals should acquire or develop for their ability to add value in their work in the future. The model is the intellectual property and a trademark of Insight222 Limited, a company registered in England and Wales with registration number 10926588.

nudge (or nudge theory) A concept in behavioural economics, political theory and behavioural sciences, popularized by Richard H Thaler and Cass R Sunstein in their book *Nudge: Improving decisions about health, wealth and happiness* (Yale University Press, 2008). The theory proposes positive reinforcement and indirect suggestions as ways to influence the behaviour and decision making of groups or individuals, such as a team, group of employees or manager, and in organizations is typically enabled by technology.

on-premise technology Software installed and run on computers physically located on-site (on the premises) at an organization.

operating model Describes how a group, team or function can be organized to operate at its best and deliver upon its mission.

organizational network analysis (ONA) A structured method for visualizing how communications, information, collaboration and decisions flow through an organization. Also known as 'relationship analytics' and 'network analysis'.

passive (**data collection**) Collecting data through a continual flow of data generated from a company's communication systems such as email, calendar and collaboration tools. It is passive because the employee does not have to be involved in order for the data to be collected. The opposite of passive data collection is active data collection.

people analytics The analysis of employee and workforce data, to reveal insights and provide recommendations to improve business outcomes.

People Analytics Value Chain An outside-in approach to people analytics in which client drivers such as business strategy and stakeholder challenges determine the work, and business outcomes such as commercial value and employee experience should be realized as outputs. The model is the intellectual property and a trademark of Insight222 Limited, a company registered in England and Wales with registration number 10926588.

people science The combining of fields such as behavioural science, organizational psychology and data science, in order to surface deeper insights about the workforce that enable organizations to make more informed decisions.

personas Descriptions of fictional characters created to represent typical users of a service that help in the understanding of the needs, experiences, behaviours and goals of these different user types.

Pet Projects Projects that are of low impact and high complexity (see **Complexity-Impact Matrix**).

pilot A small-scale preliminary study or experiment that is undertaken to test a hypothesis, or the feasibility, duration and cost of a project. The hypothesis or project is usually then evaluated prior to any large-scale implementation.

predictive analytics A branch of advanced analytics that is used to make forecasts about future events.

prescriptive analytics A branch of advanced analytics that is used to find the best course of action for a specific analytical insight.

pulse survey A type of survey with a short number of questions and more regular in terms of its frequency, which is used to gather data concerning a variety of employment-related topics. It is often used as an alternative or in addition to an employee engagement survey. Also commonly known as 'pulse'. See also **employee engagement** and **employee listening**.

Python A programming language and free software environment for statistical computing and graphics used by people analytics teams for statistical programming and data analysis. Python is a product of the Python Software Foundation (PSF), a 501(c)(3) non-profit corporation that holds the intellectual property rights behind the Python programming language.

Quick Win A project that is of high impact and low complexity (see **Complexity-Impact Matrix**).

R A programming language and free software environment for statistical computing and graphics used by people analytics teams for statistical programming and data analysis, which was first released in 1995.

raw data Data collected directly from a source that has not been previously processed.

relationship analytics See **organizational network analysis (ONA)**.

reporting The function or activity for generating documents that contain information organized in a narrative, graphic or tabular form, often in a repeatable and regular fashion.

request for proposal (RFP) A document outlining requirements requested from potential vendors who wish to deliver those requirements to the requestor (ie the customer). The vendors deliver their document as a proposal. It normally consists of, or is accompanied by, a number of questions that the customer wishes each vendor to answer as part of their proposal. Issuing an RFP document is typically a signal to invite vendors to 'bid' for the business of delivering the requirements.

request for quotation (RFQ) A document similar to an RFP but usually shorter and used as a precursor to the RFP, to request a quotation for services or products from potential vendors.

return on investment (ROI) The measure of benefit of an investment divided by the cost of the investment, usually expressed as a percentage and often converted to a monetary value.

robotic process automation (RPA) Technology that enables the configuration of computer software to digitally emulate and integrate the actions of a human to execute a business process.

scorecard A visual report that provides a consolidated, periodic snapshot of an organization's current performance compared to its targets across particular metrics.

Second Wave Technology adoption in people analytics focused on analytics dashboards. See Chapter 5 – Technology.

Seven Forces of Demand A model that identifies seven common areas of business demand that are drivers for people analytics. Used and reproduced with kind permission from the authors of *The Power of People: Learn how successful organizations use workforce analytics to improve business performance* (Pearson, 2017). The Seven Forces of Demand is the copyright of Nigel Guenole, Jonathan Ferrar and Sheri Feinzig.

Seven Types of Stakeholders A model to illustrate and provide guidance for engaging seven stakeholder groups in people analytics. The seven groups are: business executives, human resources executives, managers, employees & workers, functional stakeholders, technology & data owners and unions, works councils & employee groups. The Seven Types of Stakeholders model is the copyright of Jonathan Ferrar and David Green.

Six Skills for Success A model that captures six key skill areas required by people analytics teams. Used and reproduced with kind permission from the authors of *The Power of People: Learn how successful organizations use workforce analytics to improve business performance* (Pearson, 2017). Six Skills for Success is the copyright of Nigel Guenole, Jonathan Ferrar and Sheri Feinzig.

skills-based workforce planning The activities of workforce planning, whether strategic, operational or tactical, that focus on the skills of labour required in the future to deliver organizational outcomes. An alternative to '**cost-based workforce planning**'.

Society for Human Resource Management (SHRM) The world's largest HR professional society and leading provider of resources serving the needs of HR professionals and advancing the practice of human resource management. It is headquartered in Alexandria, Virginia, United States.

software as a service (SaaS) An approach to software licensing and delivery in which software is hosted remotely in the cloud and accessed via an internet browser.

sponsor A person or group providing support for a project or activity through financial means or personal endorsements.

stakeholder A person in the organization who has a vested interest in a project or activity and its outcomes.

stakeholder map A visual profile of the stakeholders that are most important to engage. In people analytics terms, the map is profiled across Seven Types of Stakeholders.

strategic workforce planning A process used to align the needs and priorities of the organization with those of its workforce, through understanding labour supply and demand and the long-term objectives of both the organization and its competitive environment.

SPSS A statistical package designed specifically to assist data scientists, originally in the area of the social sciences. It is a software package used for interactive, or batched, statistical analysis. Long produced by SPSS Inc, it was acquired by IBM in 2009.

statistical analysis The collection, organization and exploration of data in order to uncover patterns and trends.

statistical modelling The use of mathematical equations, based on a set of assumptions, intended to predict or explain relationships among variables.

stratified sampling A process that involves dividing the population of interest into smaller groups, called strata. Samples are then pulled from these strata, and analysis is performed to enable inferences about the greater population of interest.

talent market data The collection and analysis of external data as it relates to geographies, people, skills, jobs, salaries, functions and competitors, which, when combined with internal data, enables easier decision making. See also **labour market data**.

talent marketplace An organizational digital platform that enables companies to advertise vacant positions (such as jobs, assignments, mentorships and project-based roles), and then match them to people elsewhere in the organization who have the required profile 'match'. Analytics is used to infuse the platform with the required data and then match the talent to the open positions.

Taylorism The movement of Taylorists, which began in 1911. See also **Taylorist**.

Taylorist A person or organization that follows the practices of management as portrayed and inspired by Frederick Taylor following the publication of his book *The Principles of Scientific Management* in 1911.

terms of reference A document defining the purpose and structure of a group of people who have agreed to work together, for example, a project team or a governance committee, which enables a common understanding of the scope and accountabilities.

text analysis The process of deriving insights from large volumes of text, typically through the use of specialized software to identify patterns, trends and sentiment.

The Age of Discovery (1910s to 2010). The first 'age' of people analytics as defined in the DRIVE: Five Ages of People Analytics model. This period saw a gradual growth of interest in the field over a 100-year period from Taylorism to 2010.

The Age of Excellence (2025, onwards). The fifth 'age' of people analytics as defined in the DRIVE: Five Ages of People Analytics model. If excellence in people analytics is achieved to deliver value – at scale, among the HR profession, worldwide in multiple countries and organizations – then we estimate from 2025, we will enter The Age of Excellence.

The Age of Innovation (2015–2020). The third 'age' of people analytics as defined in the DRIVE: Five Ages of People Analytics model. This age was characterized by new models, new uses of technology, specialization, an increase in the number of practitioners entering the people analytics profession, and new approaches to creating business value.

The Age of Realization (2010–2015). The second 'age' of people analytics as defined in the DRIVE: Five Ages of People Analytics model. It is characterized by the development of maturity models and the emergence of leading people analytics practices in big companies, particularly in the technology space.

The Age of Value (2020–2025). The fourth 'age' of people analytics as defined in the DRIVE: Five Ages of People Analytics model. It is characterized by the propulsion of people analytics – due to the triple crises of the global pandemic, racial inequality and financial uncertainty in 2020 – into a new 'age', in which businesses demand more value from the activities of and investment in people analytics. Activities in The Age of Value are underpinned by the four pillars of trust, inclusion, purpose and equality in the workplace.

The Culture Pyramid A model describing the four stages of building a culture: demonstrate value, develop capability, create structure and build confidence. Adapted from an original model with permission of Kirsten Levermore (See 'About the authors').

The Four Responsibilities of People Analytics A model to describe the responsibilities of the people analytics team in providing personalized experiences to four audiences: employees, managers, executives and the workforce. The Four Responsibilities of People Analytics is the copyright of Jonathan Ferrar and David Green.

Third Wave Technology adoption in people analytics focused on specialist people analytics technologies. See Chapter 5 – Technology.

Trivial Endeavour A project that is of low impact and low complexity (see **Complexity-Impact Matrix**).

trust dividend The impact of workforce trust on financial performance when it comes to the use of employees' data. The term is used by Accenture in the 2019 study, Decoding Organizational Data: Trust, data and unlocking value in the digital workplace.

US Securities and Exchange Commission (SEC) An independent agency of the United States federal government with a mission to protect investors by facilitating capital formation and maintaining fair, orderly and efficient markets. It is headquartered in Washington, DC, United States.

workforce analytics Another term for 'people analytics'.

workforce planning Processes and techniques for analysing both the current and desired future state of the workforce. They should align with the business strategy and both current and future workers. Workforce planning can be strategic, operational and tactical in nature. See also **cost-based workforce planning**, **skills-based workforce planning** and **strategic workforce planning**.

Authors' note: Some of the above definitions are reproduced with kind permission from the authors of *The Power of People: Learn how successful organizations use workforce analytics to improve business performance* (Pearson, 2017). This is to ensure consistency for readers and standardization across the people analytics profession.

INDEX